CW00705744

DOING BUSINESS IN
CZECHOSLOVAKIA

DOING BUSINESS IN
CZECHOSLOVAKIA

KPMG PEAT MARWICK McLINTOCK
S J BERWIN & CO
NATIONAL WESTMINSTER BANK

KOGAN
PAGE

Note: This book was written on the basis of information current in June 1991.

First published in 1991

Kogan Page Limited
120 Pentonville Road
London N1 9JN

© Confederation of British Industry, 1991

British Library Cataloguing in Publication Data

A CIP record for this book is available from the British Library.

ISBN 0 7494 0471 X

Typeset by DP Photosetting, Aylesbury, Bucks
Printed in England by Clays Ltd, St Ives plc

Contents

The Contributors   9

Foreword   11
Marian Čalfa, Prime Minister of the Czech and Slovak Federal Republic

Preface   13
Alan J Lewis, CBE, Chairman, CBI Initiative Eastern Europe

PART I: A BUSINESS REVOLUTION?   **15**

---

1. Political and Economic Transformation   17
    National Westminster Bank

2. Recreating a Market Economy   27
    SJ Berwin & Co

3. Market Potential   35
    Cerrex Ltd

4. Business Culture   45
    KPMG Peat Marwick McLintock

5. Market Intelligence   51
    KPMG Peat Marwick McLintock

6. Czechoslovakia and its Trading Partners   57
    National Westminster Bank and SJ Berwin & Co

PART II: THE BUSINESS INFRASTRUCTURE   **67**

---

7. The Legal Framework   69
    SJ Berwin & Co

8. Foreign Investment   77
    SJ Berwin & Co

9. The Convertibility of the Koruna   87
    National Westminster Bank

10. Prices, Rents and Wages   93
    National Westminster Bank

11. Banking and Financial Services   97
    National Westminster Bank

12. Restitution   103
    SJ Berwin & Co

13. The Economics of Privatisation   109
    KPMG Peat Marwick McLintock

14. The Process of Privatisation   115
    SJ Berwin & Co

15. Real Estate   123
    SJ Berwin & Co

16. Commercial Law   131
    SJ Berwin & Co

17. Competition   137
    SJ Berwin & Co

18. The Fiscal Framework   145
    KPMG Peat Marwick McLintock

19. The Environment   151
    KPMG Peat Marwick McLintock and SJ Berwin & Co

20. Technology and Communications   163
    KPMG Peat Marwick McLintock

21. Transport   169
    KPMG Peat Marwick McLintock

22. The Labour Market   177
    KPMG Peat Marwick McLintock

23. Management and the Professions   187
    KPMG Peat Marwick McLintock

24. Grants and Aid   193
    National Westminster Bank

PART III: THE OPTIONS FOR BRITISH BUSINESS   203

25. Strategic Planning   205
KPMG Peat Marwick McLintock

26. Marketing   215
Saatchi & Saatchi Advertising Worldwide

27. Export and Import   223
KPMG Peat Marwick McLintock

28. Trade and Project Finance   231
National Westminster Bank

29. Countertrade   243
National Westminster Bank

30. Credit Insurance   249
National Westminster Bank

31. Agencies, Distributorships and Franchises   257
SJ Berwin & Co

32. Licensing   267
SJ Berwin & Co

33. Establishing a Presence   279
KPMG Peat Marwick McLintock

34. Forming a Company   285
SJ Berwin & Co

35. Financing a Company   297
National Westminster Bank

36. Tax Issues   303
KPMG Peat Marwick McLintock

37. Accounting Issues   311
KPMG Peat Marwick McLintock

PART IV: CASE STUDIES   315

1. Chequepoint International   317

2. Berox Machine Tool Co Ltd   323

3. Emmex Consultants   329

4. Nuclear Electric PLC   333

5. Baker Street Trading Overseas   337

APPENDICES   **341**

1. Opportunities by Sector   343
    Cerrex Ltd

2. Legislation   361

3. Bibliography and Sources of Further Information   375

Index   380

The Contributors

KPMG Peat Marwick McLintock is the UK member firm of KPMG, one of the largest international firms of accountants, tax advisers and management consultants. KPMG Reviconsult in Prague has been operational since May 1990 and is the only independent accountancy firm in Czechoslovakia. The firm is advising engineering, paper, glass, metallurgy, food processing and textile companies and is training the staff of the Czechoslovak state bank in financial accounting, internal audit and related issues.

S J Berwin & Co is a City law firm specialising in corporate finance, banking, tax, commercial property, commercial litigation, EEC and international law. From the firm's inception, its partners have advised in commercial transactions in Eastern European countries. In November 1990, S J Berwin & Co became the first UK law firm to establish an associate office in Czechoslovakia, with a Prague law firm. The firm is involved in advising both Western and Czechoslovak partners on the privatisation process and on joint ventures.

National Westminster Bank has enjoyed a long and fruitful association with Czechoslovakia and plays a leading role in promoting Anglo-Czech trade. NatWest has sponsored the Engineering Industries Association Trade Mission to Prague for the last two years and has taken part in the Brno trade fair every year since 1973. Having had such close links with Czechoslovakia over a long period of time, NatWest has built up a sizeable database on trade conditions and has offered this knowledge and expertise to assist all companies aspiring to do business in this market.

Foreword

I strongly support the CBI Initiative on Eastern Europe, which should do much to raise awareness about the many opportunities in the new markets of Eastern and Central Europe. Consequently, I warmly welcome this new book which gathers together much valuable information and offers much to help the British business-person planning their activities in Czechoslovakia.

Czechoslovakia needs foreign investment and welcomes it. We recognise the importance of a transparent and stable investment climate and have done much in a short time to achieve this. Firm economic management has ensured stable exchange rates, and inflation has quickly moderated following the liberalisation of prices. Moreover, our emerging tax and company law framework is second to none in its attractiveness to foreign investors. We aim to build on these considerable achievements with measures to further enhance business confidence, increase transparency and cut red tape.

Czechoslovakia also needs trade. With a highly educated, skilled and adaptable workforce, our country was the most industrially advanced of the old Comecon bloc and has suffered as a result of the collapse of those markets. We have, therefore, moved quickly to increase and strengthen links with the West, particularly in seeking close association with - and ultimately full membership of - the European Community. But while we have the ingenuity, skills and determination to adapt our products quickly to the demands of Western consumers, we need help in finding and establishing new markets. This book offers many excellent opportunities for those with traditional entrepreneurial skills.

Our policies are already producing results. Several very large investment programmes by foreign companies are already under way, and more will follow. Trade with the West is now increasing sharply. But in both areas, Britain, until now at least, is lagging behind its competitors. After many years of artificial imbalance, Czechoslovakia needs diversity in its economic relations. I do very much hope that this publication will alert British business to the wide range of opportunities available, particularly now that our privatisation programme is well under way.

All of us in Eastern and Central Europe are tackling something entirely new as we seek to return our economies to a free market after the distortions of the past. Czechoslovakia started this process later than others, and has learned from their experience. Even so, there may be mistakes or oversights and our Western partners can help by pointing these out. So if you meet unwelcome obstacles or difficulties when seeking to do business in Czechoslovakia, let me know, personally, and I will do my best to help put matters right.

Marian Čalfa
Prime Minister of the Government of the
Czech and Slovak Federal Republic
August 1991

Preface

The political revolution against the Communists was effected with astonishing speed in Czechoslovakia. The economic transformation of the country is going to be considerably more painful and drawn out, but there should be no doubt that the new government is building on firm foundations.

Prior to the Communists, Czechoslovakia was one of the most advanced industrial nations in Europe and played an integral role in the world trading system. This heritage was not entirely extinguished under socialist central planning. The Czechoslovak population has the highest standard of living in Eastern Europe; debt levels are relatively low and Czechoslovak companies still retain some of their traditional strengths in engineering and manufacturing.

However, a great deal has to be done to revive the economy. The government is committed to achieving this by way of a speedy transition from central planning to a market economy. Companies are being commercialised and privatised; trade and investment have been liberalised; most prices are now being set by market forces; the currency is moving towards convertibility and a commercial framework recognisable to Western executives is being put in place. This programme promises a significant improvement in economic performance and the World Bank predicts GDP could grow by as much as 6 per cent a year in the period 1993-2000.

This book is intended to help Western companies explore the potential of this developing market; provide a practical commentary on the commercial framework that is emerging and assess ways into the market from straightforward trading to direct investment. (Readers should remember that Czechoslovakia is a fast-changing environment and that this book has been written on the basis of information current in June 1991.)

This source of pragmatic business advice draws on the expertise of SJ Berwin & Co, KPMG Peat Marwick McLintock and National Westminster Bank. The CBI thanks them for the very substantial efforts they have made in putting this material together.

There are already heartening examples of companies who are succeeding in this new economic environment and this book records the experience of five of these. Chequepoint, Berox Machine Tools, Emmex, Nuclear Electric PLC and Baker Street Trading have been generous – and honest – enough to spell out the realities of operating in Czechoslovakia. The CBI thanks them for their contributions.

In addition, Saatchi & Saatchi have given us the benefit of their knowledge of marketing in Czechoslovakia, while Cerrex Ltd give an insight into the country's market potential. Important contributions have also been made by Harold Elletson, Jonathan Star, Stephanie Flanders, Mike Cronshaw and JUDr Tamara Holoubková.

Although there can be no guaranteed returns on any investment, there are undoubtedly great opportunities in Czechoslovakia. Unless businesses decide to take a long-term view and establish their presence now, the rewards will inevitably go to our trading rivals. It is our hope that this book will give British companies a competitive advantage when exploring and developing business in this new and exciting market.

Alan J Lewis, CBE
Chairman, CBI Initiative Eastern Europe
June 1991

Part I

A Business Revolution?

1

Political and Economic Transformation

National Westminster Bank

For 41 years after World War II Czechoslovakia was under communist control, notwithstanding periodic strong demands for political pluralism and true autonomy culminating most vividly in the 'Prague Spring' of 1968. Not surprisingly, when the spirit of reform swept through Eastern Europe in 1989, Czechoslovaks were at the forefront of those demanding political and economic reform – demands which led to the 'Velvet Revolution' and the peaceful introduction of a temporary, non-communist government. Although ambitious plans for economic reform were discussed, real progress had to await the general election of June 1990 in which the reformist Civic Forum/Public Against Violence won a comfortable majority in the federal parliament. Since then President Vaclav Havel and Prime Minister Marian Čalfa have begun to implement the major reforms, detailed in this book, which are intended to transform Czechoslovakia into a modern industrial country, fully integrated into the world economy.

Since World War II the Czechoslovak economy was built along the lines of the Soviet economic command system. A wide spread of investment ensured a high degree of self-sufficiency in both capital and consumer goods, although a considerable dependence on external trade with the USSR and the former GDR was characterised by participation in Comecon International specialisation. Trade with the USSR involved the bartering of Soviet raw materials, particularly imports of energy, for capital and consumer goods, including arms. Along with the former GDR regime, the communist Czechoslovak government took a cautious, conservative line towards early attempts at economic reform in both Hungary and Poland and later distanced itself from the economic and political ramifications of Gorbachev's *perestroika* and *glasnost*.

INGREDIENTS OF REFORM

Many of the economic problems faced by Czechoslovakia are shared by other East European countries, and there is a wide measure of agreement over the major structural changes required to success-fully transform command economies. Most observers anticipate that any programme would have to include:

- The creation of effective markets for capital and property and the privatisation of state-owned property and business assets.

- The removal of any monetary overhang, the result of involuntary savings in local currencies by domestic populations. These can be removed either by direct expropriation or by privatisation of state property, including the housing stock.

- The introduction of realistic pricing and costing for goods and services, including the removal of budget subsidies for basic goods. Currency convertibility, which forces realistic pricing, is a key tool.

- The acceptance of greater labour mobility. As previously protected industries are exposed to fierce competition in free markets, inevitably some will fail. The experience of former East German industry since reunification is a salutary lesson. The collapse of East German industry has been much more rapid and more comprehensive than had been forecast. The implications for industry in other East European countries are serious in that the GDR was widely regarded as being industrially the most advanced of the planned economies. Industrial closures or, at the very least, more efficient labour usage will inevitably lead to widespread and often highly concentrated unemployment.

- The provision of incentives to encourage initiative and performance. Few of the East European countries have yet come to terms with the consequences of incentives, differential incomes and the accumulation of personal wealth.

- A legislative framework providing for the full equality of all business entities, creating the conditions and regulations for the development and protection of entrepreneurial activities. Regulations for foreign business participation and investments, and rules for contractual arrangements and competition between business entities.

- Liberalisation of external trade. If the price mechanism is to take over the function of co-ordinator of economic activities which was formerly held by the centralised plan, then the conduct of foreign trade ought to shift from state trading organisations to individual enterprises and their foreign suppliers and importers. The environment in which external trade is conducted should reflect minimal state interference.

The extent to which these key provisions are being implemented are reliable proxies for the real progress of reform in individual countries. As far as Czechoslovakia is concerned, progress to date has lagged behind that in Poland, but the ultimate prospects of success are among the best in Eastern Europe.

The commitment to political reform in Czechoslovakia is now well established, and the detailed progress toward the goals listed above are enunciated in the rest of this book. It is, however, important to understand that the countries of Eastern Europe, while having some similarities, are in many important respects quite different.

Table 1.1 *Basic data (1990 estimates)*

	Area (000s sq. km.)	Population (million)	US$ GNP (billion)	GNP per capita US$
Czechoslovakia	128	15.7	124*	7,898
Hungary	93	10.6	63*	5,943
Poland	313	37.9	149*	3,931
USSR	22,402	292.0	1,466*	5,021
Denmark	43	5.1	118	23,137
UK	231	57.2	970	16,958

* Purchasing power parity

As Table 1.1 shows, the main countries covered in the CBI's Eastern Europe initiative vary considerably in geographical size and population. More importantly, they also vary in economic size and on most measures of living standards. Gross national product measures the total value of goods and services produced in an economy. Western magnitudes are generally not controversial, but in Eastern Europe measures of gross social product or net material product are difficult to translate into convertible currency measures. In the absence of a more reliable methodology, estimates can be made of East European GNPs through the use of purchasing power parities which attempt to correlate costs of production between countries.

On this basis, estimates of the absolute size of East European economies can be made which suggest that the Czechoslovak economy is about one-eighth that of the UK, or about the same size as Denmark. While too much importance should not be read into these numbers, it is clear that on a per capita basis Czechoslovakia is comfortably the wealthiest of the independent East European countries, with a per capita GNP twice that of Poland. However imperfect these statistics may be, they are supported by more empirical evidence as shown in Figure 1.1 which indicates a higher material standard of living in Czechoslovakia than elsewhere in Eastern Europe, albeit a long way behind that of the most advanced Western countries.

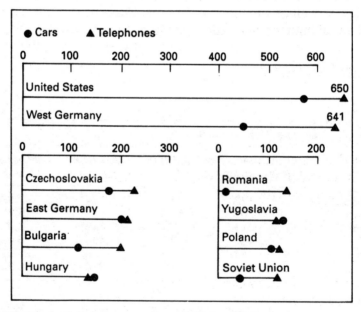

Figure 1.1 *Cars and telephones per 1000 people*

This higher standard of living does have important implications for the Czech authorities. In general, political reforms in many Eastern European countries were achieved much more quickly than had been anticipated, and rather more easily than most observers had predicted, largely because of the relatively accommodating stance adopted by the Soviet Union. One of the emerging difficulties has been that the speed of political reform has raised unrealistic expectations of equally rapid rises in the standard of living. Where living standards are already very low (notably in Bulgaria, Romania and the Soviet Union) the inability of the authorities to improve the quality of life is likely to lead to increasing popular discontent. Where living standards were already reasonably high, the risk of undue economic expectations is lower. The more realistic expectations of the Czechoslovaks toward the speed with which economic reform will raise living standards does provide the authorities with some scope for manoeuvre.

While economic reform is widely welcomed throughout Eastern Europe, and in Czechoslovakia in particular, there is recognition that full-blooded economic reform involves such substantial costs that it may be unacceptable to large segments of the population. Resistance to change remains centred around the old Communist Party bureaucracies which still exert considerable control over policy, as well as elements of the working class fearful that reform will entail higher prices and massive job losses.

EXTERNAL DEBT

Czechoslovakia's economic inheritance from communist rule is clearly in need of major reform, though in one respect it is better placed than its East European neighbours. Past governments have always been cautious about the acquisition of external debt, as a result of which Czechoslovakia is now better placed than all of its neighbours with the possible exception of idiosyncratic Romania. At end-1990, Czechoslovakia's total external debt was estimated to be some $7.9 billion, of which $2.9 billion was short term.

Table 1.2 *Convertible currency debt (1990)*

	Total debt (US$ billion)	Debt/GNP (%)	Debt service ratio (%)	Debt/exports (%)
Bulgaria	10.8	96	115	503
Czechoslovakia	7.9	18	21	109
Hungary	21.9	70	42	245
Poland	47.6	84	36	386
Romania	0.5	1	2	12
USSR	54.0	6	25	132

There are many measures of debt burden, but by nearly all of them Czechoslovakia is only moderately encumbered. Although rising, total debt in 1990 represented some 110 per cent of total export earnings. More importantly, the crucial debt service ratio, calculated as interest and amortisation of the external debt due in a given year as a proportion of export earnings in that year, has usually remained below 20 per cent.

Table 1.3 *Czechoslovakia – debt burden measures*

	1984	1987	1990	1991
Debt/GNP (%)	12.0	13.0	18.0	36.0
Debt/exports (%)	86.0	108.0	109.0	127.0
Debt service (%)	19.0	19.0	21.0	17.0
Amortisation ($bn)	0.6	0.7	0.9	0.7
Interest ($bn)	0.5	0.4	0.6	0.8

Although this means that one in five dollars generated through export earnings is already committed to servicing external debt, the burden, while high, is not unduly onerous. The risk is that it may rise higher. Most commercial lenders, given experiences elsewhere, are adopting cautious attitudes toward increasing exposures in Eastern Europe though Czechoslovakia is more likely than its neighbours to retain voluntary and significant access to the commercial markets. It is clear, however, that for Czechoslovakia to finance its future development, relations with the multilaterals will be crucial. In this respect, the rejoining of the IMF and World Bank in September 1990 and the subsequent agreement of a stand-by facility with the IMF are indicative of international approval of the progress of reform.

The generally conservative external debt management under the previous communist administration has given Czechoslovakia one of the least burdensome and manageable debt profiles in Eastern Europe. This provides the new democratic government with an unusually high degree of room for economic policy manoeuvre as it attempts profound economic reform. While the relatively moderate scale of external financial obligations does not in itself guarantee the success of economic reform, nor guarantee unqualified support from official and commercial creditors, it does provide greater leeway in the use of the country's own financial resources for reform and the ultimate achievement of economic growth targets sooner than would otherwise be the case.

Table 1.4 *Convertible currency external debt ($ billions)*

	1984	1987	1990	1991
Short-term	2.1	3.1	2.9	3.4
Medium/long-term	2.7	3.6	5.0	8.1
Total	4.8	6.7	7.9	11.5
Of which:				
IFIs	–	0.1	0.2	2.5
Official bilateral	1.3	2.1	2.3	2.9
Commercial banks	2.6	3.8	4.7	5.2
Other private	0.9	0.7	0.7	0.9

It is clear that the economic programmes and policies proposed and implemented by the authorities are already having a considerable impact. Exchange rate unification and limited internal convertibility, privatisation and financial reform have all impacted on the domestic economy, as has the changing economic relationship with the USSR. Other important but less crucial factors have included:

- Amnesty for political prisoners will increase the available workforce.

- The desire to switch production from the military sector to civilian areas of the economy.

- Reduced oil deliveries from the Soviet Union.

- Cancellation of contracts by East European partners.

- A reduced, though still good harvest.

Taken together, all these varied measures have caused substantial economic contraction and a sharp rise in the rate of inflation. Serious though these numbers appear to be, it is important to recognise that in large part they represent a one-off adjustment in a rapidly changing environment. Together with steeply rising unemployment, they may yet prove to be fairly temporary phenomena. There is considerable scope for a significant turnaround in the Czechoslovak economy. Domestic and external investment in emerging industries, and the better application of not inconsiderable labour and managerial skills should mean that by the mid-1990s the Czechoslovak economy could be showing quite rapid expansion, possibly exceeding 5 per cent per annum.

Much will depend on the external accounts. Traditionally,

Table 1.5 *Growth and inflation, 1987–91*

	1987	*1988*	*1989*	*1990*	*1991*
Real net material product growth (%)	2.0	2.6	0.4	-3.5	-10.0
Consumer prices (%)	0.1	0.1	1.4	7.0	30.0

Czechoslovakia has achieved a modest surplus on convertible currency current account (see Table 1.6). At the time of writing best forecasts indicate that a widespread change to convertible currency trading (particularly, but not exclusively, oil trade with the USSR) will result in a rapid and, over the medium term, unsustainable rise in the hard currency current account deficit. The challenge to Czechoslovak industry and commerce will be to re-establish trading links with Central and Western Europe. The generation of foreign exchange from new export markets is crucial for viability in the balance of payments if at the same time imports are to both renovate the capital base of industry and meet consumer demand. Maintaining balance in external accounts would both avoid undue accumulation of external debt and ease pressures on the country's liquidity position. How an external deficit is financed and corrected is of considerable importance to those seeking business with the country. Finance will be sought mainly from other governments, the multilaterals and from the European Bank for Reconstruction and Development. It will also come from inward direct investment,

Table 1.6 *Convertible currency current account ($ billion), 1987–91*

	1987	*1988*	*1989*	*1990 (Estimate)*	*1991 (Forecast)*
Exports	4.5	5.0	5.4	5.4	6.9
Imports	4.7	5.1	5.0	5.6	8.8
Balance of trade	-0.2	-0.1	0.4	-0.2	-1.9
Invisibles (net)	0.3	0.2	0.0	-0.3	-0.6
Current account	0.1	0.1	0.4	-0.5	-2.5
Export volume growth (%)	-2.0	0.7	8.3	1.0	22.6
Import volume growth (%)	6.0	2.3	4.2	22.0	41.7

probably from Western Europe. Correction of the deficit will result from a degree of import compression, but more sustainably from increased export earnings. It is clear that the Czechoslovak authorities have an acknowledged interest in encouraging inward investment and the development of export-oriented industries. As outlined in the following chapters, considerable scope exists for the enterprising partner of Czechoslovak businesses.

2

Recreating a Market Economy

SJ Berwin & Co

Before November 1989 Czechoslovakia's laws were the framework for a rigidly nationalised and centralised command economy. Entrepreneurial activity by individuals was illegal. Commercial activity was conducted by state-owned enterprises controlled by government ministries. All prices and wages were controlled. There were no bankruptcies and there was full employment. Foreign trade and foreign exchange dealings were the monopoly of the state.

The huge task facing Czechoslovakia's lawmakers following the revolution in November 1989 was to break up the state monopoly and to stimulate private business activity and foreign investment while maintaining basic economic stability. A transitional period was needed in which law reform measures would be accompanied by short-term restrictions and controls on such matters as prices, wages and access to foreign exchange, which would as soon as possible be phased out. It is, therefore, a mistake at the present stage to see federal or Republic laws as fixed entities. Many of those enacted under the new regime have been superseded or amended and many others will only have a short life, at least in their present form.

A two-stage approach was adopted. Before the elections in June 1990 a batch of laws was passed to make essential changes for the first steps towards a market economy. Many of these were temporary measures which have since been or are due to be replaced. From the autumn of 1990 onwards there has been intensive lawmaking activity at federal and Republic levels, as well as hundreds of decrees by government ministries implementing the legislation. The speed with which laws are being drafted and adopted means that mistakes are made and clarity sometimes suffers but there is a will to complete the basic programme and correct mistakes later. Overall, the achievement has been impressive, in spite of continuous political debate and the frequent practice of submitting to parliament, two, or even three irreconcilable drafts of the same proposal, prepared by different committees of experts!

The ultimate aim is a system of commercial law which meets advanced European standards. Due to its historical links with Austria and Hungary, Czechoslovakia naturally tends to base commercial legislation on Austrian and German models but it also seeks inspiration from other countries, including the UK, and is doing its utmost to meet EC standards, anticipating the Association Agreement with the EC now being negotiated.

PROGRESS TO DATE

Private enterprise

The first step was to remove the legal stigma attached to private enterprise and property. The Constitution was amended by a law (100/1990) which declared that property rights of individuals and legal persons (ie companies and other legal entities) and of the state are protected by the Constitution and by law, and assured all owners of property equal protection as well as prohibiting expropriation by the state without compensation.

This paved the way for the Private Enterprise Act (105/1990) which made it lawful, for the first time in 40 years, for individuals to engage in all kinds of business activity and for this purpose to form companies and partnerships, to employ staff and acquire property. Individuals were given the same economic rights, and were free to carry on business on the same basis as state enterprises and companies. As a result, thousands of small businesses have been established since the Act came into force on 1 May 1990. These will be the seed-corn for the growth and development of Czechoslovakia's market economy.

Foreign trade

Foreign trade used to be a monopoly of the Ministry of Foreign Trade, operating through agencies known as Foreign Trade Organisations (FTOs). The state's authority was cut down by legislation in April 1990 and there has since been further liberalisation. Now, most foreign trade operations can be carried out by Czechoslovak companies or by individuals registered at their local Companies' Register, without any further registration or authorisation.

Foreign investment and joint ventures

As a result of amendments to a 1988 law to encourage joint ventures with Western companies, foreign companies and individuals are now free to form wholly owned Czechoslovak companies as well as joint ventures with Czechoslovak individuals, normally without the need for special authorisation.

However, foreigners (as opposed to their wholly-owned companies) are not allowed to buy land in Czechoslovakia and, pending privatisation, state enterprises are not allowed to enter into joint ventures without permission at government level.

Foreign exchange convertibility

Czechoslovakia does not have full foreign exchange convertibility. However, a new Foreign Exchange Act (528/1990) was passed in November 1990 introducing internal convertibility on 1 January 1991.

Internal convertibility has two aspects. First, all Czechoslovak legal entities, including wholly-owned subsidiaries of foreign companies, are required to sell their entire foreign exchange to a Czechoslovak bank. The only exception allowed is for hard currency contributed as capital by a foreign shareholder to a subsidiary or joint venture. But, on the other side of the equation, all Czechoslovak companies and other legal bodies are free to buy as much foreign currency as they need from banks without any formality. This also includes currency required to repatriate the share of profits due to a foreign shareholder. So, for the first time since 1948, Czechoslovak business has virtually free access to foreign currency.

Czechoslovak companies can open accounts with foreign banks abroad with the approval of the State Bank of Czechoslovakia and may accept credit from abroad with similar approval. Internal convertibility only gives Czechoslovak companies the right to buy foreign exchange. It does not give foreign companies the right to sell their goods for Czechoslovak currency and then to exchange the proceeds into hard currency.

Privatisation

Far-reaching laws on small and large privatisations have been

enacted. Small privatisations of businesses through locally organised auctions have been proceeding since 1 January 1991. The
implementation of large privatisations awaits policy decisions,
including the basis for a voucher scheme to enable Czechoslovak
citizens to participate. The existence of a restitution claim may delay
privatisation until the claim has been resolved.

Commercial law

Before the November revolution, Czechoslovakia's internal commercial law was contained in an Economic Code which dealt with
commercial relations between 'socialist organisations'. A Foreign
Trade Code of 1963 governed (and still governs) commercial
relations with foreign enterprises.

In April 1990 the Economic Code was amended to cater for
private business in Czechoslovakia and re-introduced essential legal
arrangements such as mortgages and general and limited partnerships. These amendments were an emergency measure and a
comprehensive Commercial Code is being prepared that will
supersede the Economic and Foreign Trade Codes during 1991.
This will be a very important step forward as the interim measures
of April 1990 left many gaps and uncertainties in Czechoslovak
commercial law.

A very important new Economic Competition Act was adopted in
January 1991, introducing anti-trust law into Czechoslovakia for the
first time since 1948.

Company law

A Joint Stock Companies Act (104/1990) was adopted in April 1990,
based very closely on Austrian company law. Private limited
companies and general and limited partnerships were introduced by
the Economic Code from May 1990 onwards.

The Joint Stock Companies Act is comprehensive but the rules so
far laid down for private limited companies and partnerships are
very sketchy. All will be amplified in the Commercial Code.

Securities market and stock exchange

Regulations are expected to be included in a new Banking Act to be
adopted towards the end of 1991. At the time of writing, the Slovak
Republic has already established a stock exchange in Bratislava,
founded by four banks and two insurance companies. A grey market

in selected stocks is being operated by about 20 firms, within the existing banking system.

Removal of price and wage controls

A crucial step forward in the relaxation of price controls was taken on 1 January 1991 when the Pricing Act (526/1990) came into force. Until the end of 1990 only about 20 per cent of prices were free and 80 per cent were strictly controlled by the state. As from 1 January the situation was reversed and about 30 per cent of prices are now free and only some 20 per cent, including the prices of some foodstuffs, remain controlled. Prices rose by 100 per cent–150 per cent in January, a pain threshold which had to be passed to achieve economic progress.

Wages are, in effect, tightly controlled by the punitive tax on wage increases described in Chapter 10.

Customs law

New regulations bringing Czechoslovak customs law in line with general customs policy in Europe came into force on 1 February 1991. The basic rules governing customs duties, procedures and control are contained in the Customs Act (44/74), last amended in December 1990.

Czechoslovak tariffs and customs procedures are in accordance with its obligations as a member of GATT. Imported goods are classified according to the Harmonised System of Designation and Coding of Goods. Rates vary from zero to 70 per cent. An import surcharge of 15 per cent on a range of consumer goods was imposed in 1991 as a temporary measure.

Bankruptcy and liquidation

Czechoslovakia urgently needs comprehensive legal rules on insolvency, bankruptcy and creditors' liquidation. Currently the main legislation on bankruptcy is to be found in three paragraphs of the Civil Procedure Code. A new Act on bankruptcy and liquidation is due to be adopted.

Commercial courts

Another important law currently in preparation will change the court system for commercial disputes. Up to now, disputes based on the Economic Code have been resolved by so-called state arbitration. This is not arbitration in the normal commercial sense but a special procedure for resolving economic disputes between socialist organisations, to be found in one form or another in all the Central and Eastern European countries.

This system will be replaced, probably in 1991, by commercial courts. There has been discussion as to whether these should be branches of the civil courts or set up separately. The current view is that the commercial courts will form a division within the civil court system.

Employment law

Radical changes have been made to adapt Czechoslovakia's employment and trade union laws to the free market. A new law on employment was passed on 4 December 1990, with a separate Act concerning strikes – the Collective Negotiation Act (2/1991). In addition, Czechoslovakia's Labour Code has been extensively amended.

Under the new legislation an employer is entitled to terminate a contract of employment by two months' notice, extended to three months in certain cases. Membership of trade unions is voluntary. The power of the unions is curtailed and their role in the affairs of an enterprise or company is limited to consultation on certain matters, without decision-making powers. The right to strike exists only when negotiations for a collective agreement have broken down or if the enterprise is in breach of the agreement.

Tax reform

Much remains to be done to achieve Czechoslovakia's tax reform programme, scheduled for 1992.

Land ownership

A Land Ownership Act is planned, aimed at restoring order and certainty to Czechoslovakia's once reliable system of property law and title registration.

The environment

A proposal for a framework law at federal level is under examination and legislation is being prepared at both federal and Republic levels on air pollution, protection of water resources and a wide range of other matters. The aim is to bring Czechoslovakia's environment laws into line with EC standards.

OUTLOOK

The International Monetary Fund has set Czechoslovakia the task of creating civil and commercial legislation to European standards, adequate for the transition to a market economy. The laws adopted so far have radically changed conditions, not only for business within Czechoslovakia but also for foreigners investing and doing business in that country. But much remains to be done. The adoption of a Commercial Code and effective insolvency laws in 1991 will be an important step forward. It is, however, vital that legislation on land ownership and tax reform should not be delayed.

The momentum is there. Enough has been achieved to provide a basis to begin investigations and negotiations and – given an innovative and flexible approach and subject to suitable safeguards and guarantees – for investment. Opportunities will be lost if British companies remain on the sidelines until the legal programme is complete, while their counterparts in other countries move in.

3

Market Potential

Cerrex Ltd

This chapter provides a background to Czechoslovakia, its resources, expected priority areas under the new regime and present trade patterns with the UK. Businessmen should also examine Appendix 1 which elaborates on the prospects mentioned briefly in this chapter and looks in more depth at some 20 economic sectors.

GENERAL BACKGROUND

Czechoslovakia is situated in the heart of Europe. It has a maximum length of some 465 miles and a maximum width of about 170 miles. The country is about 40 per cent the size of Poland and one-third larger than Hungary. Land-locked, it is bordered to the north by Germany and Poland, to the east by the USSR, to the south by Hungary and Austria and to the west by Germany.

The country is made up of two separate Republics – the Czech lands of the western two-thirds of the country and Slovakia in the east. Tensions do exist between the Czechs and minority Slovaks, but are well below the explosive ethnic and regional differences apparent in many other East European countries.

Czechoslovakia's main cities are Prague (the capital), Ostrava (heavy engineering and metallurgy) and Brno, best known for engineering in the centre of the country and, in the south, Bratislava which is the capital of Slovakia. There are a number of lesser but important cities, each a major industrial area: Plzen (beer, paper and engineering); Kosice (heavy metallurgy), Ceské Budejovice (brewing), Lucenec (ceramics); Karlovy Vary (ceramics); Trinec (metallurgy); Olomouc (pharmaceuticals); Kladno (steel); Zlín (shoes); Svit (leather and textiles); Paskov and Ruzomberok (paper); Teplice (textiles and glass); Trnava (power generation); Ziar nad Hronom (aluminium); Otrokovice (tanning); Banská Bystrica (wood processing); Hlohovec, Litvinov and Sala (chemicals and pharmaceuticals); and Martin (engineering).

Geographically, there are many rivers including the Vltava on which Prague is situated, the Danube in the south of the country, the Morava which divides the country into two and the Váh in Slovakia. There are two major mountain ranges. The Bohemia highlands in the west rise to over 5250 feet. The chief feature of the south west is the Forest of Bohemia and, in the centre, the Moravian plateau. The eastern part of the country is dominated by the Carpathian mountains and the High Tatras, whereas the south is flat as it approaches the plain of the Danube.

Czechoslovakia's population (15.7 million) – some two-thirds of whom live in the Czech lands and a third in Slovakia – is less than half that of Poland, but 50 per cent larger than Hungary. Of the total, 70 per cent are estimated to be Roman Catholic and about one million Protestant. The two principal languages, Czech and Slovak, are closely related (eg *prumysl* is Czech for 'industry' and *priemysl* is Slovak), while Hungarian and Ukrainian are also spoken in some parts of Slovakia.

CZECHOSLOVAKIA'S RESOURCES

Agriculture

Some 50–60 per cent of land is used for agriculture. Chief crops have traditionally been barley, wheat, sugar, maize and fodder (in the fertile lowlands) with rye, oats and potatoes (in the highlands). A wide variety of pasture animals are reared.

Diversification took place in the early 1980s when the authorities began to encourage private fruit and vegetable cultivation and animal breeding. Agricultural has on the whole been one of the more successful sectors in Czechoslovakia. Production has risen over the past 20 years due mainly to the large amount of investment during the 1980s when it was estimated that half of all budget subsidies went into agriculture. Agricultural exports have been a considerable currency earner accounting for 7 per cent of total visible exports.

Raw materials

Czechoslovakia is one of the most heavily wooded nations in Europe with about 40 per cent of the country covered by forests. Some two-thirds of timber is coniferous (mainly spruce) and the country has developed an important pulp and furniture industry. About 25 per cent of woodlands are, however, affected by sulphur and other emissions from coal-fired power stations and this will continue to reduce the value and quality of timber that can be produced. A forest maintenance and improvement programme is continuing which will help Czechoslovakia to extend its already considerable exports of timber.

There are extensive mineral deposits of soft and hard coal mainly in northern Bohemia, west of Prague and in northern Moravia. In 1990 hard coal extraction was about 22 million tons per year, brown coal about 82 million tons (but declining) with reserves well into the next century. Iron ore deposits supply only about one-fifth of requirements. In addition there are varying deposits of graphite, copper, silver, gold and uranium and there has been a drive to mine other metals including tin, lead, refined mercury, zinc and aluminium.

Energy

Hydroelectricity constitutes a small part (about 1.5 per cent of the country's total energy supplies) with power stations on the Vltava and Váh rivers. As there are minimal oil and gas deposits, large amounts have had to be piped from the USSR (Ukraine). Much of the coal has been used for thermal power stations and the country has turned progressively towards nuclear power. Plans to reduce coal-powered stations by building new nuclear stations are sensitive because of environmental objections.

Communications

Communications expanded rapidly during the 1960s and early 1970s but then slowed down in line with economic growth patterns and in response to higher fuel prices. Emphasis has been on the provision and improvement of cheap and plentiful mass transport. Railways developed in the second half of the 19th century to join together the major cities of the Hapsburg empire.

Modern communications have been aimed at improving the transport systems in the cities and the east–west routes. Electrification of railways (especially the line to the USSR) started in the 1970s, and there are about 11,500 miles of track. Although roads are historically of good quality, there are few motorways (about 500 kilometres) and maintenance outside the cities needs to be improved to accommodate increasing private car ownership. There is a very sophisticated internal air network joining most of the major cities with regular daily services. The small proportion of the rivers that are navigable are used for both passenger and commercial traffic including the carrying of heavy products from the USSR along the Danube.

Industry

Industrial production is characterised by a wide product range, a spread of industry throughout the country and the relative neglect of consumer goods (see Tables 3.1 and 3.2). Czechoslovakia has developed a narrowly based economy with emphasis on heavy engineering, mining and certain outdated products, although it has a very skilful and well-educated workforce as well as a world-wide reputation for glass, ceramics and brewing. Iron and steel production has for many years been the second largest in Eastern Europe after the USSR, employing about one-quarter of all the workforce and responsible for some 30 per cent of total output.

Textiles, hides and skins and leather industries employ about 14 per cent of total manpower although, in terms of turnover, chemicals and metallurgy are more important. Chemicals had been

Table 3.1 *Share in total industrial production, 1988/9*	
Sector	Share (%)
Chemicals and rubber	13.5
Clothing	1.3
Construction	3.4
Electro-technical products	8.9
Food and beverages	14.1
Fuel	4.4
Glass, ceramics and porcelain	1.3
Iron metallurgy	9.0
Leather processing	2.1
Machinery	22.0
Non-ferrous metals	2.3
Paper and cellulose	1.9
Power	3.9
Printing	0.6
Textiles	4.3
Wood processing	2.9
Others	4.0
	100

Source: Czech and Slovak Federal Authorities

Table 3.2 *Employment, 1988/9*	
Sector	*Numbers employed (000s)*
Working population	8,162
Of which:	
Industry	3,051
Agricultural and forestry	961
Construction	811
Commerce	801
Transport/communications	522
Arts/education/culture	630
Health and social welfare	426
Housing/local administration	315
Science research	186
State administration and finance	162

the most dynamic sector in the 1970s but was affected by the sharp increase in oil prices. Energy, metallurgy, agricultural processing, electro-technical industry, chemicals and the wood and timber sectors each account for some 6-9 per cent of employment. Between 1985 and 1990 glass and ceramics showed increases in output and may prove to be among the most dynamic in the future.

SOME MAJOR OPPORTUNITIES

The Czechoslovak authorities have limited financial resources of their own and to achieve their aims require a mixture of substantial investment, transfer of technology, international aid and goodwill.

The main category where initial sales could be expected are where access to currency earnings locally is less important. Aid funds are concentrating on environment, energy, industry modernisation and technical know-how and budget support schemes. Also in this category are sales to Western firms wanting to set up or invest in Czechoslovakia and those industries where there has been a long history of hard currency export earnings - eg glass, textiles, beer and some engineered products. However, this category is also the most competitive - some of the most promising opportunities, for example in flat glass, motor cars, telecommunications and other sectors, have already been snapped up and parts of tourism and the service sector are likely to follow.

Czechoslovakia can be used as a centre for research or component manufacture and as a springboard for sales to other markets in

Eastern Europe and perhaps beyond (such as the Middle East and North Africa) where the UK presence has to date been small. Other activities require a major commitment by UK industry without any clear indications as to when a return may be achieved or at what level this might be. A substantial number of such opportunities are now available as many Czechoslovak firms are looking for co-operation and partners in the West to update technology, make them more competitive, and during mid-1991 several thousands of such firms will be announced as ready for foreign shareholdings and sale. The Czechoslovak authorities have identified four major priority areas for foreign assistance and investment – energy, engineering conversion, tourism and the environment.

Problem areas

The country has the dubious distinction of consuming more energy per head than the US and taking far more energy to produce a ton of steel then any of its Western neighbours. Unless an active energy conservation policy including the introduction of a more modern industrial framework and updating of power generation can be achieved, it may fail in one of its primary aims of becoming competitive in world markets. The cessation of special trade links with the USSR will mean that the fuel bill will be an increasing burden on foreign exchange earnings and the country will need to diversify its energy resources (eg via international pipelines with Austria, possibly the Middle East and North Africa and the Northern European network).

Another major area of difficulty will be the conversion of the armaments industry to civilian use. Armament production fell by 50 per cent between 1988 and the beginning of 1991. Modern equipment is already available in abundance in this and other sectors and there is a highly qualified workforce.

To achieve modernisation of its infrastructure Czechoslovakia is looking towards the telecommunications and transport sectors, including the establishment of fibre optics, a modern communications network dovetailing with Western systems, modernised railways and motorways to the western frontiers. The aim is that Czechoslovakia will become the hub of communications between East and West. Substantial resources will be put into passenger transport and large transport projects as one of the ways of developing Czechoslovakia as a European business and tourist centre.

The service sector, including tourism, is also a major area for development and is seen as an opportunity for re-employing unemployed workers from other sectors. In 1990, over 21 million people visited the country and it was estimated that in Prague alone there was a need for an additional 10,000 beds every night. Concentration has to date been on luxury developments, although the authorities see a need to move to three-star hotels, motels and other tourist accommodation, with restaurants and other tourist attractions up to Western European standards. This is not a sector which the government intends to fund or where aid funds might be deployed and therefore an injection of money by private organisations will be needed.

The sector that appears to have received most publicity has been environmental protection. This will be encouraged by government legislation and international pressure and will benefit from international aid. Water treatment is already well developed but hazardous waste and air pollution equipment is required.

Traditional industries, including glass making, ceramics, paper and wood, remain profitable and all are good export earners. In only a few of these industries is it easy to introduce modern technology, but it will be possible to apply modern energy saving techniques and to secure more efficient use of basic materials.

UK TRADE WITH CZECHOSLOVAKIA

UK trade with Czechoslovakia has been at a low level. For example, exports from the UK to Czechoslovakia are on average 15 per cent of those to Finland which has one-third of the population. During the late 1980s the level of bilateral trade barely kept pace with inflation. There is a lack of natural trade links with the country and also the fact that English has not been a major language in Czechoslovakia – until the last two years, generally German and Russian have been studied after the national languages. Czechoslovakia's trade has tended to gravitate towards the Comecon block rather than the West. Competition too from Austria and Germany has been very strong – the UK can claim only one-fifth of the level of visible exports supplied by Germany.

Latterly, attempts by the Czechoslovaks to sell exports of machinery and machine tools have not been successful, but they sell large volumes of glass, ceramics, footwear, clothing and timber to the UK, and are expected to put increasing effort into the marketing of

Table 3.3 *UK exports to Czechoslovakia by broad sector, 1988–91 (£000s)*

Sector	1988	1989	1990	Jan/Feb 1991
Office machines and automatic data processing equipment	13,298	15,359	15,413	1,322
Machinery specialised for particular industries	13,607	12,132	10,905	1,202
Professional, scientific and controlling instruments	11,693	7,906	9,108	1,106
Organic chemicals	7,315	8,206	8,939	1,106
Textile yarn, fabrics	5,917	9,045	8,683	726
General industrial machinery and equipment	4,700	5,716	7,788	N/A
Hides, skins and fur skins (raw)	6,788	8,055	7,270	1,077
Chemical materials and products	7,646	8,225	6,447	1,481
Miscellaneous manufactured articles	2,689	2,844	5,778	1,215
Plastics in primary forms	5,677	6,250	5,663	683
Total exports	130,420	131,418	133,158	17,394

Source: UK Department of Trade and Industry.

electronic parts and components. The Czechoslovaks have none the less managed to sustain a positive balance of payments with the UK over many years.

Table 3.4 *UK imports from Czechoslovakia by broad sector, 1988–91 (£000s)*

Sector	1988	1989	1990	Jan/Feb 1991
Cork and wood	22,059	23,209	19,353	1,416
Miscellaneous manufactured articles	10,720	10,298	13,613	1,451
Textile yarn, fabrics	10,450	11,098	11,645	1,909
Iron and steel	5,736	4,663	8,584	1,241
Footwear	8,082	7,933	8,289	754
Non-metallic mineral manufactures	8,314	8,663	7,475	962
Rubber manufactures	5,293	5,735	7,274	872
Road vehicles	18,683	24,299	6,328	N/A
Articles of apparel and clothing accessories	4,621	5,301	6,184	831
Furniture	5,061	4,875	5,388	1,122
Total imports	148,248	156,649	135,988	16,861

Source: UK Department of Trade and Industry.

Table 3.5 *Bilateral trade levels, 1986–90 (£m)*					
Sector	*1986*	*1987*	*1988*	*1989*	*1990*
UK exports to Czechoslovakia	108.8	114.1	130.4	131.4	133.1
UK imports from Czechoslovakia	125.4	141.5	148.2	156.6	136.0
Balance	–16.6	–27.4	–17.8	–25.2	–2.9

Source: Derived from Department of Trade and Industry figures.

Despite CoCom constraints, the UK's major exports have been office, electronic and scientific equipment and, with a gradual liberalisation in CoCom rules, it could be expected that these exports will continue to expand. Another major category has been raw materials, primary plastics and other products for further processing. Additional important growth areas will be services and sectors designated as priorities under the aid and funding arrangements such as energy saving, environmental equipment, medical goods, financial and scientific services, and transfer of technology. Although initially high, demand in the longer term for exports of consumer goods will be determined very much by the availability of foreign exchange and a continuation of the present import deposit scheme.

4

Business Culture
KPMG Peat Marwick McLintock

Czechoslovakia has a long history of entrepreneurship. Before World War II the country was the most industrially advanced in Eastern Europe and it had enjoyed almost 20 years of uninterrupted democracy. It had developed a diversified industrial base under the Austro-Hungarian Empire and, on its formation in 1918, Czechoslovakia became a major trader in Europe. In the inter-war period, the country continued to develop its heavy industries of iron, industrial machinery and coal mining, but also specialised in lighter industries such as clothing.

Since then, 40 years of centralised planning has done its best to smother the entrepreneurial spirit of the country. The Stalinist model of development was adopted which emphasised heavy industrial growth as a prerequisite of growth for the whole economy. The USSR had immense influence over the country and saw Czechoslovakia's role within Comecon as the country specialising in heavy industries.

The system did not encourage business managers to think about profitability or efficiency: with central allocation of every input necessary for production there was no incentive to innovate, especially as any improvement in efficiency went unrewarded. However, Czechoslovak managers were under pressure to increase output to make growth rates look strong which encouraged the production of goods of any quality to meet targets. Nevertheless, free enterprise is reviving as businesses return to being privately run. It will be further encouraged as price reform goes through, allowing the market to compete freely. By comparison with the other Eastern European countries Czechoslovakia is quite efficient, although the division between the Czech and the Slovak Republics means that investors must think regionally.

Amendment of the laws governing private business and foreign participation have allowed entrepreneurs to start new businesses unfettered by prohibitive requirements. Already the early results of the auctions of smaller state-owned enterprises under the Small Privatisation Act are indicating that the country's entrepreneurial spirit is not dead.

The market economy in Czechoslovakia is currently in its infancy. Under the communist regime, poor management, inadequate investment and energy inefficiency combined to make the industrial sector fairly unproductive and inefficient with respect to the West. Many of the old state enterprises which exported within Comecon countries have reduced production considerably since the reforms started, inducing redundancies and growing numbers of unemployed. Therefore, labour shortages *per se* are unlikely to constrain the nascent market economy, but there will be a considerable delay while labour is retrained to meet the demands of a market economy. Many people are involved in more than one business activity, and small businesses are growing, aided by the small privatisations.

Other factors working in favour of the market economy include the relatively cheap capital and labour costs which encourage foreign participation. The country's debt burden is not as great as that of most of the other Eastern European countries and Czechoslovakia regularly meets its debt and interest payments.

CURRENT PLAYERS

Private enterprise's share of Czechoslovak output was around 3 per cent in 1989. This is similar to that of the former GDR but lower than all other Eastern European economies. In 1989 Hungary and Poland both stood at 14.5 per cent. However, estimates of the black market suggest that the private sector share may have been more significant and that official figures may reflect state attitudes towards the private sector's activity rather than actual figures.

State enterprises

Most state-run enterprises are currently involved in the process of privatisation. In the past, they were usually monopolies with their raw material supplies, production targets and markets determined by the central planners. Management was appointed after approval by the local party officials. Workers were all represented by one national trade union which was mainly concerned with pensions and housing. As the trade union was run by the Communist Party, and strikes were illegal, it was not a trade union in the Western sense.

Now modern trade unions are slowly evolving as the structure of industry changes. Many monopolies will be split up in the large privatisations and management will have to learn to manage without central control.

The private sector

The private sector is currently in a state of some flux. After years of suppression it is finally being recognised as an important source of wealth creation. However, Czechoslovaks lack experience of the free market and business decisions are generally not made as quickly as in the Western business environment.

The government is similarly cautious. It will not be rushed into finalising legislation until it has been thoroughly researched and debated. There is the added problem posed by the federal structure of the country which means that regulations can differ between the Czech and Slovak Republics. Business deals may require complex negotiations with federal and republic governments or industry representatives and this may be frustrating for firms wishing to move quickly. Overall, however, the legal conditions are now virtually fulfilled to allow the creation of a private sector. The problems arise as a result of management inexperience and a lack of investment funds.

FOREIGN INVOLVEMENT

Joint ventures are being registered in Czechoslovakia at a rapid pace. With large privatisation now scheduled to come on stream at the end of 1991 or early 1992, foreign investment should increase dramatically as the government expects such investment to play a significant role in most of the large privatisations. Joint ventures are possible with private Czechoslovak companies and privatised state enterprises, and new legislation permits up to 100 per cent foreign ownership. Joint ventures with state companies before privatisation are only possible when a dispensation is granted by the government. There is no restriction on the form or extent of investment for foreign firms. Firms can enter licensing agreements, purchase shares in joint stock companies and take part in training pro-grammes and exchanges.

The process of setting up a joint venture involves:

- a total initial investment of at least Kčs100,000;

- development of a company charter; and

- registration with the Federal Ministry of Finance.

Generally, new enterprises will need modern technology, management assistance and capital from foreign firms. So far, most of the joint ventures have been in the Czech Republic, 80 per cent of the capital has come from the foreign partner and most ventures have involved one-person enterprises with commitments of less than Kčs500,000.

Investment opportunities exist in nearly all sectors of the economy. The Agency for Foreign Investment, the Association of Entrepreneurs and several local consultancies can assist companies to find suitable joint venture partners. Foreign firms are attracted to Czechoslovakia by the country's extensive experience of operating in other former communist countries. As the country is ideally situated for both East and West European markets it is seen as a good place to invest for access to the growing markets in the East. Prague is seen as a business centre and, with several Western banks and many consulting firms setting up there, this creates a favourable climate for investment. There are also a number of substantial regional industrial centres which are increasing in importance.

The Commercial Section of the US Embassy in Prague lists 30 products or services which are the most immediately required by the country. These are: pollution control equipment; computers and peripherals; computer software and services; telecommunications equipment and services; information services; education and manpower training services; management consulting services; financial services; travel and tourism services; aircraft and parts; avionics and ground support equipment; medical equipment; building products; accounting services; drugs and pharmaceuticals; railroad equipment; food processing and packaging equipment; hotel and restaurant equipment; air conditioning and refrigeration equipment; employment services; industrial process controls; mining industry equipment; insurance services; scientific laboratory instrumentation; franchising; materials handling machinery; advertising services; textile machinery and equipment; and agricultural services.

MANAGEMENT CULTURE

Many Czechoslovak companies are short of modern equipment and most lack the financial capital to improve the situation. Therefore many businessmen are very keen to do business with Western companies. However, the business ethics of the country are very different from those of the UK and a lot of misunderstanding can be avoided if it is understood that decisions take some time and that it is very unusual to complete a business deal before many meetings and several months have expired. Initial contacts between a foreign company and a Czechoslovak one should be broad, encompassing several levels of management: the Czechoslovaks place great weight on personal contact. It is important to balance negotiations with both federal and regional government and to establish that interest in the country is long term and not, as some Czechoslovaks fear, merely a quick profit-making exploit. Besides, it is unlikely that a reasonable return on investment will be seen for several years.

5

Market Intelligence

KPMG Peat Marwick McLintock

Market intelligence on Czechoslovakia is not readily available. What data there is quickly becomes outdated because the political and economic reforms are changing the market situation so rapidly. Some of the sources of information available to UK firms considering an approach to the Czechoslovak market are discussed in this chapter which covers statistical information, trade fair information, market research and surveys and various other useful sources.

SOURCES OF STATISTICS

The statistics produced by the Czechoslovak authorities are contained in *Statisticka Rocenka*, the statistical yearbook, which has been produced annually since the 1950s. The latest edition of this book was published in 1990 and gives annual data from as far back as 1937 (in some cases) up to 1989. Its contents range from the national income growth rates to categories which are unknown to Western statisticians, such as internal trade by sector and investment in infrastructure by type of input. The book itself is a vast collection of data on Czechoslovakia. The main categories are the following: national income growth; geographical and climatic data; environmental facts; population; various macroeconomic variables; state budget data; labour statistics; prices; sectoral outputs; trade figures; standard of living statistics; education and health statistics; and international comparisons.

The data contained in the yearbook is in Czechoslovak – an English translation is not available – and the figures themselves are rather misleading. It must be remembered that they have been prepared as part of a centrally planned economy and are a reflection of such a system. The detailed price indices do not represent market prices as the current price data reflects price setting by the authorities. For example, in recent years statistics for tonnage and growth may be accurate in terms of what they are actually measuring, but the products represented are not directly comparable. The collation of the data also creates problems. In comparison with Western figures, Eastern European national income:

■ includes intermediate production in final output figures (double counting); excludes non-productive services such as education and health;

■ does not fully account for official price increases to allow for quality improvements; and

■ deducts depreciation from gross fixed capital formation.

Future statistics are going to be produced on a different basis, more in line with the EC, so there will be a lack of continuity in comparing current with past data once the next statistics book is published. The publication date is not yet known.

More recent statistics are estimated by organisations such as the Economist Intelligence Unit and PlanEcon in the United States. These organisations also forecast the main macroeconomic variables for several years hence. Over time the statistics available should become more reliable and the forecasts more accurate.

There are other ways of obtaining current information on particular market sectors. These include attending trade fairs in the country, and commissioning market research and market surveys.

TRADE FAIRS

Trade fairs are held in several cities in Czechoslovakia, with most taking place in Brno, South Moravia, which saw around 5500 exhibitors from more than 50 countries presenting to some one million people in 1990. A comprehensive list can be found in the *Exhibition Bulletin,* a monthly publication which lists exhibitions world-wide up to a year in advance. The John Hague Exhibition Service deals with the major trade fairs and is very helpful in providing advice and information. The fairs are also publicised in the relevant trade journals and Eastern European magazines. Their themes range from tourism, through engineering to dog shows. Eleven exhibitions have been planned for Brno in 1991.

MARKET RESEARCH AND SURVEYS

Market research is, as yet, limited in Czechoslovakia. Several companies have set up some market research capability, but none are as yet market research companies on a Western European scale. In the past all research has been conducted by state-owned research institutions on a planned basis. Currently the Ministry for Science and Investment co-ordinates all research, but each ministry has its own research institute. One way for foreigners to approach the problem would be through Gallup, MAI, or the trade directory, *Esomar*, according to the information required.

A firm which offers market research as part of its services is Ecoma, a state-run organisation set up in 1989, which is about to be privatised. It is primarily a market survey and public polling organisation and co-operates with foreign companies such as Gallup, but more frequently other Comecon companies. The British Embassy in Prague will conduct small surveys in response to enquiries. International marketing firms such as Saatchi & Saatchi are setting up in Czechoslovakia.

INFORMATION SOURCES

In the UK

The best point of first contact for any firm interested in getting involved in Czechoslovakia is the Department of Trade and Industry in London. The Czechoslovak desk will send out a *Country Profile* which encompasses a map, political and economic background, information on UK/Czechoslovak trade, business tips, legislation, financial information, statistics on trade and a comprehensive list of other published information and useful contacts. The DTI also organises trade missions.

The DTI appoints an advisory body, the East European Trade Council, to advise on trading and trade opportunities. This independent, grant-aided group provides advice to businessmen and stocks a large number of journals and other publications on Eastern Europe in its library. The literature ranges from regular journals such as *Business Eastern Europe* and *PlanEcon*, to smaller publications such as the Czechoslovak Chamber of Commerce's (CCC) *Economic Digest*. The library also contains the most up-to-date versions of books such as the CCC's *Your Trade Partners in Czechoslovakia*, DTI *Country Profiles* and various product catalogues. It maintains a book of press cuttings, a monthly update of the *Economic Supplement* from the British Embassy in Prague, product files, foreign trade organisation lists, market research information and offers of contracts and joint ventures from enterprises in Czechoslovakia. To use the library, which is very compact, it is necessary to telephone for a booking.

Another approach should be through the Chambers of Commerce network, particularly the London Chamber of Commerce's Eastern European Desk. They can provide members and non-members with advice and information. They carry out their own trade missions, hold conferences and seminars which non-members may attend, keep updated copies of trade directories and receive information from the British Embassy in Prague. They publish their current activities and events in Eastern European markets in their magazine *London Commerce*. Their Czechoslovakia Committee, which comprises businessmen who spend a lot of time in the country, is able to give advice on the current market situation and trading practices. The London Chamber also has an Exhibitions Section which organises occasional trips to Czechoslovakia. The Birmingham Chamber of Commerce can also help directly with useful information on Eastern Europe. Through Chambers of Commerce or trade directories it should be possible to identify businesses which have traded similar products with Czechoslovakia and, provided they are not rival competitors, they should be willing to discuss their experiences.

EC databases – BC-NET and BRE – have particulars of companies wishing to trade with Czechoslovakia and also contain details of Czechoslovak companies wishing to trade with EC companies.

There are many other sources of information in the UK. These include the following:

- The Czechoslovak Embassy in London has a Commercial Section which will provide a limited amount of advice to firms interested in doing business in Czechoslovakia, on subjects such as import duties.

- The Department of Trade's Export Market Information Centre has trade statistics and trade directories and keeps a product database.

- The British International Freight Association gives advice on the transit of goods and documentation.

- Customs and Excise which is the authority on UK customs and tariffs.

- The Export Credits Guarantee Department advises on credit insurance for exports.

- The Export Intelligence Service sends computerised intelligence of trading opportunities and market pointers to subscribers.

- The Law Society can provide details of solicitors practising in Czechoslovakia.

- The Ministry of Agriculture gives advice on trade in agricultural products and machinery.

- The Simpler Trade Procedures Board (SITPRO) can advise on documentation requirements.

- Technical Help to Exporters gives information and advice on legal and technical requirements, regulations and standards.

- The Know-How Fund for Eastern Europe, the Overseas Development Agency and the Foreign and Commonwealth Office are also good sources of information.

In Czechoslovakia

In Czechoslovakia there are several sources of information. The major ones are the British Embassy in Prague and the Czechoslovak Chamber of Commerce and Industry.

The British Embassy in Prague

The Commercial Section of the Embassy is housed in a different building to the rest of the Embassy, close to the centre of Prague. The Embassy staff are well informed on the current situation in the country and produce monthly round-ups of information which are sent back to the DTI in London. They have a card index of useful contacts and, while initial advice is normally free, enquiries that require more detailed research such as obtaining product catalogues and information on firm size and turnover are charged for under the DTI service card scheme at rates ranging between £30 and £180. The Commercial Section is not responsible for making appointments to meet contacts.

It is advisable to contact the Commercial Section before arriving in Prague and to arrange an appointment at the beginning of the visit. It is also advisable to brief them in as much detail as possible on objectives and the various options available to achieve them. The more specific and detailed the briefing, the more effective the help that they will be able to provide.

The Czechoslovak Chamber of Commerce and Industry

The CCC's membership has increased dramatically over the last year and it is decentralising with the aim of becoming a regional organisation. The Prague office will continue to be a useful source of information. The CCC has a customs division, a legal and consulting division, an information division, a publishing division and a foreign relations division. It also produces a number of publications that provide contact names and addresses of businesses in particular industries. The *Czechoslovak Enterprises Directory* is published in English, German and French, and gives the names and addresses of companies divided alphabetically by industry group. The CCC has also launched a computerised database of Czechoslovak companies which will go further than the *Enterprises Directory* and include details of a company's assets.

Further sources of information include three Czechoslovak journals – *Economic Daily, Profit Weekly* and *TOP Weekly* – which give business information. The Agency for Foreign Investment (part of the Ministry for Economic Policy and Development of the Czech Republic) gives information on the current state of the economy and legislative changes and has a database of potential Czech candidates for joint ventures. Each of these companies is profiled by financial information, capacity, number of employees and related data. However this database is being constantly superseded by events which may have a major impact on a company in the short term. The Ministry will supply contacts and direct enquiries to relevant product catalogues and to EC-produced market research on such broadly based categories as infrastructure, services and banking. In response to an enquiry from a potential foreign investor the Ministry will compile a profile of companies, updated to take into account the most recent events. There are likely to be several offers for any joint venture proposal and firms are advised to use experienced consultants to help choose the best offer. The Slovak Republic also has a similar agency. The Institute of Management in Prague is able to give assistance with any queries about management skills and availability. It is involved in the improvement of knowledge of management skills through personnel training.

6

Czechoslovakia and its Trading Partners

National Westminster Bank and SJ Berwin & Co

RELATIONS WITH EASTERN EUROPE

The dramatic political and economic changes evident throughout Eastern Europe have had a significant impact on relations between the East European countries, with much of intra-East European trade now collapsing. As with other former communist countries, Czechoslovakia's foreign trade has traditionally fallen into two categories:

1. Trade in convertible currencies with non-communist countries outside the Comecon region. The Czechoslovaks, in an endeavour to obtain hard currency, have in the past directed better quality production to these markets. However, by Western standards even these goods were often uncompetitive and were sold instead to developing countries financed by trade credits.

2. The bulk of Czechoslovakia's trade has traditionally been in non-convertible currencies, mainly with fellow Comecon countries, but also with non-socialist developing countries under bilateral agreements.

Table 6.1 *Exports to other Comecon countries, 1989 (% of total)*

Bulgaria	83
Czechoslovakia	56
Soviet Union	46
GDR	43
Romania	41
Hungary	40
Poland	35

Non-convertible currency trading has formed a comfortable majority of Czechoslovakia's trade in recent years, but it was highly inefficient. Comecon was never intended to be a large free market on the EC model; rather it was originally intended to be a conduit for trade between East European countries and the Soviet Union. Trade was bilateral and included no effective means of offsetting surpluses with one country with deficits with another. Furthermore, trade was denominated in inappropriately named 'transferable roubles' so that prices bore no sensible relationship to the cost of production or to world market prices. This failure to link costs with prices led to great inefficiencies and distortions, the removal of which is at the core of the economic reform programmes.

The withdrawal of Soviet domination of Eastern Europe has sharply reduced pressures to continue intra-Comecon trade, which has further declined as political and economic pressures throughout the region have brought the cancellation of many long standing trading agreements. Furthermore, supplies of raw materials from the Soviet Union, especially but not exclusively oil, which have in the past been delivered at preferential rates well below free market prices, were expected to have to be paid for in convertible currency from the beginning of 1991. This change of Soviet policy is still largely extant, though there are signs that it could be modified in exchange for a degree of political support.

The extra costs of energy imports to all Eastern European countries are a significant burden to the balance of payments and will add further impetus to changes in the direction of trade. Czechoslovakia has already substantially reduced its trade with the Comecon region as shown in Table 6.2. This trend will now accelerate, particularly if accommodations can be reached with the EC for complete access to the wider European market.

Table 6.2 *Geographic distribution of trade (% share)*

	1985	1989	1990
Non-socialist	35	39	48
Industrial West	26	31	40
Socialist	65	61	52
Comecon	57	56	46
(of which USSR)	(35)	(31)	(25)
Total	100	100	100

There are, however, good reasons why intra-Comecon trade will not disappear altogether. Much of Eastern Europe's stock of physical

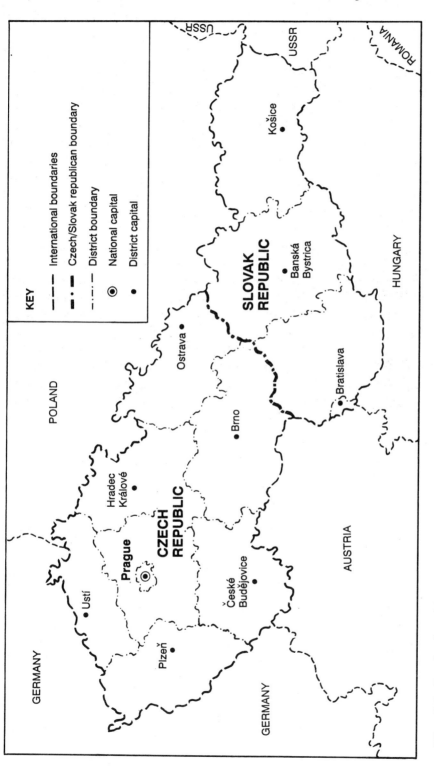

Map 6.1 *Czechoslovakia and its neighbours*

assets, particularly those of the Soviet Union, are manufactured to unique standards which are not easily replicable in the West. Secondly, given the extent of past trade and the current reliance on Soviet markets, many East European countries will be reluctant to shut down industries dedicated to supplying the Soviets because of the social costs involved. As long as these factories generate some tangible earnings, possibly on a barter basis, it may well prove better in the short term for production to continue. Thirdly, while industry and consumers alike have a large appetite for Western goods, the lack of convertible currencies will inevitably slow the rate at which purchases from the West can expand.

Over the medium to long term, therefore, the likely course of events is that trade between East European countries will quickly collapse to a basic level of raw material trade, buttressed by bilateral agreements to continue the supply of goods manufactured to East European standards, the replacement of which is not easily possible in the West. Thereafter, as economies reform and move fully into convertible currency trading, intra-East European trading should begin to recover as a natural result of physical proximity. The speed with which this trade recovers depends on the rapidity with which economic reform is embraced, with countries quickest to reform being those most likely to succeed in a new trading environment. On this basis, Czechoslovakia ought to be in the forefront of any recovery in East European trade.

RELATIONS WITH THE EUROPEAN COMMUNITY

The remainder of this chapter is about the dramatic change in Czechoslovakia's relations with the EC and reviews the Association Agreements currently being negotiated with Czechoslovakia, Hungary and Poland.

Relations with the EC: a new direction

In seeking aid from the 'Group of 24' donor countries of the Organisation for Economic Co-operation and Development (OECD), Czechoslovakia's provisional government declared its policy to 'return to Europe where they have always belonged geographically, and civilisationally, as well as spiritually'. With the decay of the Warsaw Pact and Comecon, it was inevitable that Czechoslovakia and the other countries of Central and Eastern Europe should turn to the EC as their future partner, offering political stability, financial aid in rebuilding their economies and a market of 320 million people for their goods and services. The Community responded with equal enthusiasm to this unique opportunity to achieve the reintegration of Europe.

The EC's response was two-fold. The first was to provide funds for specific aid programmes to lay the foundations for a market economy with emphasis on training, privatisation and improvement of the environment. Details of grants through the PHARE programme and other sources of financial assistance are reviewed in a later chapter of this book.

Secondly, the EC opened negotiations for Association Agreements with Czechoslovakia, Hungary and Poland, regarded as the most firmly committed to democracy and the return to a market economy. The new agreements will be of a different order from the existing Trade and Co-operation Agreements entered into with these countries in 1988. They will be designed to build an entirely new economic and political relationship comprising:

- an institutional framework for an ongoing political relationship;

- a free trade area, to be introduced over ten years;

- extensive economic, social and cultural co-operation; and

- a framework for future financial assistance.

It was decided to opt for a free trade zone as opposed to a customs union as the latter would have entailed the creation of a common external tariff and the adoption of much Community legislation as well as other necessary political measures.

However, it is the declared aim of Czechoslovakia, Hungary and Poland (the Associated Countries) to become full members of the EC, though it is premature for either side to make any commitment to full membership. The present EC member states are determined not to destroy the cohesion of the Community by premature expansion. Having regard to the problems of absorbing the European Free Trade Area (EFTA) countries, the admission of the Associated Countries is unlikely to be feasible before the end of the century. However, after initial resistance, the EC negotiators have agreed that the preamble to the Association Agreements will refer to full membership as an ultimate, but not automatic goal.

Association Agreement structure and institutional framework

The EC Council of Ministers gave the Commission a mandate to negotiate the Association Agreements with the Associated Countries on 18 December 1990 and negotiations started immediately in that month.

The legal basis for the agreements is Article 238 of the Treaty of Rome, under which such agreements require the assent of an absolute majority of the members of the European Parliament and a unanimous vote of the EC Council of Ministers. The agreements will have a common framework but are being negotiated separately and will be adapted in detail to the particular needs and priorities of each country.

The institutional framework, a key feature of each Association Agreement, will consist of:

- an Association Council;

- an Association Committee; and

- a Parliamentary Association Committee.

The Association Council, the highest political body, will supervise implementation of the agreement and will meet periodically at ministerial level. It will be a forum for dialogue on major issues and broader international questions and for settling disputes. It may establish subsidiary bodies for particular aspects of co-operation.

The Association Committee will consist of senior officials. Its task will be to prepare the work of the Association Council and deal with administrative and technical matters. The Parliamentary Association Committee will enable members of the European and national parliaments to meet regularly and make recommendations to the Association Council.

Free movement of goods

A free trade area will gradually be established over a period of ten years, on the basis of reciprocal and balanced obligations and with due regard to the General Agreement on Tariffs and Trade ('GATT'). The Community will move more rapidly towards free trade than the Associated Countries, thus assisting their economic recovery.

Over this period, trade between the parties will benefit from the gradual removal of customs duties and of charges and quantitative restrictions and other measures which obstruct the free movement of goods. Paradoxically, the Associated Countries must first *erect* trade barriers to take the place of the state control of foreign trade and foreign exchange which formerly protected their markets. The USA is concerned about the prospect of overall tariff increases, followed by reductions over ten years which will selectively benefit the EC. The solution will have to be found within the context of the GATT negotiations.

Trade in industrial, agricultural and fishery products
Liberalisation of trade in industrial products will take place in two broad phases, each lasting, in principle, for five years. It was originally proposed that the passage to the second phase would be reviewed, having regard to the Associated Countries' economic situations and the progress of reform. However this condition has been abandoned.

As regards trade in agricultural and fishery products, basically the EC will continue to protect its markets under its Common Agricultural and Fisheries Policies subject, of course, to the outcome of the GATT negotiations. However, special concessions to promote trade in these products with the Associated Countries are being negotiated individually.

Special arrangements are also being negotiated for textiles, steel and processed agricultural products, in view of EC sensitivities in these areas.

Back-up provisions
There will be back-up provisions regarding 'stand-still' (no new trade barriers), anti-dumping, safeguard (emergency) measures, competition and state aids and rules of origin. The EC recognises that the Associated Countries will need time before their systems of state aids and subsidies to industry can be dismantled.

Free movement of workers, services and capital
Due to the fear of a mass migration from Eastern Europe, the EC is adopting a cautious stance. The ultimate goal of eventual free movement of workers is acknowledged but without any commitment to a timetable. During the first five years the EC will concentrate on improving the situation of workers from the Associated Countries already legally employed in EC member states. Further improvements will be considered later.

Concerning free movement of services and capital, here again there will be a phased approach. The Associated Countries will be given time to adapt to EC rules as their market economies develop and strengthen.

Economic co-operation
The Association Agreements will provide for co-operation in many areas, including industrial co-operation with a view to achieving

conformity of standards and certifications; investment promotion and protection; and co-operation in science and technology, education and training, agriculture, energy, environment, transport, telecommunications, health and safety, tourism and related services, customs, statistics, economics, regional development and culture. The agreements will also provide the framework for future EC financial assistance, superseding the PHARE programme at the end of 1992.

Some key issues

Approximation of laws

For the EC, it is an 'essential precondition' that the laws of the Associated Countries must be made compatible with those of the EC. Particular areas mentioned in the Commission's mandate are company law, company accounts and taxes, intellectual property, health and safety of workers, financial services, competition rules, consumer protection, indirect taxation, technical rules and standards, transport and the environment.

For the EC member states the 'harmonisation' of laws required by the Treaty has proved immensely slow and difficult: the drive for a single market at the end of 1992 has only been made possible by adopting the principles of majority voting and the mutual recognition of laws which are equivalent though not identical. But, on the other hand, as the Associated Countries are having to rewrite their entire commercial legislation, it is easier for them to make their new laws conform to EC standards. Czechoslovakia's new law on competition and its proposals for the environment are good examples.

State aids and anti-dumping

It is a vexed question for how long and in what form the Associated Countries will be allowed to subsidise their industries. The Association Agreements will recognise that the transition will have to be gradual. This is relevant to the nature of the anti-dumping measures which will apply to protect the EC against unrealistically costed goods while these measures continue. The Associated Countries would like to see the immediate application of the more lenient anti-dumping regime for market economy countries while the EC wishes to retain the strict regime for countries with planned economies. A 'tailor made' compromise is likely.

Financial assistance

Operation PHARE will be the main channel through which EC

financial support will be provided to Associated Countries until the end of 1992. Thereafter, the Community envisages that the amount and nature of further assistance should be decided on within the framework of each Association Agreement – scaling down grants as soon as economic progress allows.

The Associated Countries, on the other hand, are seeking a commitment to provide finance over at least five years. They also want a bigger say in the allocation of funds.

The future

A solid European foundation is being laid for Czechoslovakia's emerging market economy, which has every prospect of flourishing in an extended single European market. Business people contemplating a direct investment or joint venture in Czechoslovakia will be reassured by this prospect, irrespective of whether Czechoslovakia's association with the EC ripens into full membership.

Part II

The Business Infrastructure

7
The Legal Framework
SJ Berwin & Co

LEGAL SYSTEM

Czechoslovak law is based on the continental civil law system and is therefore predominantly codified. The roots of the Czech system can be found in Austrian law and the Slovak system in Hungarian law. Each system developed separately until 1918 and the Czech system was codified whereas the Hungarian system, upon which the Slovak system was based, was built more on case law precedent. The two systems maintained their national status after 1918, although there was a movement to unification between 1919 and 1938 which was largely, although not totally, achieved.

The Czechoslovak Civil Code contains provisions regulating the relationships and activities of individuals. The law regulating relationships and activities in the course of business is currently contained in the Economic Code. The provisions of the Economic Code, brought into force during the socialist republic, are intended to govern relationships between state-owned enterprises and individuals. There have been recent amendments to the Economic Code so as to enable the transition to a market economy. There is also currently a draft of a Commercial Code (expected to come into force during 1991) which will contain comprehensive provisions regulating business transactions and replace the Economic Code.

All this creates difficulties for the business person in that during the period of transition to a market economy the law is a collection of socialist principles and *ad hoc* amendments and is continually being modified. Nevertheless, one aspect is certain and that is the constitutional laws which declare basic human and economic rights. The provisions of other legislation cannot be contrary to these fundamental rights; if they are, for example because they have not yet been amended, they cannot be applied by the courts which are strictly bound by the constitutional laws.

The structure of the Czechoslovak codes (whether Civil, Economic or Commercial) is important. They contain two types of provisions, mandatory and dispositive (distinguished by the use of the words 'shall' or 'may'). Every term which is contrary to the mandatory rules is either null and void or unenforceable depending upon the provisions of the code itself. Dispositive rules will provide the terms for a contract if the parties do not agree otherwise. This means in commercial transactions that every undesirable or impractical dispositive rule must be clearly and expressly excluded or substituted by an appropriate contractual term; otherwise it will apply.

THE CONSTITUTION

The Constitution and constitutional laws have a predominant position in the hierarchy of the Czechoslovak legal system. At present, the situation is rather complicated and in transition in that the 1960 Constitution and the major Constitutional Law of the Czechoslovak Federation of 1968 are still in force although substantially amended by legislation adopted by the newly democratically elected parliament. The President is proposing a new Constitution embodying these changes. The provisions of the Constitution and constitutional laws are entrenched, in that amendments require a three-fifths majority of both Slovak and Czech deputies in the federal parliament.

Czechoslovakia has a federal form of government with a federal parliament and a legislature for each of the Czech and Slovak Republics (the Czech and Slovak National Councils). The Constitution states the basic division of competence between the federal state and the two Republics. Apart from the division of competence between the federal parliament and the Republics, the Constitution also sets down the rights to be accorded to individuals.

The federal parliament consisting of 200 deputies is directly elected. The current length of a parliament is 24 months, but a proposal of the current President will extend the period to 4 years. The parliament elects the President who holds office for 5 years, while the Prime Minister and members of the government are appointed and dismissed by the President. There is no requirement for the Prime Minister and members of the government to be members of parliament. The members of the government appoint a 'Presidium' (or Cabinet) from among themselves which co-ordinates government policy. There are two houses within the parliament, one made up of elected representatives on a territorial basis (and there is therefore an imbalance between Czech and Slovak deputies) and the other on a parity basis. To be passed, a law requires a majority of both houses. Once a law has been passed by parliament it comes into force after signature by the President. Prior to such signature, it can be ruled as being unconstitutional by the recently established Constitutional Court. Otherwise, the civil courts merely interpret legislation.

THE RELATIONSHIP OF FEDERAL AND REPUBLIC AUTHORITIES

There are certain areas of policy within the exclusive competence of the federal parliament, other areas in which both the federal parliament and the Republics have shared competence and areas which are totally within the competence of the Republics.

The areas of exclusive competence of the federal parliament are:

- foreign affairs;

- defence and protection of frontiers;

- currency;

- customs;

- federal reserves;

- the federal budget;

- nuclear security;

- protection of the Constitution; and

- fulfilment of international commitments.

The implementation and administration (but not legislative competence) of any of these may be delegated to the Republics.

The areas of shared competence (that is where the federal parliament is primarily competent but in which the Republics may be charged with the implementation by passing secondary legislation such as decrees, ordinances and regulations) are:

- economic strategy;

- taxes and duties;

- the rules relating to the budget;

- legal status of the Czechoslovak State Bank and the regulation of commercial banks;

- prices;

- foreign economic relations;

- production, distribution and consumption of electricity, gas and heating;

- traffic;

- post and telecommunications;

- major environmental questions;

- employment;

- levels of remuneration;

- social security, health and pensions;

- property of enterprises, individuals and other legal persons;

- internal public order and security;

- press and media; and

- control activities.

All other matters are within the exclusive competence of the Republics including industry, agriculture, building and construction, forestry and water, domestic trade and tourism, education, culture, health and justice.

The structure of ministries and other organs of state administration in Czechoslovakia is based on the practical application of the constitutional principles of division of competence between the federal state and the Republics. Some ministries exist only at federal level (in areas of exclusive federal competence), some exist only in both Republics (in areas of exclusive competence of the Republics) and some exist in both the two Republics and the federal state (in the areas of shared competence of the federal state and the Republics).

State enterprises, responsible for production in a centrally planned economy, are controlled by a founding ministry which exercises broadly similar functions to a shareholder. Ministries, therefore, have a much more direct role in the economic life of Czechoslovakia than in Western countries and will continue to do so until the completion of the government's privatisation programme.

LEGISLATIVE PROCESS

A legislative proposal can be submitted to the federal parliament only by bodies authorised by the current Constitution. These are:

- the federal government;

- the Czech National Council;

- the Slovak National Council;

- the committees of the houses of parliament; and

- the President.

The proposer of the legislation submits the written proposal, including the full text of the proposed law and the reasons for it, to the President of the federal parliament, who arranges for it to be considered by standing committees and ultimately to be debated in each house. The President of the federal parliament sends the proposal to each of the two houses of parliament, to the government and other relevant organs of state administration and to the Czech and Slovak National Councils. Unless the Czech and Slovak National Councils have proposed the law themselves they are able to make representations in relation to it.

More than 90 per cent of legislative proposals are initiated by the government. Whether the federal government or the government of one of the Republics is the proposer depends upon the subject matter of the legislation and whether the legislative competence in the matter belongs to the Republic or the federal state. A federal proposal initiates from the relevant ministry or other organs of administration. The ministry undertakes a consultation exercise involving other ministries and departments and it then passes on the proposal to the government's legislative council where the principles of the legislation and detailed wording of the text are worked out. The law is then submitted to the President of the federal parliament.

One practical problem for parliament is that often two or even three entirely different proposals on the same matter are submitted at the same time which makes it extremely difficult to predict the form in which the legislation is to emerge. Bearing in mind the complexity of the legislative process it is remarkable how much legislation has been passed since the elections in June 1990.

Local government

Local government is competent to pass legislation for its territory if it is given the power to do so by legislation. The *obec* or municipality is a legal entity which can own property. It is a body comprised of citizens who take decisions in meetings of the municipality, by referendum or through elected representatives of the municipality.

The government of each Republic manages and controls the activities of the municipality in relation to the administration of matters concerning the Republic. Otherwise the municipality is independent.

THE COURTS

The Constitutional Court

As mentioned previously, recent legislation has established the Constitutional Court to ensure conformity with the Constitution and constitutional laws, the protection of human rights and the resolution of disputes of competence between the federal state and the Republics.

The civil courts

The court system comprises the Supreme Court of Czechoslovakia, the Supreme Court of the Czech Republic, the Supreme Court of the Slovak Republic and local courts at two levels – regional and district.

The Federal Supreme Court decides appeals against the decisions of the Supreme Court of the Republics, examines the legality of decisions of federal organs, interprets federal laws and other laws, enforces decisions of foreign courts, and adjudicates on competence disputes between courts and state notaries. The judgments of the Federal Supreme Court, if acting as a court of appeal, are binding on the lower courts. The Supreme Courts of the Republics decide on appeals against decisions of local courts.

The judiciary is composed of professional judges and lay assessors. Judges in Czechoslovakia are career judges, moving straight into their training after completion of their legal education. They are independent of parliament and government but are subject to the rule of law. The President of the Federal Supreme Court and other judges are nominated by the President.

Until the new Commercial Courts are established there are no courts to deal with commercial disputes. Generally, the relative inexperience of the judiciary in Czechoslovakia will make the courts an uncertain place in which to try disputes, even after the new system of Commercial Courts has been established, until a body of experience has been built up.

State arbitration

The pre-revolution legal system contained the concept of state arbitration to adjudicate upon disputes between the state and enterprises and between state enterprises. This system is totally unsuited to dealing with disputes on commercial matters and is expected to be abolished during 1991. At present the competence of the organs of arbitration is extended by post-revolutionary amendments to include cases where private entrepreneurs and private commercial companies are involved.

Cases where foreign partners are involved can be decided by the Court of Arbitration of the Czechoslovak Chamber of Commerce and Industry. It will apply only if the parties agree in advance on this means of settling their disputes, or where such resolution is included in international bilateral agreements. Although the Court of Arbitration is part of the Czechoslovak Chamber of Commerce and Industry, it is entirely separate from the system of state arbitration.

8

Foreign Investment

SJ Berwin & Co

Even though the command economy is in the process of being dismantled, doing business in Czechoslovakia still involves many dealings with bureaucracy at government and local level. But the business person will be pleasantly surprised to find that the *establishment* of a company or other business entity is now no more difficult than it is in any other European country.

Any type of company or partnership available to Czechoslovak residents can now be used. No official authorisation is normally required, whether the foreign party chooses to form a wholly-owned subsidiary or a joint venture with Czechoslovak individuals or a company which they control. Privatisation has put a brake on joint ventures with state enterprises, which have to be approved at government level unless they form part of an agreed privatisation project. But foreign companies and individuals are now free, as they have not been for many decades, to set themselves up in Czechoslovakia and to establish links with its new class of entrepreneurs.

This chapter will explain the legal framework for foreign investment and joint ventures and will touch on key issues, some of which are dealt with in more detail in other chapters. These are:

- what authority is needed to invest;
- the form of foreign participation;
- the acquisition of Czechoslovak assets;
- employment law;
- auditors and accounts;
- reserve fund;

- investment protection;

- customs-free zones;

- dispute resolution; and

- negotiating joint ventures.

THE FRAMEWORK FOR FOREIGN INVESTMENT

Foreigners investing in Czechoslovakia do so within the framework of the pre-1989 joint venture law. Inspired by *perestroika*, its purpose was to create capitalist islands in the Marxist ocean, to entice Western companies to bring their capital and expertise to joint ventures with Czechoslovak enterprises.

The original joint venture law, adopted in 1985, did not allow foreign parties to hold a majority interest. It was replaced in 1988 by the Enterprise with Foreign Property Participation Act (173/1988) – often known as the Joint Venture Act (JVA) – which allowed foreigners to control joint ventures but still insisted on a token, although unspecified Czechoslovak shareholding. This requirement was abandoned by an amendment to the law in April 1990 which allowed 100 per cent foreign ownership and made other important changes. Further relaxations were introduced in 1991 by government decree.

Enterprises involving foreign ownership, whether they are wholly-owned foreign subsidiaries or joint ventures, are still classified as a separate category from those in which there is only Czechoslovak participation. Now that private enterprise is legal, the distinction has become redundant. In due course, the JVA will no doubt be given a decent burial but, in the meantime, it continues to be the framework for foreign investment.

An 'enterprise with foreign property participation' has a wider meaning than that of a joint stock company. It is a body, whether incorporated or unincorporated, carrying on business and with its registered office in Czechoslovakia, which a foreign party wholly or partly owns – whether it acquires its interest at the time of formation or by a later purchase. For ease of reference, all such entities will be referred to in this chapter as Foreign Property Companies, or FPCs. A 'foreign party' is a corporation with its registered office, or an individual whose permanent residence, is outside Czechoslovakia. 'Czechoslovak party' has the opposite meaning.

Main features of FPCs

An FPC has the following features:

- It can be wholly-foreign owned.

- There are no minimum requirements for Czechoslovak representation in the management.

- The Czechoslovak party may be an individual registered as an entrepreneur or a corporate body.

- An FPC is a Czechoslovak company for all purposes, even if it is wholly-foreign owned. For example, it is not affected by the rule which prevents foreigners buying land in Czechoslovakia.

- As a Czechoslovak company, an FPC is subject to the foreign exchange internal convertibility rules. It must therefore sell all its foreign exchange balances to a Czechoslovak bank and is entitled to purchase foreign currency for all its commercial requirements.

- The foreign party's profit share can be converted into hard currency and transferred abroad: this is covered by the internal convertibility system.

Following the changes in company law which came into force on 1 May 1990, an FPC may be established in any of the legal forms open to Czechoslovak residents. The forms now available are as follows:

- joint stock company (*Akciova spolecnost*);

- private company limited by shares (*Spolecnost s rucenim omezenym*);

- general commercial partnership (*Verejna obchodni spolecnost*);

- limited partnership (*Komanditni spolecnost*);

- partnership limited by shares (*Komanditni spolecnost na akcie*); and

- association (*sdruzeni*).

OBTAINING AUTHORITY TO INVEST

Under the JVA in its original form, an application to set up an FPC had to be made to several ministries, supported by a feasibility study and evidence to show that the joint venture would benefit the Czechoslovak economy. The procedure was simplified in April 1990, when the requirement for a feasibility study was dropped and only one ministry – normally, the Federal Ministry of Finance – was made responsible for issuing consents. Finally, a government decree streamlined the process further by removing the need for Ministry of Finance consent where:

- the FPC will be wholly-foreign owned;

- the proposed Czechoslovak party is an individual, or a company whose participants are exclusively Czechoslovak individuals or foreign persons; or

- the proposed Czechoslovak party is a co-operative founded after 1 July 1988.

The position is different if the Czechoslovak party is a state enterprise. Under the new privatisation law, such a joint venture will require specific approval at government level, unless it is established within the context of an approved privatisation project.

In the field of banking, the formation of an FPC still requires the authority of the Czechoslovak State Bank. Also, some activities such as insurance, mining and casinos require a licence from the ministry responsible, irrespective of whether there is a foreign investor.

FORMS OF FOREIGN PARTICIPATION

The foreign party may invest either in cash or in kind. If convertible currency is used to subscribe for shares, the FPC is allowed to keep this in a foreign currency account – an exception to the rules for internal convertibility which normally require such currency to be sold to a Czechoslovak bank.

Alternatively, the foreign party's subscription may be wholly or partly in kind – for example by providing machinery or technology rights. Non-monetary investments in a joint stock company must be valued by an expert whose name appears on the official lists kept at the district and regional courts, or who otherwise has official approval. The names of approved experts can be checked through the relevant Chamber of Commerce and Industry. Difficulties can arise with the Companies' Registry when intangible assets such as know-how are included in the valuation of a contribution in kind.

Capital may also be contributed in the form of a loan. Currently, loans exceeding Kčs50 million require the approval of the Czechoslovak State Bank.

Acquisition of Czechoslovak assets

A foreign party is generally free to buy shares in a Czechoslovak-owned company and Czechoslovak assets, other than real estate (which may, however, be acquired by a wholly-foreign owned FPC). Business assets may also be acquired as part of an approved privatisation project.

EMPLOYMENT LAW

Czechoslovakia has very detailed and complex laws on employment and the rights of trade unions, as well as a system of collective agreements. New laws were introduced, and the Labour Code extensively amended, in December 1990. Some salient points are as follows:

- Employees do not now have to belong to a trade union.

- Employees may be dismissed on two months' notice of termination (or, in certain cases, three months).

- The role of trade unions has been greatly reduced. In many areas where there was previously a requirement to obtain the approval of trade unions, this has been confined to a mere duty to 'discuss' these matters.

- Employees may exercise the right to strike only on grounds that negotiation of a collective agreement has broken down or that the strike is conducted to enforce performance of the conditions of an existing collective agreement.

- While there is provision for employee representation on the supervisory boards of joint stock companies with more than 200 employees, employee representation has been abolished for state enterprises.

- Working hours vary from 40 to 42.5 hours per week.

- Paid holiday ranges from three to five weeks (depending on age and profession).

- The probation period for employees may be agreed, with a maximum of three months.

ACCOUNTING PRACTICE

An FPC is required to appoint two auditors to approve its annual balance sheet and financial statement. This contrasts with the requirement for a 'domestic' joint stock company to appoint only one auditor. The auditors must act independently and rules regarding their appointment and functions are laid down by the Federal Ministry of Finance. There is no objection to the auditors being two individuals from the same accounting firm.

Accounts and records must be kept in Czechoslovak currency and in accordance with general rules applying to the business concerned, laid down by the Federal Ministry of Finance, and there is an obligation to supply accounting and statistical data.

Reserve fund

A reserve fund must be established with a minimum of 10 per cent of the issued capital, built up by payments of at least 5 per cent of the after-tax annual profits. The distribution of dividends is subject to payment of taxes and contributions to the reserve fund.

INVESTMENT PROTECTION

The JVA guarantees that the property of an FPC on the territory of Czechoslovakia will not be expropriated by the state except in accordance with rules of law and subject to compensation at full market value. There is no machinery for enforcing this guarantee. A Foreign Investment Act containing more comprehensive rules is planned for the end of 1991.

British investors will benefit from an Investment Protection Agreement between the UK and Czechoslovakia, signed on 10 July 1990 and due to be ratified shortly. The agreement guarantees fair and equitable treatment for investments of each country's investors on the territory of the other. Each undertakes to refrain from unreasonable or discriminatory measures affecting the management, maintenance, use, enjoyment or disposal of investments on its territory. These guarantees are coupled with undertakings that investments from the other country will be no less favourably treated than those from any third state; and that no nationlisation is to take place except on a non-discriminatory basis and for full compensation. Notably, the agreement gives investors and the governments of each country the right to enforce the agreement by international arbitration.

CUSTOMS-FREE ZONES

Czechoslovakia's customs legislation, as most recently amended, provides for customs-free zones to assist in regional development, to be treated as foreign territory for the application of customs procedure, foreign exchange and trade rules and outside the system of price regulation and supervision. At the time of writing, no such zones have yet been established.

APPLICABLE LAW AND DISPUTE RESOLUTION

The JVA lays down that Czechoslovak law governs the establishment, legal form, legal relationships and liquidation of an FPC. Pending the introduction of the new Commercial Code and the establishment of Commercial Courts, the Economic Code applies to commercial relations within Czechoslovakia and disputes are settled by the present system of state arbitration.

This does not prevent the parties from choosing a foreign system of law to govern the *contract* which establishes an FPC and lays down the terms of the relationship between them. An arbitration clause may also be included, conferring jurisdiction on a foreign arbitration tribunal. The practice is growing for the use of neutral systems of law and arbitration. The law of Switzerland is frequently chosen; arbitration under the rules of the International Court of Arbitration, the International Chamber of Commerce and the Zurich Chamber of Commerce is also common.

NEGOTIATING JOINT VENTURES

A joint venture is an arrangement where two or more parties come together to participate in an enterprise. It should be distinguished from a wholly-foreign owned company, which some officials and lawyers in Czechoslovakia persist in calling a 'joint venture' because it is still governed by the JVA, which originally required Czechoslovak participation.

There are three main types of legal structure for carrying out joint ventures – contractual joint ventures, partnership arrangements and corporate joint ventures.

Contractual joint ventures

In a contractual joint venture, the relationship between the parties is governed entirely by contract without the creation of a partnership or company. This may be appropriate where parties are co-operating on a defined project, such as a property development, or bidding to carry out a particular engineering contract or some other project which will continue only for a limited period of time.

Partnership arrangements

If the joint venture is structured as a formal partnership, the partners will share directly in the profits or losses in the proportions which they agree. They will also each be potentially liable for the whole of the obligations of the business.

Partnership joint ventures are, therefore, comparatively rare unless set up to achieve taxation benefits, as in the case of the well-known German hybrid, the GmbH & Co KG. This is a form of limited partnership with a limited liability company as the general partner and may be favoured in Czechoslovakia by German and Austrian investors.

Corporate joint ventures

In Czechoslovakia, as in the UK and the USA, it will be the company which is most often chosen as the medium for a joint venture. The joint venture will then take the form of a relationship at shareholder level between the shareholders, and a relationship between each of them and the jointly-owned company.

The two basic documents governing these relationships will be the Shareholders' Agreement and (in the case of a joint stock company) the Statutes. It may be convenient to have more than one Shareholders' Agreement, so as to deal separately with formal matters affecting the structure of the company and the commercial terms. The documents should cover:

- the object and scope of the joint venture;

- capitalisation and financing of the company;

- the basic rights of the parties, including transfers of shares, protection of minority shareholders and provisions to apply in case of deadlock;

- termination of the joint venture;

- composition of the management and supervisory boards and the scope of authority to be granted to managers;

- other arrangements regarding management; and

- agreements not to compete.

Additional documents

Further agreements are likely to be needed covering, for example, the following matters.

Contracts for the purchase of assets If any of the shareholders are to sell property such as land or plant to the new company, a contract for the sale and transfer will be required. A joint venture company will want warranties regarding the values of what is being purchased and protection against undisclosed liabilities.

Funding arrangements Agreements will be required for the funding of the joint venture, for example if any of the shareholders are to provide loans to the joint venture company or if any part of the price to be paid for assets is to be left as a debt. A joint stock company may issue bonds, secured on the property of the company. Guarantees may be required from shareholders for bank borrowings.

Property rights Contracts will be needed for the purchase or lease of the factory, office, shop or other premises where the joint venture company is to carry on its business.

Contracts for the supply of goods If a joint venture company is to manufacture or market goods, it may need to contract to purchase parts or materials from one of the parent companies. The basis for calculating the price and the period of the contract will be very important.

Provision of services If any of the shareholders are to provide services, separate agreements will be needed. For example, the Czechoslovak shareholder may be acting as agent or distributor, or the foreign shareholder may agree to provide management services by seconding managers or technicians.

Intellectual property Licence agreements will be required if the joint venture company is carrying out any form of manufacture or other activity which involves the use of know-how, patents, trade marks or other rights that belong to one of the shareholders. The joint venture company itself may develop improvements or know-how to which the shareholders will want access through cross-licences.

Some key questions

Every joint venture is unique but the Shareholders' Agreements and other documents should provide answers to the following questions:

- Will the joint venture company have the property and rights it needs to carry on its business as contemplated by the Shareholders' Agreement?

- Is each participant clearly and satisfactorily committed to providing the assets, facilities and rights which it is to contribute to the joint venture?

- Can each participant compel the joint venture company to enforce its rights against a defaulting shareholder?

- If a participant wishes to sell its interest, what will the consequences be, and who will take over any loan stock or other securities?

- What will happen if the joint venture is terminated? Will the participants be able to 'recapture', and prevent others from using valuable know-how which they have provided to the company? Will they have access to rights which other participants have provided to the company or which have been developed by the joint venture itself?

9

The Convertibility of the Koruna

National Westminster Bank

RATIONALE

The rationale behind a free exchange rate system with a convertible currency is not only that it facilitates the liberalisation of foreign trade but that it extends the market allocation of resources within the economy to external prices. A free exchange rate system effectively opens up the economy, exposing it to external markets, to the extent that regulations are withdrawn. Internal competition is enhanced as a consequence and the structure of domestic prices is influenced by prices prevailing externally. In this way, a formerly protected economy adjusts and finds a new position in wider world markets.

Both the liberalisation of internal trade through the deregulation of domestic prices and the freeing of the exchange rate are consistent and integral to a functioning open market economy, and currency convertibility becomes a tool for the goals of establishing such an economy. In practice, convertibility means that the state relinquishes control over resource allocation and prices and foregoes its monopoly over the supply of foreign exchange for the conduct of foreign commerce. Private individuals and enterprises correspondingly become autonomous, free to make their own resource allocation decisions in the light of prevailing prices under conditions of competition.

The actual transition from a fully administered exchange rate regime, as is typical under a command economy, to a market determined exchange rate system is not abrupt and would normally involve transitional stages. A market influenced exchange rate and domestic prices determined by conditions of supply and demand acknowledges state decontrol in the economy. However, the government would normally retain foreign exchange reserves for intervention purposes to influence the exchange rate as is the case in Western industrial countries. This would also be crucial in the management of the difficult transition phase in order to avoid undue instability during a period of profound economic change and uncertainty.

The stated goal of koruna (Kčs) convertibility has been part of the economic restructuring process since 1988. Up until the end of 1988, the central bank managed several exchange rates, or 'coefficients for internal reproduction price balances'. Surcharges were levelled on the lowest official rate, depending on the nature of the transaction and entities involved. The exchange rate was essentially pegged to a basket of five currencies – those of Austria, France, Germany, the USA and Switzerland – for the purpose of establishing commercial and non-commercial exchange rates vis-à-vis convertible currencies.

THE ROAD TO CONVERTIBILITY

The move towards convertibility began on 1 January 1989 when the multi-tiered exchange rate regime was streamlined to include only a commercial, a non-commercial and a third, special tourist rate. Throughout 1989, monthly foreign exchange auctions were held setting the various exchanges rates. On 1 January 1990 the koruna was devalued to Kčs17 against the US dollar. The commercial and non-commercial rates were merged though the special, higher tourist rate was retained. The tourist rate was based on foreign exchange auctions and their frequency was increased to twice a month.

In March 1990 the authorities announced their intention to introduce limited internal convertibility by 1 January 1991. As a prelude, the koruna was substantially devalued to reduce divergence with anticipated lower market rates. On 15 October 1990, it was devalued by nearly 50 per cent to Kčs24 to the dollar, although devaluation expectations persisted and pressure on foreign exchange reserves continued. A single rate was introduced on 28 December 1990 at Kčs28, representing a further 16.7 per cent devaluation from previous, commercial and non-commercial rates, although a 7 per cent revaluation from the now defunct tourist rate.

Apart from discrete changes in the exchange rates, the koruna has been pegged to five currencies (see Table 9.1) commonly used in invoicing for exports and imports and the weights have changed each year.

Table 9.1 *The Koruna basket*

Currency	%
Deutschemark	40.94
US dollar	32.88
Austrian schilling	12.32
Swiss franc	9.05
French franc	4.82
	100.00

Limited internal convertibility was introduced on 1 January 1991. This allows legal persons (that is, registered local and joint venture enterprises) to freely exchange korunas for convertible currency for current account transactions. However, the obligatory surrender requirement to the banking system of all newly received foreign exchange was raised from 40 per cent to 100 per cent. Under the new system, exchange rate auctions were discontinued and foreign exchange accounts allowed with the permission of the State Bank. Private individuals are currently allowed to purchase a maximum of only Kčs5000 (around $180) worth of foreign exchange each year, although there are now more opportunities for individuals and enterprises to hold foreign exchange accounts. Like 'legal entities', a full surrender requirement applies to all new foreign exchange received. The new single exchange rate is set daily and 'maintained', if necessary, by central bank intervention.

Although these new measures represent a partial and limited liberalisation from previous exchange rate regimes, the authorities have maintained a high degree of caution in the evolution to a convertible currency. Additional administrative measures were imposed with a 20 per cent tariff on imports of consumer goods. A low absolute limit imposed on individuals' entitlement to foreign exchange is likely to cap a high degree of latent demand. While this situation exists a black, or parallel, market will continue to operate. In a freely determined market, the gap between official and other markets is virtually non-existent. For this to occur, however, citizens and enterprises must feel confident that a regular and

Table 9.2 *Koruna convertibility – diary, 1989–91*

Date	Event
January 1989	Streamlining of exchange rates to commercial and non-commercial Monthly foreign exchange auctions
January 1990	Commercial and non-commercial rates merged Higher tourist rate introduced Twice-monthly auctions Koruna devalued to Kčs17 = US$1
October 1990	Koruna devalued by almost 50%
December 1990	Single exchange rate at Kčs28/$ (a 16.7% devaluation for commercial and non-commercial rates, but 7% revaluation of tourist rate)
January 1991	Limited internal convertibility introduced Single exchange rate set daily

assured supply of foreign exchange is available at a moment's notice and at a familiar rate.

THE RISKS OF CONVERTIBILITY

The path to a convertible currency involves a number of potentially destabilising risks for the authorities. The foremost risk entails the potential for inflationary pressures that are likely to ensue once the full impact of prolonged and effective devaluation and depreciation is absorbed into the economy. Internal economic structural adjustment is likely to add volatility to exchange rates. Latent consumer demand for imports will cause strong demand for foreign exchange, which will also be required as a hedge against inflation. In the interim, the authorities will need to retain sufficient reserves both at hand and 'on call' for daily intervention purposes to meet foreign exchange demand.

For this objective, the authorities will need, and have already requested, international bilateral and multilateral official finance to support an exchange rate stabilisation fund. Czechoslovakia has already been granted several credit facilities from the IMF, World Bank and the EC to ease economic and financial reform. In particular, a 'stabilisation' fund is in place specifically for currency convertibility which can be drawn on to supplement reserves. The IMF has so far provided a comprehensive $1.78 billion loan and the EC a further $667 million. Unlike the full conversion of the former

Ost-Mark, the Czechoslovak authorities wish to retain their own currency and do not have equivalent access to the full range of support facilities offered by the Bundesbank in the replacement of the Ost-Mark by the Deutschemark.

The levels at which a market determined exchange rate will stabilise, and the extent of effective devaluation involved, will have a crucial bearing on the competitive viability of enterprises in the Czechoslovak economy. The importance of an appropriate rate of exchange is critical in determining the longer-term international success of Czechoslovak industry and commerce. Too high a rate of exchange will tend to increase the attendant social costs of readjustment by costing resources, including labour, at relatively uncompetitive rates. Investment inflows are also likely to be deterred. On the other hand, too rapid and deep a devaluation would tend to heighten inflationary pressures and dislocate import sensitive industries.

Adopting a middle course with an appropriate exchange rate policy should minimise, although not eliminate, both higher inflationary and unemployment eventualities. The appropriate exchange rate is nevertheless exceedingly difficult to determine in advance, but in the longer term is a level which can command both foreign and domestic confidence in the koruna as a secure means of exchange and store of value. However, the realisable competitiveness of Czechoslovak industries has essentially been untested in world markets, thereby providing an inadequate track record that could underpin a more stable convertible currency. The rate of exchange will nevertheless have to be at a level which the market believes that the authorities are both able and sincere in defending and at the same time needs to reflect the real economic and financial strengths and weaknesses of the Czechoslovak economy. In practice, full convertibility of the koruna will depend on how quickly the government wishes to introduce comprehensive market reforms. Current indications are that the former cautious position is being superseded by calls for more rapid change. The situation remains, however, a vexed political issue.

10

Prices, Rents and Wages

National Westminster Bank

Czechoslovakia has had a history of stable prices under the previous communist regimes. Consumer prices rose by slightly more than one per cent a year on average over the period 1970-89. However, as in other former planned economies, the official indices did not fully capture inflation. Considerable 'hidden' inflation exists both in terms of suppressed demand and widespread state transfer pricing: through the state budget alone, almost 75 per cent of the national income created was redistributed by means of taxes and subsidies. Among the immediate problems for monetary policy will be to tackle the greater transparency in prices once market reforms are introduced.

The new Eastern European governments have all expressed the desire and need to restructure the basis of their economies from central planning to that of open markets. Individual countries like Hungary and Poland have made more headway than others, but all started from different positions and are proceeding at varying speeds. A crucial distinguishing systemic feature between these two types of economies remains the role of prices. Under a command economy prices are set by central state authorities and need not bear any relation to true costs of production because of the overriding importance of the central plan. In a market economy, however, prices are decided by buyers and sellers in markets under conditions of competition. Prices should reflect relative scarcity of goods and services. Profitability criteria ultimately govern the viability of firms which determine their own resource allocation and decisions for investment, purchase of inputs and sale of output.

Liberalisation fundamentally alters the role of prices in the economy, with the price mechanism taking over the function of co-ordinator of economic activities which the centralised plan once had. The transition from command to market economy involves widespread price liberalisation in all sectors of the economy – for goods, services and property. All these sectors have been heavily regulated in the past. The initial focus of deregulation, however, will affect the retail sector and consumer goods. State controls over prices are in the process of being lifted and subsidies on goods and services removed. This process can be gradual or instant, as in the recent case histories of Hungary and Poland respectively. Prices then become subject to conditions of supply and demand in markets and any rationing systems are disbanded.

However, freeing prices alone is not sufficient to ensure that prices will indeed reflect true costs and relative scarcity. Above all, competition in markets has to be ensured and this requires the break-up of state industries, presumably through privatisation and a revival of the private sector, in tandem with price liberalisation measures. However, the long established distortions through administered prices in Czechoslovakia is likely to lead to a wide divergence from new market prices. This is particularly the case where final consumer prices have diverged substantially from the prices paid to producers, entailing large government subsidies, or where domestic prices diverge substantially from external prices for similar goods.

PRICE, RENT AND WAGES REFORM: THE RECORD

Consumer prices

Price reforms undertaken in 1990 largely involved increases in, but no changes in the determination of, administratively set prices. This was largely in anticipation of higher market-determined prices, particularly where heavy subsidies had been applied. The latter had been particularly the case with foodstuffs where, on 9 July 1990, retail prices were raised to reduce government subsidies.

The move to widespread market determination of prices began in January 1991. Prices of goods sold in retail stores increased between 80–100 per cent since the previous Ministry of Trade survey taken in September 1990, compared with 10 per cent inflation for 1990 as a whole. However, the process of breaking down retail monopolies is lagging, creating insufficient competition to stem price rises. Czechoslovak officials anticipate around half of former state retail outlets and a smaller proportion of the wholesale distribution network will be privatised by mid-1991. In the main, however, the near doubling of prices of retail goods reflects greater transparency in the relationship between final prices and costs of production, rather than unsatiated demand which had obscured previous price setting. However, an interventionist rearguard approach to reform remains, particularly in areas where price reform becomes politically sensitive to social welfare concerns. In February 1991, the federal Finance Ministry and regional Finance Ministries issued a joint decree listing goods and regulated prices. The decree stipulates maximum trade price margins on selected consumer goods in an attempt to manage the rate of price increase.

Rents

The property market in Czechoslovakia has traditionally been strictly controlled by the state with the apportionment of property for housing, commerce and industry governed by central administrative authorities. Rents are typically set by central authorities and bear little or no relation to market demand or supply. The housing sector is an area where heavy subsidy by the state has been a social priority. However, as part of wider liberalisation measures, the property sector will become subject to reform, although a strong element of subsidy is likely to remain for the least well-off.

The position prior to attempted liberalisation in the property sector has effectively barred foreigners from directly owning property. The possibilities are emerging, dependent on new legislation, for foreign participation through joint ventures. Although there is currently no commercial lease structure in place, foreign tenants are entering into three to five year rental agreements in hard currency which are modelled on those in Germany. In general, there is a severe shortage of international standard office accommodation in the main urban areas which has tended to push up rents for prime space. It is likely that further lease type arrangements will be modelled on those existing in Germany.

In February 1991 the Czechoslovak parliament approved a Restitution Bill for the return of state-confiscated property to Czechoslovak citizens which will involve the return of some 75 per cent of houses in Prague alone. The Bill excludes property legally nationalised before and after 1948. Accommodation costs are set to increase substantially by mid-1991: the Czech and Slovak authorities expect a 180 per cent and 100 per cent increase in rents during 1991 in their respective regions. Current legislation, pending parliamentary approval, will clarify rent in three forms:

1. 'Economised' rent for authority-owned flats and flats rented by enterprises to their employees.
2. 'Regulated' rent applied to flats left vacant in reprivatised houses or flats where state financial support was provided in their construction.
3. 'Free' rent applied to apartments and houses built without state participation or where flats in family or private houses are concerned.

It is generally expected that rent will take up an increasing proportion of average expenditure, at around 20–25 per cent of the total.

Wages

Under the previous planned economy the allocation of labour was administratively determined with salary structures set by government across various sectors. Gradual decentralisation over wage determination emerged from 1987 onwards, giving enterprises greater control over labour management: wages began slowly to reflect individual enterprises' profitability. Within limits, enterprises can make payments related to performance around par, or basic wages. In 1990 the government set strict limits on the growth of personnel costs. In general, the highest wages have historically been paid to those in construction (11 per cent above the national average) and in agriculture (4.5 per cent above the national average). Those in 'non-material' production were on average remunerated at below the national average. The implications of a largely de-regulated labour market will include allowing enterprises and industries with greater competitive leverage to offer higher wage rates. However, considerable rises in nominal wages can be anticipated under union pressure and in response to rising consumer prices and rents. Real wages are, nevertheless, likely to fall during an (indeterminate) interim period of economic restructuring and contraction, with the role of government policies critical in preventing a wage-price spiral.

The new nature of the labour market assumes critical importance for the Czechoslovak economy. Essential legislation remains to be determined and is likely to be highly contentious in striking a balance between the needs of a flexible market economy and the protection of labour interests.

11

Banking and Financial Services

National Westminster Bank

Reform of the Czechoslovak banking system only really began in earnest following the tumultuous political changes subsequent to the overthrow of the communist regime. Prior to 1990, the Czechoslovak banking system was in large part modelled on the Soviet command system. The central bank – *Statní Banka Ceskoslovenska* – oversaw and underpinned the entire credit allocation mechanism, one that was essentially geared to the needs of a centrally planned economy and its resource directing five-year plan. Credit allocation followed the dictates of the five-year plans, irrespective of commercial criteria. Compared with other Eastern European countries, particularly Hungary and Poland, Czechoslovakia lagged even the piecemeal attempts at restructuring of the financial system during the 1980s.

The new democratically elected government of Czechoslovakia has set out to transform radically the economic structure, with the general objective of placing the economy on an internationally competitive, market basis. A crucial part of this process involves a transformation of the financial system – attuned to a market economy – one that involves a high degree of decentralisation, competition and incorporation of commercial business practices with the creation of differentiated financial markets. In short, the financial system is to be reformed and transformed, reflecting the institutions and functions common to the Western model and Western practices.

The first significant banking reforms were introduced on 1 January 1990 resulting first in the state central bank shedding its commercial functions. A clear two-tier system is now in existence, with the central bank performing functions typical of its Western equivalent, namely, banker to the government, refinancer for commercial banks, the executor of monetary policies, maintainer of the exchange rate and fiduciary issue. The central bank's former commercial operations were handed over to two new commercial banks, the largest of which is the *Komercní Banka* and the other being *Vseobecná Úverova Banka* (General Credit Bank). *Komercni Banka* is headquartered in Prague, having taken over half the available assets of the former central bank and all 84 of the central bank branches in Czech lands. The General Credit Bank took over the remaining 38 central bank branches in Slovakia and is headquartered in Bratislava.

In the former system, all the state-owned banks filled specific niches – associated with a particular sector of the economy – whether industry, agriculture, external trade or personal/household financial needs. The banks collected savings and allocated credit in accordance with annual credit plans.

SPECIALISED BANKS

The five specialised banks are as follows.

1 Ceskoslovenska Obchodní Banka

The foreign trade bank and joint stock company with 51 per cent of the shares owned by the central bank and the remainder by foreign trade enterprises. It supervises all foreign transactions in both domestic and foreign currencies, and undertakes short- and long-term credit operations in connection with Czechoslovak imports and exports. It grants credit to foreign customers for Czechoslovak goods, either directly or through intermediaries.

2 Zivnostenská Banka

This bank has a representative office in London and handles financial transactions for private individuals and non-profit institutions. It accepts deposits from foreigners in domestic and foreign currencies, and keeps accounts for Czechoslovaks abroad. The bank was formerly an arm of the Obchodni Banka, but is now a fully independent, competing commercial bank dealing with foreign traffic.

3 *Investicni Banka (Investment Bank)*

This bank grants investment credits and is responsible for the holdings of the state budgets of the Federation, Republics and other state funds of securities that were mainly foreign and had been originally acquired by the government when such assets were nationalised in 1948.

4 and 5 *Savings banks*

There are two savings banks, one for each of the Czech and Slovak Republics, largely dealing with the general public's financial requirements. Each savings bank operates a large, local network of small offices channelling household deposits to the central bank. Lending activity centres primarily on housing loans to newly married couples with fixed and heavily subsidised interest rates. The lending rate for house purchase varied very little between 1984–89 at between 3.15 per cent to 3.34 per cent, some 5 per cent below the prime discount rate. This practice of interest rate subsidy is currently under review.

Since 1990, all banks and savings banks were permitted to operate anywhere in the country and in all fields of lending other than foreign borrowing and lending. Customers are now in theory free to choose branches or banks, introducing competition into the new system. In practice, however, for the time being the geographic concentration of bank branches precludes effective choice.

One serious problem that emerged with the 1990 banking reforms was that the banks set up were not recapitalised when they were turned into commercial banks. Old loans to large state enterprises comprise the majority of portfolios for several of the banks. *Komercni* bank, for example, reports that outstanding credits, mostly medium and long term, account for 98.9 per cent of its total Kčs328 billion in assets. With no new capital having been brought in as a result of the 1990 reforms, the capital/asset ratios are very low. Moreover, the quality of the loan portfolios has not been properly assessed and is likely to be impaired. Capital adequacy is a source of concern to the monetary authorities with average capital/asset ratios of 1–2 per cent well below the 8 per cent required by the Basle international guidelines. The requirement is stricter for new banks at 5–10 per cent.

Although most banks are still state owned, profits are no longer automatically surrendered to the central bank, but are subject to a tax of around 55 per cent. In principle, loan decisions are to be taken on purely commercial criteria but, in practice, banks are not entirely free to choose their clients. When banks are unwilling to provide credit to certain state enterprises, the Federal Ministry of Finance can provide guarantees in certain cases, even to unprofitable enterprises.

FOREIGN BANKS

Recent legislation provides for the establishment of further banks and limited foreign involvement, but the government is proceeding slowly in introducing full competition, allowing time for adjustment. The authorities fear that domestic banks would not be able to compete given their lack of commercial experience and weak capital base. Foreign capital is currently allowed up to 35 per cent of total, in general, but other than through joint ventures, foreign bank activity is severely curtailed for the time being. The central bank and the Ministry of Finance authorise and provide licences to new banks and joint ventures, and by the end of November 1990 the total number of banks had increased to ten, with five applications pending. Despite the current restrictions, there is substantial foreign interest in the banking sector. At least 15 foreign banks have established representative offices. The most significant joint venture so far in the banking sector has been with Société Général (with a 70 per cent stake) and *Komerční Banka*. Some foreign banks have found that leasing arrangements are attractive to both their clients at home and to Czechoslovak companies.

THE FINANCIAL SYSTEM

The banks dominate the Czechoslovak financial system. No true capital market exists yet, although banks and companies may now issue bonds with the permission of the central bank. The government intends to issue treasury bills and/or bonds as a means of developing financial management techniques in the emerging decentralised system. So far, the central bank has only issued bonds sold to the general public while those companies that have issued bonds have largely done so for their employees. There are plans to establish a stock market in Prague eventually, to trade in these and other securities, but the real stimulus for such an exchange would have to coincide with the planned privatisation of state enterprises.

Since 1990, inter-bank deposits are permissible and a small

market in such deposits has begun to emerge. Rates for these transactions have been in the 5 per cent to 5.5 per cent range and promissory notes are rarely used except in cases where inter-enterprise supplier credits are required.

In general, the development of a sophisticated financial system trading in various forms of credit will emerge in line with changes in sectors outside the financial system itself. In particular, proposed state enterprise privatisations and general deregulation in the economy will in tandem stimulate the emergence of stock markets and greater financial intermediation. The Czechoslovak authorities are being advised in this process by both multilateral agencies and private consultancies from the West.

MONETARY POLICY

Monetary management is currently conducted largely by means of direct credit controls. This is the inheritance of practices from the past. The lack of existing financial intermediation means that indirect monetary controls are underdeveloped.

In the past, monetary policy was implemented through the monetary plan as part of much wider macroeconomic policy. It had a direct influence on state budgeting and exchange rate policy, and had a greater importance than in other Eastern bloc countries. The monetary plan was largely drafted by the central bank, which sought to ensure that the overall stock and circulation of money was kept in prudent line with developments in the field of production and resource allocation targets. After government seal of approval, the monetary plan was dissected to meet specific sector needs, allocating credit and foreign exchange for each sector. Interest rates were essentially fixed, taking a passive, secondary role, and in the case of housing loans rates of repayment were heavily subsidised. The last monetary plan was drafted in 1990, but the concept of an all-embracing and all-controlling monetary plan has now been discarded by the new political authorities.

The main method for implementing monetary policy has been moral suasion whereby the central bank closely advises the two main commercial banks. In addition, and in preparation for an expanded financial system, the central bank has established guidelines and prudential rules for the emerging proliferation of financial institutions. These include limits on capital/assets ratios, credit/deposit ratios, foreign credits and excessive concentration of credits. In an attempt to begin to enforce minimum reserve requirements, banks have had to increase, from zero, their obligatory minimum reserves kept with the central bank by 5 per cent of the growth of all koruna deposits, excluding inter-bank deposits.

Apart from changes in the nature of monetary control, the direction of monetary policy has been to maintain overall macroeconomic stability while structural reforms are implemented. This task will be made more difficult as the economy is progressively liberalised. The key danger remains that of inflation as restructuring is undertaken. Consumer credit has largely been frozen and commercial credits are expected to remain constant in real terms.

INTEREST RATES

Credit and interest rates have not played a significant proactive part in the allocation of credit and thus resources within the economy, which has largely been controlled from above by plan. In general, the interest rate structure has been fixed according to type of deposit or credit, with different rates for enterprises and households. These rates have largely been arbitrary, irrespective of commercial criteria or conditions of supply and demand. In general, the longer the term of the loan the higher the interest rate. Most deposit and credit rates have been both stable and positive in real terms until recently. The prospect of rising inflation entails an erosion of real rates of deposit return without nominal adjustments in line with price increases.

The central bank discount rate to the commercial banks remains the principal rate for banks seeking refinancing. This rate has been progressively raised throughout 1990 from 4 per cent at end-1989 to 8.5 per cent at end-1990. The discount rate rose to 10 per cent by January 1991. A more rapid increase in nominal discount rates is anticipated if they are to remain positive with respect to rising inflation forecast for 1991. All other rates for deposit and lending are derived from the prime discount rate and it is envisaged that rates of interest will become progressively flexible to reflect variations in demand and supply in each discrete sector.

12

Restitution
SJ Berwin & Co

The question of whether to return property which belonged to individuals and their families and was confiscated by the earlier socialist regimes presents major political issues and commercial ramifications. Restitution was felt necessary by many in the new democratic order, to purge Czechoslovakia of the very essence of the old regime: if a new property owning and entrepreneurial democracy was to be developed, then the vestiges of the earlier market economy had to be re-established.

It was well appreciated that restitution of property could be a negative influence on possible foreign investment, unless effected quickly and clearly and with the maximum degree of certainty as to what property belongs to whom and, to the extent possible, for it to be known which properties were in question. This is largely what the Czechoslovak restitution laws have aimed to do.

In Czechoslovakia, land and the means of production were controlled by the state for over 40 years. Czechoslovak property owners first experienced confiscations in 1938 by the Germans and, after World War II, the country had several socialist governments which carried out confiscations or nationalisations in 1946, again in 1948 and the years that followed, and once more after the Dubcek spring of 1968.

POLITICAL AND COMMERCIAL CONSIDERATIONS

Having decided soon after the 'Velvet Revolution' that confiscated property should be returned to its earlier owners, the Czechoslovak government was faced with several factual issues which it needed to resolve:

- What land and businesses were previously confiscated, in what circumstances, and who by?

- Who owned the confiscated properties and businesses and where are they now? Can they or their descendants be traced? Are the owners interested in or able to retake the property or businesses in question?

- What, if any, compensation was paid in respect of those earlier expropriations? There were certain bilateral state-to-state commissions which existed and under which compensation was paid, primarily to ex-Czechoslavaks living in other countries.

- What is the status of that land and the businesses now? In some cases, buildings have become dilapidated; others have been demolished or rebuilt and modernised. Some businesses no longer exist and others have been expanded and improved.

The question of whether property should be returned to its original owners gave rise to various problems. Property which has not been looked after will inevitably have deteriorated. The original owners may wish to use the property for their own purposes or even sell the property, and there could be no certainty they would maintain it in its present use, for example, as apartments or as a factory. The original owner may also be unwilling to repair and maintain property that is not paying a real return.

The alternative was to pay financial compensation. This would overcome the difficulties of the attitudes of the original owners, and how and whether they would maintain and use the property. However, there were two main commercial objections: Czechoslovakia needs all its available money for the regeneration of its economy rather than to pay compensation for the misdemeanours of earlier governments; and, secondly – particularly relevant in respect of original owners now living outside Czechoslovakia – payment of compensation would be a drain on Czechoslovak hard currency resources if paid in hard currency or freely convertible Czechoslovak koruna.

Another policy issue was whether restitution should be limited to those still living, whose property was confiscated, or should also be allowed to pass to the children or grandchildren of the original owners. Should existing and former Czechoslovaks be treated equally? Or should only Czechoslovak citizens and residents be entitled to recover property or receive compensation? Should

Czechoslovak nationals and residents perhaps be able to recover property and foreigners only compensation? Furthermore, what property should be restituted? The intention was to return property confiscated by the socialist regimes, but issues also arose as to whether this should extend to property confiscated in the 1938–46 period and under the criminal law (eg, for leaving Czechoslovakia or for collaborating with the Germans).

The major practical difficulty, still an important factor, relates to the valuation of property. There is still only a limited property market in Czechoslovakia and, therefore, no easy way to determine market value for properties. Until there is free use of land and it is possible to transfer land freely to any purchaser, it is difficult to calculate real values.

THE LEGISLATIVE FRAMEWORK

The Czechoslovak government has adopted two laws dealing with restitutions. The Act on Relieving the Consequences of Some Property Injuries, the so-called Small Restitution Act, came into effect from 1 November 1990 and aims to cover property that was seized by the state without proper compensation to its original owners in the period between 1955 and 1959. The Act on Out of Court Rehabilitations, the so-called Large Restitution Act, was adopted in February 1991 and came into effect on 1 April 1991. It has more general application and encompasses not only matters listed in the Act but also cases of injury covered by other Acts including those resulting from political persecution or action contrary to acknowledged human rights. It applies to injuries and confiscations in the period 25 February 1948 to 1 January 1990. Both Acts apply to moveable as well as immovable property and there are no limitations as to further management of recovered property by its owners.

The Small Restitution Act

Under this law the owners of property seized by the state between 1955 and 1959, and under certain subsequent government decrees, may recover the property or receive financial compensation on the purchase price or the difference between financial compensation and the purchase price.

Claims under the Small Restitution Act had to be submitted by 1 May 1991. Many potential claimants had difficulty identifying the property and who owns it now. Properties had been destroyed or their very nature altered, and in many cases there was uncertainty whether a particular property was covered by the Large or Small Restitution Acts. To overcome uncertainty many parties have filed protective claims which the Czechoslovak authorities will have to consider and resolve in time. Claimants who have, for whatever reason, not been able to recover property, have until 15 April 1992 to submit their claims to the Czechoslovak courts. Where the original owner of property has died, his legitimate heirs are entitled to claim. There is no need for a claimant to be either a Czechoslovak citizen or resident.

To recover property, a claimant was required to submit a written demand to the person or organisation which presently possesses the property. The intention was for the claimant and the organisation then to agree the return of the property. This agreement is then registered with the state notary. Where the claimant is a foreigner, then a declaration of the State Administration for Foreign Exchange and Property Matters that the property is not subject to international agreement is required (ie, that compensation was not previously paid under one of the bilateral treaty arrangements to which Czechoslovakia was a party). Where the present owner of the property fails to hand the property back the claimant may enforce his claims by court action.

Where property has been demolished or is no longer fit for its purpose, financial compensation will be paid to the original owners. The compensation will be calculated on the basis of the value of the property on the date when it was seized and the price of the property calculated according to a regulation of the Ministry of Finance in 1964, with a 3 per cent per annum value added since the property was seized. Property on which a new building has been constructed or which is subject to 'rights of personal use' (eg, a lease) may not be recovered and financial compensation is the only remedy.

Where land has been sold to a third party prior to 1 October 1990, the original owner will be entitled to recover the purchase price from the organisation that sold the property. If that organisation no longer exists, then it is up to its legal successor or the Ministry for Privatisation to repay that original owner. Even if the property has been sold to its original owner, he is entitled to the same rights.

It is of great importance to foreign investors that rights of purchasers of property will be respected and upheld. This applies to the cases when purchasers are either physical persons, joint ventures or commercial companies and the property was sold before 1 October 1990. In practice this means that, for example, a foreign partner entering a joint venture need not be concerned that property belonging to or purchased by the joint venture will be taken away in order to satisfy restitution claims.

If immovable property, land or buildings are claimed and other moveable items are already attached to such property, the organisation in possession must offer these items first to the claimant for their residual value. Where flats and commercial premises are recovered, the original owner must respect the right to use them by those currently in possession, and the normal landlord and tenant rights under other regulations will apply.

Where property is claimed under the Small Restitution Act the organisation in possession of the property must complete the contract on delivery of the property or the purchase price and fulfil any resulting duties within 30 days of the claim being accepted. The Ministry for Privatisation must pay financial compensation or the surcharge between the price and compensation within one year from 15 April 1991. However, with some of the uncertainties which exist, it is likely to be some time before all outstanding claims are resolved. None the less, for the foreign investor there will be a degree of certainty as to ownership of such property, at least for the purpose of negotiations leading to the purchase or lease of such property.

The Large Restitution Act

The Large Restitution Act covers a far wider selection of property confiscated and is therefore likely to involve many more claims. As under the Small Restitution Act, legitimate heirs of an original owner can claim. However, the major restriction is that property will only be restored and compensation paid to claimants that are Czechoslovak citizens and residents.

Under the Large Restitution Act, to recover property previously confiscated the claimant must send a written demand to the organisation which presently owns or is in control of the property, giving details of his right to the property and specifying the way in which the property was acquired by the state. The written demand should be made before 1 October 1991, six months from the date on which the Large Restitution Act came into effect. As under the Small Restitution Act, only if the organisation does not comply with its duties need the claimant seek to bring an action in court to recover his property, but any claims must be brought within one year from 1 April.

If the property has deteriorated to such an extent that it cannot be used for the purposes of living, manufacture, sale or other services, the claimant may apply for financial compensation instead of delivery of the property. If immovable property is of a higher value than at the time when it was acquired by the state, the claimant can decide whether he will claim delivery of the property, pay the difference between the purchase price and compensation, or whether he will claim financial compensation from the relevant ministry. If the property subject to the Large Restitution Act was sold by the state to a legal person, this entity is obliged to deliver the property to its original owner and then to claim the purchase price paid from the relevant organ of state administration. This does not apply to cases when the purchaser was a commercial company, a foreign state or a joint venture.

There is a special regime for rented flats and commercial premises in recovered immovable property. Under the Large Restitution Act, the person recovering the property takes over all rights, duties and obligations of previous owners who made the agreement on the use of these flats and premises with their present users. If either party is dissatisfied with the rent or other conditions and they are unable to agree, they can refer the case to a special local national committee to fix these terms. There are exemptions where the person recovering the property is obliged to make a new agreement on the terms and conditions of use with tenants. This agreement must be maintained for at least ten years from 1 April 1991.

The effect of the Large Restitution Act is to facilitate not only justice being done for those who lost property to confiscations in earlier regimes, but also – and of equal importance – that ownership of land becomes certain. There remains for the present some insecurity for investors in Czechoslovakia, but this should in large part disappear when the deadline for claims passes on 1 October. However, the rules for compensation also give some security to investors that property which becomes part of a joint venture will remain within the transaction and any legitimate claimant's remedy will be in damages.

13

The Economics of Privatisation

KPMG Peat Marwick McLintock

In the first phase of Czechoslovakia's political and economic liberalisation, privatisation seemed a noticeably lower priority than in Poland and Hungary, the two Eastern European countries most advanced in their efforts towards reform. In many other respects Czechoslovakia, among the newly liberalised states, seemed the most attractive to foreign investors. Its general level of development and per capita GDP were higher than all the others, and its infrastructure and industrial development were perceived by most outsiders to be well ahead of its reforming neighbours. Yet while Hungary and Poland pursued the goal of transforming their economies with relentless haste, there appeared to be a question mark over privatisation in Czechoslovakia. Privatisation nevertheless has a major role to play in the following areas:

- the growth of the market economy;
- the development of capital markets; and
- the encouragement of foreign investment.

THE MARKET ECONOMY

One of the main roles of privatisation in the overall regeneration of the Eastern European countries is in developing a market-oriented economy, a process which had hardly started in Czechoslovakia before the fall of the communist regime. Unlike Hungary, Czechoslovakia had not begun a steady process of encouraging private enterprise, and unlike Poland it had no significant privately owned agricultural sector.

The plans for privatisation have been the subject of more debate in Czechoslovakia than elsewhere, and concern about selling off major parts of the economy to foreign interests has delayed the passage of legislation. Hence, while Hungary's and Poland's privatisation laws were well in train and the first privatisations were undertaken during 1990, Czechoslovakia's principal law on major privatisations was not passed until February 1991. While a large number of smaller enterprises have now been privatised in auctions, Czechoslovakia still has not really started large privatisations. However, it is now seriously embarking on that process.

CAPITAL MARKETS

Privatisation aims to develop capital markets which can potentially supply capital to firms either in the form of debt or equity. To the extent that there are private sector savings, it will act to mobilise them and channel them to enterprises promising a high rate of return.

Czechoslovakia lags behind Hungary in developing its capital markets, with the establishment of a stock exchange still some way off. There is, however, more progress than in Poland in that a number of investment funds have been established. *Investicni Banka* was the first bank to launch investment funds, with two subsidiaries establishing five funds between them: three of the funds are close-ended property funds, the other two are open-ended Czech and Slovak funds which will eventually be 70 per cent invested in shares and bonds. *Komerční Banka* is planning similar funds. However with no stock market and major privatisations only just beginning, the market is clearly still in its infancy.

The extent to which capital can be mobilised through a stock exchange will depend largely on the volume of private sector savings. If the private sector lacks savings, new capital can only be raised abroad with the corresponding implications of foreign ownership. Even if there are substantial private savings, these may be difficult to mobilise and may not be available for newly privatised firms if they are absorbed by the state in the initial sell-off. There is no consumer experience in dealing with shares or products offered by investment funds, while accelerating inflation has made households more concerned over protecting their savings. Savings banks, in which people have always deposited their money, have raised their rates considerably. The longer-term and higher-risk return of equity investment will take time to be accepted.

Privatisation will undoubtedly encourage the establishment of equity markets although it may do so to the detriment of the banking sector. Financial systems based on equity finance as opposed to bank (or debt) finance can encourage short-termism. Many observers believe that the rush to establish a stock exchange is diverting attention away from a thorough reform of the banking system.

FOREIGN INVESTMENT

Another vital role of privatisation is in encouraging foreign investment. Czechoslovakia is not burdened by the same level of external debt as some other countries in the region. Its debt totals about $8billion, ($500 per capita) compared with Hungary's $21billion or $2000 per capita. It is recognised that foreign investment will have a regenerating influence on the Czechoslovak economy and there has been substantial interest from outside investors. Well before the law on major privatisations was approved a number of significant, one-off deals with foreign investors had been negotiated and approved. Notably, these included an agreement between Sklo Union, the country's leading producer of industrial glass, and Glaverbel of Belgium, which allows the latter to acquire a 40 per cent stake in the company's flat glass division, and the investment by Volkswagen in the car manufacturer Skoda, which was originally a minority stake but with provision for a majority shareholding. A number of similar projects are in the pipeline and approaching fruition. These major deals are signalling not only a strong interest by foreign investors in Czechoslovakia but also the fact that privatisation is now gathering pace.

PROGRESS TO DATE

The small privatisation

Small business units, such as shops, restaurants, hotels and workshops are to be sold to private individuals or companies through a series of auctions. In the first batch of small privatisations in January 1991 all 18 businesses were sold, while the following month only one of the ten remained unsold. By mid-April 1991, more than 1000 enterprises had been sold. However, there has been controversy about the apparent success in selling businesses to domestic rather than foreign entrepreneurs. Some of the prices paid were very high by local standards and there were accusations that Czechoslovak bidders had foreign backing, with few constraints to prevent this happening.

Another problem was last-minute claims on the properties under the restitution law, which led to the Moskva Restaurant in Prague being removed from the list to allow a claim to be investigated. Clearly the system of auctioning will be a protracted process and it will take time before a significant effect is felt on the economy. However, alongside the process of transferring existing state-owned businesses to private enterprise, there is also the setting up of entirely new small businesses which is already showing its presence in the streets and shops all over Czechoslovakia.

The large privatisation

According to government plans, 3000–4000 enterprises are to prepare privatisation plans under the large privatisation legislation as a prelude to their disposal. Since the legislation was passed so recently, practical experience of the mechanics of the privatisation process is limited. The first privatisation through foreign purchase to be finalised under the terms of the Act took place in June 1991, when Procter and Gamble took 100 per cent control of Rakona, a detergent company in the Czech Republic.

The Czech government has issued a timetable and guidelines for selecting businesses to be privatised. Detailed projects for those enterprises to be included in the first round of privatisation must be submitted to the Ministry for the Administration of National Property and its Privatisation by the end of November 1991, and those to be included in the second round by the end of May 1992. Sales under the voucher scheme are scheduled to start in February 1992. The Slovak government has not yet announced similar details.

The voucher scheme

A distinctive aspect of large privatisation is that it embodies the concept of the investment coupon or voucher, which will be distributed to all Czechoslovak citizens and with which shares of any joint stock company can be purchased. This mechanism is essentially to ensure that the people at large will be able to participate in the privatisation process, which would otherwise be limited to domestic institutions and foreign investors. (The minimum value of a share is set at Kčs1000, which compares with an average monthly salary of Kčs3500.) However, precisely how this will operate and whether it will be applied in all cases still seem to be open questions. Clearly shares distributed gratis do not raise capital and therefore satisfy financially neither the government nor the enterprise. There are some suggestions that the voucher scheme might not be used in all cases, particularly where it is not essential in order to ensure distribution of the shares. The dilemma here is that this would inevitably leave the less attractive enterprises (from an investor's point of view) to be distributed to the people as a whole.

14

The Process of Privatisation

SJ Berwin & Co

One of the key elements in the development of a market economy is Czechoslovakia's privatisation programme. The importance of this can be illustrated by the fact that it is the intention of the Federal Ministry of Finance to transfer into private ownership about 70 per cent of the enterprises which are currently state owned. The successful regeneration of the Czechoslovak economy and its conversion to a market-driven system is considered by many to be closely tied to the success of the privatisation programme.

There are two interlinked but distinct levels to the privatisation process: the 'small privatisations' and the ' large privatisations'. The former are principally concerned with small properties and business such as shops, houses, restaurants and small factories. It is the intention of the Czechoslovak government, embodied in the legislation, that these small properties and businesses should, in the first instance at least, be offered to Czechoslovak citizens. The large privatisations concern enterprises of a much more substantial nature, such as large properties, factories and commercial enterprises (eg trading companies) where there is no specific intention that Czechoslovak citizens should have priority. On the contrary, the Czechoslovak government is anxious to encourage and attract foreign investment.

THE SMALL PRIVATISATION ACT

Small privatisations are governed by the law dated 25 October 1990 which became effective on 1 December 1990. This Act provides for the sale of economic or property units, including both moveable and immovable property, which have been or are still operative parts of organisations acting in the field of services or trade. Property which is not subject to the Act includes the following:

- Property used by foreign citizens or persons domiciled or resident outside Czechoslovakia.

- Property that is involved in agricultural production.

- Property that may be subject to restitution claims pursuant to the laws on restitution (see Chapter 12).

Mechanics of small privatisations

The operative units are being sold on a local basis in public auctions all around Czechoslovakia. The auctions are organised by the local committees in the regions where they are situated, under the control and regulation of the governments of the Czech or Slovak Republics. Each of the appropriate bodies is obliged to produce and has produced lists of operative units which are to be put up for sale. The list is drawn up in accordance with the policies established on a Republican basis by the Ministries of Privatisation of the Czech and Slovak Republics. Each list contains, in relation to each operative unit, details of its name and location, a completed inventory of all its assets, the name of the organisation that currently operates it, the asking price and the time and location of the auction. Other relevant details will also be included, such as the manner and deposition of the auction security and, where appropriate, details of the credit presently allowed to the organisation in relation to supplies and any proposals for fresh credit to be made available to it. The selection of operative units to be auctioned is based on either the policy of the local committee or on interest expressed by particular individuals or entities.

Any person who wishes to participate in an auction has to deposit security for his or her participation. This will be at least 10 per cent of the asking price for an operative unit with a minimum deposit of Kčs10,000. The person that is successful at the auction will have the deposit credited against the purchase price and unsuccessful participants will have their deposits returned. In addition, each participant has to pay for the right to bid at the auction at a rate of Kčs1,000, which is not recoverable. If at the auction no bids are received at the asking price, the auctioneer may reduce the asking price in stages by 10 per cent at a time, but not below 50 per cent of the asking price.

Ownership of property and small businesses, together with all benefits and risks, passes at the time of the purchase at auction, although the purchaser has a further 30 days in which to produce payment. For two years following the auction, the property or business may only be transferred to Czechoslovak citizens or to individuals who were Czechoslovak citizens after 1948. If the business purchased had previously been used for the sale of basic food stuffs then the purchaser is obliged to continue supplying food from the premises for at least one year. Failure to comply with these provisions renders the purchaser liable to a continuing fine.

THE LARGE PRIVATISATION ACT

This law dated 26 February 1991 took effect on 1 April 1991. It sets out the philosophy of large privatisation and the conditions for the transfer of property and assets by state enterprises, state monetary institutions, insurance houses and other state organisations, to Czechoslovak and foreign partners.

The types of property that may be privatised include the financial resources which an enterprise has the right to manage or which are under its control, together with all other rights, proprietary values and obligations. The process of privatisation may cover all or part of the enterprise's property. The property to be transferred is stated to have been managed by existing enterprises due to the uncertainty about ownership of assets under the previous system.

Certain property is excluded from the Large Privatisation Act and is, therefore, not capable of being transferred. For example:

■ National property which is obliged to remain, according to the Constitution of Czechoslovakia, under the sole ownership of the state (eg, natural resources, historical monuments and public transport facilities).

■ Property to be returned to juristic persons such as churches, religious orders and congregations by special rules of law.

■ Property which may be subject to the restitution laws. However, even property which is *prima facie* subject to restitution claims may be sold in the privatisation process unless the restitution claims have been made within a specified time.

■ Property to be privatised under the Small Privatisation Act.

The Federal Ministry of Finance, together with the Ministries of National Property Administration and Privatisation of the Czech and Slovak Republics, have produced guidelines for the preparation of privatisation plans. The Ministries have and will continue to evaluate industrial and commercial enterprises which they consider are particularly appropriate for privatisation. It will then be for the managers of these enterprises to prepare a privatisation project. It is anticipated that as many as 4,000 of the largest enterprises will be privatised by direct sale to the managers and employees through the voucher scheme and, in some cases, by auction. In many cases the larger enterprises are to be broken into smaller commercial entities in order to make them more suitable for privatisation. Foreign participation in this process will be actively encouraged.

The privatisation project

The central feature of the Large Privatisation Act is that the privatisation project, which is the first stage of the privatisation process, is the primary responsibility of the managers and/or the founder of the enterprise. The founder of an enterprise is the organ of state administration responsible for the enterprise, and will generally be the relevant ministry (eg the Ministry of Industry) or the sectoral ministry (eg an enterprise involved with health care products will be controlled by the Ministry of Health and by certain national committees). The privatisation project should contain an extensive analysis of the enterprise and its business and will include all relevant economic, technological and other information, including the following:

- A description, valuation and assessment of the property designated to be privatised, including that property not considered suitable for sale, such as bad debts, obsolete stock and other unusable assets.

- Information about the manner in which the state acquired the relevant property.

- A method of transfer of the property to be privatised including settling claims by authorised persons.

- If a commercial company is to be formed, the nature of that company.

- If a joint stock company is to be formed, the division of its share capital, the percentage of each type of share and the extent to which investment vouchers will be used.

■ In the event of a sale, the form and method of determining the price, and the conditions of payment.

■ The method of transfer of intellectual property rights, although this has to be subject to discussion with the Federal Bureau for Inventions if these rights belong to the enterprise.

■ The timetable for completion of the project.

Further information which the privatisation project should contain include details of the future activities of the enterprise, details of the persons who have expressed interest in either purchasing the enterprise in whole or in part or in establishing a commercial company to use the property of the enterprise, details of the present and expected market share of the enterprise, and the number of staff and their qualifications. The project may be concerned with either the whole enterprise, a part of the property of the enterprise only, or the combined property of several enterprises.

Preparation of the project

Although the Act states that the founder is responsible for the preparation of privatisation projects, in practice it will usually be the managers of the enterprise who will prepare the plan. This will invariably involve assistance from outside professional advisers, but will often also mean involvement by foreign prospective purchasers or joint venture partners. In the event that somebody other than the enterprise does prepare the project, the founder will seek the views of the enterprise itself on the proposed project.

Approval of a privatisation project is a matter for the Federal Ministry of Finance, or the Czech or Slovak Ministries of Privatisation, depending upon whether the enterprise is a federal- or Republic-based and controlled entity. The federal government or the Czech or Slovak governments, as the case may be, may reserve the right to approve specific projects which they consider essential to the interests of the economy generally. In all cases, a direct sale of property will be subject to governmental approval.

Transition of privatised property to funds

One of the central features of the Large Privatisation Act is the establishment of funds into which all the assets of the state enterprises to be privatised are to be placed after the project has been approved. It is from these funds that assets will be purchased by those participating in the privatisation programme. The enterprise can cease operating, its assets be removed to the fund, and its business passed to some other entity, without the need for liquidation. The assets that come within the privatisation project will then be removed and either returned to the ownership of the privatised entity or transferred to the newly established company that is taking over the enterprise's business.

The property of the funds may only be used for the purposes defined by the Large Privatisation Act, which are to establish joint stock companies or other commercial companies, to sell part or all of their property, to transfer the properties to municipalities or to transfer the property for the purpose of pension and health insurance funds. In addition, it is possible that funds may be used to settle restitution claims or to fulfil the continuing obligations of enterprises which are privatised. Property sold from the funds will either be sold on the basis of private contract or at public auction.

There are three funds: federal, Czech and Slovak. Essentially, assets of enterprises controlled by federal organs will be placed in the federal funds, while enterprises controlled locally in a particular Republic will transfer their assets to the Republic's fund. Enterprises operating in both Republics will transfer their assets to the Republic fund where it has its base, but the fund will be divided two-thirds to the Czech fund and one-third to the Slovak fund.

Intellectual property

The only assets not transferred to the fund relate to intellectual property (ie patents, trade marks, trade names, industrial designs, copyrights, etc.). Instead, these rights are transferred directly from the enterprise to the successor or purchaser by contract. The method of their transfer, or at least outlines of the proposed method subject to contractual negotiation, must be indicated in the privatisation project.

The problem is to determine whether the enterprise is, in fact, the owner of the particular right. The main difficulties arise with patents and industrial designs and their improvements, as in some circumstances such rights may belong to the employee who developed them, even though this was done in the context of his employment, subject obviously to registration. (The enterprise has two months to claim and register such right or any improvement by an employee, or the employee could claim the right.) The situation is similar for copyright and software.

Another difficulty, which is still unclear, concerns where only part of an enterprise is privatised. In such circumstances, it is important for the investor to ensure that the relevant Czech or Slovak ministry has approved the privatisation plan *including* the transfer of any relevant intellectual property rights.

Effective purchase

On the contract becoming effective, ownership of the property, both movable and immovable, being transferred under the privatisation project, as well as other rights and obligations related to the privatised property, will pass to the purchaser. It is not necessary for the creditors of the enterprise to approve the assignments of any debts, although the fund out of which the property is sold is obliged to guarantee the fulfilment of the obligations which had been acquired by the purchaser. If the entire property of the enterprise is being privatised, (unless a specific provision to the contrary is stipulated in the contract and subject to the Act on Trade Names) the use of the name of the enterprise will automatically be transferred to the purchaser.

Investment vouchers

The voucher system is one of the most controversial aspects of the Czechoslovak privatisation scheme. It was introduced in order to maximise the number of participants in the privatisation process and to try to involve as wide a part of the Czechoslovak population as possible. The aim is not only to transfer ownership of the many enterprises to the public, but also to establish a share and property owning populace, because it is believed that people who own part of the business and will enjoy the fruits of its success will work harder and show more initiative. Another objective is to help the creation of a financial and securities industry.

Due to the limited amount of private savings, a sell-off to Czechoslovak citizens alone was not considered practicable. It was also felt that if assets were sold to the highest bidder then 'tainted money' would be attracted (ie, those who benefited most from the previous communist system would acquire the majority of the assets). Accordingly, the Czechoslovak government has proposed a scheme under which it will sell 1000 investor points to all Czechoslovak citizens and residents. The cost at which they will be offered will be substantially less than the value of the shares which can be purchased with these investment points. The vouchers will be non-transferable, other than to heirs. Vouchers can then be used to buy shares in the privatised companies offered to the public.

Each voucher, which will be issued by the Federal Ministry of Finance, will contain the name and date of birth of the citizen, the name of the authority which issued the voucher, the acquiring price, the period of validity, and the date of issue. However, the net proceeds of sale of the vouchers will be transferred to the relevant fund according to the residence of the purchaser of the voucher. The vouchers will be used for the purchase of shares of any joint stock company included in the list of privatisation projects, or for acquiring a participation in the commercial companies founded especially for this purpose, after the necessary consents have been obtained.

Miscellaneous provisions

There are special rules about the valuation of the property of an enterprise and, in particular, where there is participation by foreigners in the privatisation process, the Federal Ministry of Finance will request a market evaluation by internationally recognised specialists.

Article 45 of the Large Privatisation Act contains a provision which is designed to prevent enterprises avoiding the privatisation process. An enterprise is unable to dispose of assets over which it has control, other than in the ordinary course of business, unless special governmental approval is obtained. It is possible that this may cause delay for certain foreigners wishing to establish joint ventures.

15

Real Estate

SJ Berwin & Co

Foreign investors in Czechoslovakia need to be familiar with the basic principles of property law (here meaning land as opposed to personal property) applicable there. The land occupied by the enterprise in which the foreign investor intends to invest or the land to be acquired by the enterprise for the purposes of its business is of fundamental importance to the well-being of that business. Not only is it important to be sure that the enterprise has good title to the land but also that the use of the land is not restricted in any way by rights which other persons may have over it. Furthermore, the foreign investor contemplating establishing an office in Czechoslovakia will wish to know whether he can in fact own or occupy land himself or through a Czechoslovak company and, if so, how the ownership or occupation can be best effected.

The law covering this area is complex and is in transition between the previous system of socialist ownership and the new property legislation to be enacted in response to the needs of a market economy. It is expected that a new property law will be passed shortly. Until it is passed, the principles will continue to follow those of the pre-revolution era. This chapter therefore covers ownership, use and dealings in land as the law currently exists.

Following the establishment of the socialist state in 1948 large areas of land were expropriated or confiscated by the state without compensation. The restitution laws attempt to restore the position and clear up uncertainties relating to title to land.

The co-operative form of ownership still plays an important role in the Czechoslovak economy, not only in agriculture but also in production of consumer goods and in the construction industry. The ownership of land must be clarified at the outset when dealing with property in Czechoslovakia as only state property is subject to privatisation and many of the laws relate only to state property. Furthermore, the ability to use and dispose of property depends upon the legal status of the bodies who own it.

On the other hand the significant change in property law after the revolution in November 1989 was to put all forms of ownership on equal footing. This particularly involved removing the state's favoured position in relation to property and enabling private owners or private enterprises to exercise property rights in the same way as former socialist enterprises. Property law principles are contained in the Economic Code as amended by subsequent legislation. The Act on Letting and Sub-letting of Business Premises is a major piece of new legislation affecting property to be let for business purposes.

OWNERSHIP

As a result of recent legislative changes, land in Czechoslovakia may be owned by the state, a co-operative, socialist organisations or other legal persons or individuals. The provisions covering owner-ship by the state, co-operatives and socialist organisations are likely to be temporary due to the privatisation of state property and amendments to the legislation covering co-operative ownership. Any legal entity, including a joint venture with foreign participation and, indeed, a 100 per cent foreign-owned subsidiary, is entitled to acquire land. Generally a foreign individual may not acquire land (other than a business lease). Land may however be obtained by a foreign person in ways other than purchase such as, for example, the restitution of property rights under the Small Restitution Act (foreigners are excluded from the Large Restitution Act). Further-more, the second round of public auctions within the Small Privatisation Act are open to foreigners as are acquisitions of shares of enterprises covered by the Large Privatisation Act (excluding the acquisition of vouchers).

State property generally includes property owned by the state, property rights of the state and property rights of state organisa-tions. A state enterprise or other state organisation has the 'right of management over such property'.

Co-operative property is a collective form of ownership of a group of citizens who are voluntarily associated for agricultural, social, production, distribution or other common needs. The major difference between state and co-operative ownership is that state entities only manage property whereas co-operatives own the land (unless they occupy property acquired from the state free of charge).

Property ownership by social organisations is still acknowledged by law. The organisation can only use state property given to it to achieve its objectives, although it can use its own property as it wishes.

Rights and duties of ownership

The following are the rights and duties flowing from the ownership of land:

- An owner has a right of possession and is entitled to have the right protected.

- The owner or manager (in the case of state property) or any user of the land must refrain from doing anything that would seriously threaten the exercise of another person's rights over the property.

- A building is owned by its builder unless the builder is a state organisation, in which case the owner is the state.

- The land may be in co-ownership, including co-ownership with the state. The use and disposal of the land must be agreed between the co-owners. The approval of the other co-owners must be obtained for any transfer of a share in the land.

- There are detailed rules in the Civil Code as to the rights and duties of private owners of land covering such matters as rights of entry on to adjoining land.

LAND DEALINGS

Land registration

Land in Czechoslovakia is subject to a system of registration. Any dealings in land must be entered in the Land Register before they can take effect.

However, the current shortcomings of the Land Register cannot be overemphasised. It originally applied to land throughout Czechoslovakia and was maintained by the district courts. However, in 1957 the registration system was taken over by the Office of Geodesy and Cartography and, as a result of many old documents being lost during the transfer, records of ownership are, to say the least, unclear. The foreign investor needs to be aware of this possible complication.

Transfer and use of state land

The Economic Code governs transfers of land to entitities, and the Civil Code to individuals. Specific provisions are likely to be replaced in a new property law. It is important to ascertain whether state land is subject to restitution rights or is the subject of privatisation (particularly under the Small Privatisation Act where the first round of auctions was not open to foreigners).

Currently, state land can be put to the permanent use of entities other than state organisations, such as co-operatives or societies. It is uncertain whether these arrangements will continue under the new property law and therefore whether they will apply to the activities of foreign business people.

The manager of state property may let surplus property to individuals under the Civil Code. Such a contract of letting must contain:

- a description of the property;
- the term of the letting;
- the payment due for the use of the property; and
- an agreement on the maintenance of the property and the sharing of maintenance costs.

The letting terminates by agreement of the parties, the expiry of the term or, if the letting was for an indeterminate period, upon one month's notice. These arrangements do not apply to business premises which are covered by separate legislation explained later in this chapter.

Transfer of co-operative land

Co-operative land is owned collectively by the members of the co-operative and may be transferred or let with the agreement of all its members. Such land is not subject to restitution rights. The law in relation to co-operatives will shortly be amended and a different legal regime will then apply.

Letting and sub-letting of business premises

Business people looking for premises in Czechoslovakia should know about the new law on the letting and sub-letting of business premises. This law applies whether the tenant is a foreigner or a Czechoslovak entity or individual. Different types of property must be distinguished because they are treated differently. Residential property is subject to a different law – the Act on Management of Flats.

Business premises can only be let for specific purposes for which they are approved by the building construction authority. For selling and offering of services a government permit is required. The lease must be in writing. If the parties fail to observe the provisions of the Act, or if a government permit is not obtained the lease is null and void. The mandatory provisions of the lease are:

- a description of the property and the purpose of the lease;

- the amount of the rent (if this is not fixed by law then it is open to agreement by the parties);

- if the lease is to be for a fixed term, the length of the term.

The lease expires at the end of the term. A periodic tenancy may be determined by the landlord or tenant giving three months' notice in writing without proving any grounds. The landlord may determine a lease for a fixed term before the expiration of the term by giving three months' notice in writing and by proving any of the following grounds stated in the Act:

- The use of the premises by the tenant is contrary to the terms of the lease.

- The tenant is in arrears on the rent by more than one month.

- The tenant is obliged by the lease to perform certain services to the landlord (in order to cover part of the rent) and the tenant has not performed those services.

- The tenant's behaviour has caused nuisance or annoyance to other occupiers.

- The letting was in conjunction with the use of a flat and the tenant has been required to vacate the flat.

- The landlord intends to redevelop the building in which the premises are situated.

- The tenant has assigned or sub-let the premises to another person without the approval of the landlord.

- The tenant is unable to carry on the business for which he took the premises. A tenant may determine a fixed term lease by giving three months' notice in writing and by proving any of the grounds stated in the Act.

- The premises have become unusable other than due to the fault of the tenant.

- The landlord is in breach of the duties imposed on him by the lease.

Following termination of the lease, the property must be given up in its original state. This is particulary significant in relation to alterations undertaken by the tenant. The rights and duties of landlords and tenants are governed by the following principles:

- The landlord is obliged to hand over the premises in such a state as to enable them to be used for the agreed purposes and it is the landlord's duty to keep the premises in that state at his own cost.

- The tenant is obliged to pay the maintenance costs on the premises.

- The tenant is under a duty to notify the landlord of disrepair. The tenant must allow the landlord necessary access to undertake the repair, otherwise he is liable for any consequent damage.

- A tenant can take a further lease of the premises only with the approval of the landlord.

Other than these principles contained in the Act, the landlord and tenant are free to negotiate the remaining terms of the lease. However, under Czechoslovak law as it currently stands, it is not possible to assign the benefit of a lease. This is because the Economic Code only permits the assignment of one particular contractual relationship, a claim to a debt, and a lease clearly does not come within this. Czechoslovakia does not as yet possess a sophicated market in the letting of business premises. There is obviously no recognised 'institutionally acceptable' form of lease and each letting tends to be in an *ad hoc* form. Certain lettings have been linked to a lease on the German model with the rent payable in Deutschmarks.

MORTGAGES AND OTHER FORMS OF SECURITY

The concept of security for the performance of an obligation is a relatively new one in Czechoslovak law and was introduced by an amendment to the Economic Code. As such, therefore, the main principles are very bare, evidencing the lack of a sophisticated property investment market.

Mortgages and other forms of security only exist alongside the obligations which they secure, and are ancillary to those obligations. The benefit of security over property is that it enables a creditor in the case of default to obtain satisfaction from the property given as security. The security is taken generally to secure a monetary claim but it is also possible to secure a non-monetary obligation, for example a supply of products.

Security can be taken over both movable and immovable property: security over land is a mortgage. It is possible under the Code on International Trade for a foreign claim to be secured. The security can be taken either by agreement or by law. If taken by agreement, it must be in writing and, in relation to land, its existence must be registered in the Land Register. The principal means of enforcing the security involves the sale of the property in accordance with the principles contained in the Economic Code. The security may be redeemed on repayment of the debt. When the security is redeemed the assets must be returned and the reference to the mortgage deleted from the Land Register.

EASEMENTS/SERVITUDES

The owner of one property may obtain rights (an easement/servitude) across another person's property. This may be obtained for access, drainage, supply of services, support to a building or for a similar purpose. The existence of such a right must be entered in the Land Register of the property affected by the right. The right attaches to the land and may not be sold separately. Such a right may be granted in a document or may be obtained through prescription after it has been exercised continuously for a period of ten years.

BUILDING PERMISSIONS

Prior to commencement of building works the builder/owner must obtain a building permit. This permit is issued by the local organs of state administration (the national committee for dealing with building activities within the relevant territory).

16

Commercial Law

SJ Berwin & Co

The principles of Czechoslovak commercial law are regulated by the Economic Code, as amended in 1990. The Economic Code was designed to govern relations between socialist organisations and, at the time of writing, commercial relations between state organisations, companies and individual entrepreneurs are governed by the Code. Relations between Czechoslovak parties and foreign parties are governed by the International Trade Code of 1963. This chapter deals with some of the most important aspects of commercial law such as the formation, interpretation and determination of contracts, the liability for damage to others, unjust enrichment and product liability.

The federal parliament intends to adopt a new Commercial Code during 1991. This code will replace the Economic Code and the International Trade Code and therefore will contain provisions relevant to commercial relations within Czechoslovakia as well as relations arising from international trade. The new Code will include substantive as well as procedural provisions. A system of commercial courts will be introduced, although it has not been decided whether this will be included in the code or will be in separate legislation.

The provisions relating to contracts between individuals are to be found in the Civil Code. However, it is proposed in this chapter to concentrate only upon those provisions affecting contracts in the course of business which are found in the Economic Code. The Economic Code contains both mandatory provisions (distinguished by the use of the word 'shall') which are binding and cannot be excluded, and dispositive provisions (distinguished by the use of the word 'may') which will be binding unless excluded by the parties to the contract.

A company incorporated in Czechoslovakia (including a joint venture or wholly-owned subsidiary) is not permitted to chose a foreign system of law or foreign arbitration. However, in relation to contracts between foreign parties and companies incorporated in Czechoslovakia, foreign law and arbitration may be chosen. For the foreseeable future the latter will be the preferable route for the foreign investor due to the inexperience of the Czechoslovak judges in dealing with commercial matters.

THE LAW OF CONTRACT

The paramount principle of the law of contract is freedom of contract. This is a considerable departure from previous limitations upon contracting parties arising from state interference and central planning.

However, the new commercial environment has not yet fully stabilised due to the continued existence of state-owned enterprises. It is essential for business people who wish to contract in Czechoslovakia to know exactly what they can expect from their contractual partners, from both a legal as well as psychological point of view. Foreigners may be faced with Czechoslovak contracting parties with little experience of the notion of freedom of contract. As a result the Czechoslovak contracting party may have relatively few negotiating skills and limited flexibility. The problems facing the Czechoslovak contracting party can best be illustrated by a brief indication of the pre-revolution notion of a contract:

■ There was a restricted choice of contracting parties. In many areas of the economy the law stated with whom a contract could be made and what kind of obligations could be concluded.

■ The law listed, exhaustively and restrictively, who could carry out economic activities including making contracts. Private entrepreneurs, associations, and companies were excluded. Those empowered to enter into contracts involving foreign trade were particularly restricted. Organisations were permitted to contract only within the framework of economic activities stated in the constitution prepared by their founding ministry. They could not extend production or sales outside their permitted fields.

■ Even within their permitted activities, organisations were also subject to legal constraints requiring, for example, that, for national interest reasons, certain areas of their production had to be provided for nominated persons or for particular purposes.

■ Only certain unimportant contract terms were freely negotiable. The price, for example, was not: it would be fixed under existing price regulations. The quality of the goods was also governed by specified technical standards and not by agreement of the parties.

The current draft of the Commercial Code does not contain any mandatory provisions relating to the formation of a contract and will, therefore, leave it to individual contracting parties to formulate their own agreements. The draft only contains provisions regulating what is termed as a 'public offer', meaning an offer of goods or services to the public generally rather than to specific parties.

Czechoslovak contract law requires a contract to be in writing unless the Economic Code or any other law or agreement specifically states otherwise. A contract not in writing is void. However, unless the parties previously agreed that the contract should be in writing, an oral contract can, under certain circumstances, be valid if it has been partly performed (eg goods partly supplied). The current draft of the Commercial Code leaves the contracting parties free to negotiate their own forms of contract in that a contract need only be in writing if the law specifically requires it.

There is a general rule which allows the parties to negotiate and agree the terms of contract provided that such terms are not prohibited by Czechoslovak law. The minimum essential terms of a contract are an agreement on:

■ the object of the contract (eg the goods or services to be provided);

■ the terms of fulfilment of the contract (eg delivery of the goods or services); and

■ any other item stated by either party as being an essential term.

If the price is not negotiable (ie it is fixed by existing law) it is not an essential term of a contract. However, the law relating to prices has been relaxed recently by the Law on Agreed Prices, and parties are now free to agree market prices in the majority of cases.

If there are any doubts as to the meaning of a contract it will be interpreted in accordance with the actual intentions of the contracting parties. The circumstances under which the contract was made and principles of good faith will also be taken into account. Ambiguous terms will be interpreted against the persons who drafted them.

A contract may be void because of its form or content. If the reason for the contract being void is only applicable to part of the contract then only that part will be void and the remainder will remain in force unless the underlying substance of the contract has been lost. A contract may be void for the following reasons:

■ If a term is contrary to the law or the purpose of a contract is to circumvent restrictions imposed by the law.

■ If its object is incapable or impossible of performance. Performance is considered to be still possible if it can be effected only under more difficult conditions, or at an increased cost, or after a delay.

■ If it is founded upon a basic mistake by either party and the other party knew or ought to have known of the mistake.

■ If one party is induced into entering into it by illegal threat or by fraud.

A contract may only be avoided by the aggrieved party. Alternatively, that party may also affirm the contract subsequently, in which case it is treated as valid from the outset.

The Economic Code contains the notion of a 'preparatory contract' in which the parties make a preliminary agreement to enter into a future contract (ie a contract to contract). This is of importance in respect of the negotiations leading up to the formation of a contract. Business people should therefore take care when reaching agreement in principle to make clear the non-binding nature of the commitment or the 'heads of terms', unless they are intended to be binding.

Specific types of contract

The current Economic Code contains specific provisions relating to specific types of contract and it is likely that the Commercial Code will contain similar provisions. The most important categories of contract contained in the current draft of the Commercial Code are:

■ contracts for the sale of property;

- contracts for the purchase of an enterprise;

- leasing contracts;

- loan agreements;

- licence agreements for intellectual property; and

- agency agreements.

UNJUST ENRICHMENT

Czechoslovak law has a general principle of unjust enrichment which is wider than anything comparable in English law. Where a person acquires a pecuniary advantage from property to which he does not have title and at the expense of another person, the advantage must be refunded or paid to the person who is properly entitled.

LIABILITY FOR DAMAGE TO OTHERS

Product guarantees and breach of contract

A supplier is responsible for the quality of the goods, which is either stated in a technical specification or agreed in the contract. The duration of the guarantee depends upon the nature of the products, although the parties may vary this in the contract.

A contracting party is obliged to perform his or her part of the contract within a certain period. No delay is attributed to a party in performing a contract where the delay is due to the person benefiting from the performance.

If a contracting party does not perform his or her part of the contract on time, the other party is entitled to withdraw from the contract. Before exercising the right to withdraw, the party in breach must be given notice of his failure to perform and a sufficient additional period to perform appropriate to the nature of the obligation. If the party in breach remedies the breach during this period then the innocent party may not determine the contract.

Damages

Following the latest amendment to the Economic Code, Czechoslovak law recognises three types of damages:

1. damage caused by operations, including environmental damage;

2. damage caused by property;

3. damage caused by breach of contract.

A person can avoid being liable for damage caused by his or her operations if the damage was caused by *force majeure* or by another person (including the person suffering the damage).

17

Competition

SJ Berwin & Co

UNFAIR COMPETITION

Like France, Germany and most countries in the civil law tradition
(and unlike the UK), Czechoslovakia has a collection of rules under
the general heading of 'Unfair Competition'. They are based on the
principle that a person must not behave in a way which is
incompatible with fair competition and is calculated to damage a
competitor.

The Economic Code classifies as unfair competition:

- Passing-off – ie acting in such a way as to lead to confusion
  about the identity of the products or industrial or trading
  activities of a competitor.

- False information which could harm the reputation of the
  products or industrial or trading activities of a competitor.

- Misleading information, the use of which could deceive the
  public with regard to goods.

The draft Commercial Code attempts to provide more specific and
detailed standards of behaviour for the cut and thrust of free
competition. Its targets include misleading advertising and labelling;
parasite competition (designed to steal the reputation of a competitor); corruption (getting unfair advantage by suborning employees
and others in a position of trust); discredit (spreading damaging
information about a competitor without justification); and under-
cutting competitors by marketing products which do not meet
public health or environmental requirements.

Remedies for unfair competition will be through court proceedings claiming an injunction to stop the wrongful behaviour,

damages or unjust enrichment. Damages for loss of reputation can be claimed in addition to financial loss. Trade associations and consumer groups will have the right to bring unfair competition proceedings.

ANTI-TRUST LAW

The Act on Protection of Economic Competition ('the Act') was passed on 30 January 1991 and came into force on 31 March. It grapples with the difficult task of laying down and enforcing principles of free competition in an economy which still consists substantially of state-owned monopolies.

The Act affects privatisation, joint ventures and (in some cases) commercial contracts such as licence and distribution agreements. The following is a brief overview.

Purpose and scope

The purpose of the Act is to protect economic competition and create conditions which are favourable for its continued development and unfavourable to monopolies and dominant positions which prevent or restrict competition.

The Act applies to:

- Private enterprises – all entrepreneurs engaged in business within Czechoslovakia, including foreign entrepreneurs who have a permanent base there.

- State enterprises – state administration and community organs with activities that are relevant to competition.

- Activities which take place abroad, so far as the effects of such activities impact on the home market.

Private enterprises and state enterprises are referred to together in the Act as 'entrepreneurs'. The law does not apply to the effects of acts which are only manifest in a foreign market.

Jurisdiction is exercised by Offices for Economic Competition at federal and Republic levels. The federal Office has jurisdiction in cases where more than 40 per cent of total supplies to the relevant market in Czechoslovakia is involved. In other cases, jurisdiction belongs to the Republic Office of the territory in which the matter may have an impact. The appropriate office (or offices) is referred to here as 'the Office'.

The Act reproduces many of the concepts of EC anti-trust law, developed under Articles 85 and 86 of the Treaty of Rome. It targets five areas for achieving its purpose of protecting competition:

1. cartel agreements (anti-competitive agreements and practices);

2. mergers adversely affecting competition;

3. the abuse of a monopoly or dominant position in the market;

4. state aids; and

5. lack of competitiveness following denationalisation and privatisation.

Cartel agreements

Cartel agreements are agreements or understandings which result, or may result, in preventing or limiting competition. Such agreements are null and void (ie unenforceable in the courts) and punishable by a fine of up to 5 per cent of each party's turnover for the previous financial year (or the amount of any actual financial benefit gained through the illicit behaviour).

Examples of cartel agreements given in the legislation are:

■ price fixing;

■ agreements which restrict or control production, sales, technological development or investment;

■ sharing of markets for goods or services;

■ agreements on different commercial terms for different customers under contracts for the same goods and services, whereby certain buyers will be placed at a disadvantage;

■ agreements to block access to the market by third parties;

■ unwanted 'ties'; and

■ improper restrictions on the right to terminate an agreement.

So far as intellectual property rights are concerned, a restriction on competition which goes beyond their 'object and scope' is null and void, unless an exemption is granted.

Exemptions

As in the case of EC anti-trust law, the Office has power to grant an exemption where the restriction on competition is essential to achieve a benefit in the interest of the public and the consumer. Examples mentioned in the Act include standard conditions of sale, manufacturing specialisation agreements and non-discriminatory discounts. Exemptions may be granted on a conditional basis.

An exemption will also be given where the market share of the parties is less than 5 per cent of the market of a Republic, or 30 per cent of the local market which they regularly supply.

All cartel agreements must be registered at the federal Office. There is no exception, even for agreements which are too small to affect the market, unless an exemption is actually applied for.

Applications for exemption are treated as granted unless the Office notifies its refusal within two months. The Office retains wide discretion and presumably expects, in most cases, to take no action so that exemptions will be granted by default – the two-month time limit would otherwise be unworkable. The policy seems to be that the Office should get as much information as possible and then decide selectively which relationships pose significant dangers to competition and call for special scrutiny.

Escape clauses

A dissatisfied contracting party can take advantage of two escape clauses. First, everyone is given the right to terminate an agreement which is for longer than two years, by giving six months' notice at the end of the second or any subsequent year. Agreements about pricing can be terminated by two months' notice at the end of the first year, or at the end of any subsequent six months. 'Agreement' in this context almost certainly means 'cartel agreement', namely a *restriction on competition* (eg an undertaking not to deal in competing products), and *not* the whole agreement – provided the agreement is economically viable without the restriction.

Secondly, a party can withdraw from such an agreement if it has become burdensome due to unforeseen circumstances which are 'so serious that he or she may not be justly asked to suffer such detriment notwithstanding any detriment the other parties to the agreement may suffer by the withdrawal'. The right to give such a withdrawal notice may be challenged in court.

These escape clauses must be borne in mind when negotiating any joint venture, licence or distribution agreements to which the Act applies. Both could operate harshly against the party which entered into, say, a ten-year licence agreement, only to find that some of the most important protective clauses – such as those designed to preserve exclusivity for the licensor – were brought to an early end.

Control of mergers

Mergers are subject to control by the Office if they are likely to result in a limitation of competition in the relevant market. An agreement whereby one entrepreneur acquires the legal or *de facto* possibility of control of the whole or part of another, counts as a merger for this purpose.

If the participating enterprises control more than 30 per cent of the relevant market, this is to be treated as automatically threatening to limit competition.

Mergers must be approved by the Office in advance. Failure to obtain approval means that the merger will be legally invalid. The Office is required to approve a merger if it is established that any detriment through restrictions on competition is outweighed by economic benefits. The Office may also tie its approval to conditions and may limit its duration. If a decision is not given within three months, the agreement is treated as approved.

Abuse of a monopoly or dominant position

The Act does not prohibit the acquisition of a monopoly or dominant position as such, but – like Article 86 of the Treaty of Rome – the *abuse* of such a position.

A monopoly position in the relevant market means that an entrepreneur faces no competition at all. A dominant position arises where it delivers not less than 30 per cent of the total supplies of identical, comparable or interchangeable goods. The 'relevant market' is the entire market of a Republic, or the local market which the parties to the agreement regularly supply. It could, therefore, be very small.

An enterpreneur may not abuse his or her monopoly or dominant position to the detriment of other enterpreneurs, customers or against the public interest. Abuse involves particularly:

- forcing the acceptance of unfair terms in contracts;

- forcing acceptance of a contract with the condition that the other contracting party will accept an additional contract which is unrelated to the original contract;

- inserting arbitrarily different terms in contracts with different contracting parties; or

- suspending or reducing production, sales or technical development of a commodity in order to obtain a benefit to the buyer's detriment.

The Office: extent of powers

The federal and Republic Offices maintain cartel registers and have extensive powers, not unlike those of the EC Commission, in relation to competition matters. These include imposition of fines (discussed earlier), obtaining information and documents, taking interim measures to safeguard the position before a final decision is made and ordering correction of infringements. The latter would, presumably, include power to order a merger carried out without the necessary approval to be unscrambled. The procedures of the Office are treated as a matter of administrative law but are open to judicial review by the courts.

There is a general obligation for Office personnel to maintain confidentiality about commercial secrets of enterprises.

The Office has the following functions in relation to state administration organs:

- It is empowered to 'demand' correction of state aids which interfere with competition, but without any machinery for enforcing its will.

- State bodies involved in the transfer of state property in, or in preparation for privatisation projects, must evaluate the competitiveness of the future operating body and must submit their evaluation to the Office for an opinion.

- Community organs (eg municipal bodies) are required to establish a 'competitive medium' for the relevant regional or local market when state enterprises are being divided up or transferred. If competition is not protected at that time, the community organ must produce proposals to remedy the situation within two years. There is an exclusion for 'services where citizens cannot influence the choice of their supplier in view of transportation distances as they relate to extensive time loss and real transportation costs'.

Some general comments

1. It cannot be too strongly emphasised that the operation of the Act depends almost entirely on how the officials at the Office exercise their discretion.

2. The Act probably does not apply to foreigners without a permanent base in Czechoslovakia. A representative office is probably a permanent base for this purpose. It remains to be seen whether the Office will invoke the 'effects doctrine' in relation to acts done abroad, so as to catch agreements to which foreigners are parties.

3. It also remains to be seen whether a distribution or licence agreement under which the Czechoslovak party undertakes not to export outside Czechoslovakia, will be treated as being outside the Act because its effects are only manifest in a foreign market. More probably, a restriction on exports will be found to have a potential effect on competition within Czechoslovakia and therefore to fall under the Act.

4. The jurisdiction of the federal and Republic Offices is ill-defined. It depends on the market shares involved and, as it is difficult to get two economists to agree on what constitutes a 'relevant market', this is a potential for jurisdictional disputes.

5. The exemption procedure may operate arbitrarily because, on the one hand, it will be necessary to apply for exemption even for very small cartel agreements and, on the other, exemption will automatically be treated as having been granted if no refusal is given within two months, even if the restrictions involve blatant market sharing or similar abuses.

6. Fines can be imposed only within one year after a breach of duty has been ascertained but not later than three years after the end of the year when the breach occurred. This places a premium on concealment and may be compared to the EC where fines are often imposed for events which took place many years previously.

7. All mergers which may result in limitation of economic competition must be approved in advance. As this criterion is impossible to determine without a decision, all merger agreements, including agreements to acquire control of part of a business, will have to be submitted (but will be treated as approved if no decision is given within three months).

8. The Act applies both to state and private enterprises. However, the activities for which a state enterprise was formed fall outside the Act to the extent that these activities will, by their intrinsic nature, limit competition.

9. The Act is likely to be amended to make it fully workable. Meanwhile, careful consideration will be needed as to whether a notification and application for exemption should be made in an individual case, even where one of the parties involved is based outside Czechoslovakia.

18

The Fiscal Framework
KPMG Peat Marwick McLintock

The information on taxation in the book has been divided between two chapters. The Czechoslovak tax system, the main taxes, their administration and collection, and likely future developments in the tax system are discussed in this chapter. The taxation issues that will affect decisions to invest in Czechoslovakia, such as tax planning, tax structures, and the tax treatment of joint ventures are covered in Chapter 36.

THE CZECHOSLOVAK TAX SYSTEM

Under the Czechoslovak Federal Constitution, taxation may only be imposed in Czechoslovakia under an Act of Parliament. Such powers are given to both the federal and the republic parliaments.

As there was no equivalent to the capitalist concept of making profits under the communist, centrally planned economic system no concept of the taxation of such profits developed. At the same time, the Czechoslovak accounting systems are rudimentary when compared with Western systems and are still largely geared to providing measures of compliance with state reporting requirements. The combination of these factors means that the Czechoslovak tax system is comparatively unsophisticated by Western standards.

The direct tax system includes all forms of receipts as income (and, in most circumstances, makes little distinction between capital and revenue receipts). All income from domestic sources is treated as taxable income, apart from a very few items such as compensation and damages. All persons physically present in Czechoslovakia and companies having a headquarters or a place of business within the jurisdiction of the state are treated as taxable subjects (including foreigners resident on Czechoslovak soil). Dividends received from Czechoslovak companies are taxable as ordinary income (ie, there is no domestic relief from double taxation in the form of a credit for the tax already paid by the company). Foreign dividends received by a Czechoslovak company are also taxable, except where exemption relief is provided for under a double taxation treaty. There is provision for double tax relief on a credit basis under Czechoslovak law – the foreign tax credit being allowed up to a maximum of the Czechoslovak tax on the foreign source income.

The principal taxes which apply in Czechoslovakia at the present time are:

- For enterprises:
  - profit tax
  - payroll tax;

- For individuals:
  - wage tax (withheld from wages)
  - citizens' income tax;

- Turnover tax.

There are a number of other taxes covering such areas as the transfer of property, gifts and agricultural taxes, but these are unlikely to be important investment considerations. Withholding taxes are looked at in Chapter 36.

Profits tax

It is as well to remember that until 1989 no private enterprise was permitted in Czechoslovakia other than the activities of individual small traders, craftsmen and joint ventures with foreign participation. In the latter case the Czechoslovak participants had to be state enterprises. Profits tax has applied to all Czechoslovak private enterprises since 1 January 1990 and is payable on profits at the rate of 20 per cent on the first Kčs200,000 of income and 55 per cent on the balance. The tax treatment of joint ventures is dealt with in Chapter 36.

Profits are computed on the basis of gross income less all expenses incurred in conducting the activities giving rise to the profit. The profit and loss account follows a standard chart provided for under the accounting law and is basically only prepared for tax return purposes. The accruals concept is recognised but items which are not allowable for tax purposes are not brought into the profit and loss account. The allowable expenses include depreciation allowances computed on a straight-line basis in accordance with the rates laid down by the Ministry of Finance in Decree 586 of 1990 (1.3 per cent for buildings and between 6 per cent and 13 per cent for various categories of plant). The payroll tax of 50 per cent of the wages bill, which is looked at in more detail below, is also treated as a deductible expense in arriving at taxable profits.

Certain items such as entertaining or excess costs of motoring are not deductible. Provisions for doubtful debts or for obsolescent stocks may not be made without specific permission from the Ministry of Finance. Similarly, excessive salaries (ie over and above that provided for under the plan), including under this heading items such as bonuses, staff welfare payments and holiday pay, are also not deductible, though the wages tax is still payable in respect of all payments of remuneration whether or not it is tax deductible. Previously these categories of payments were required to be provided out of the remuneration fund but since the requirement to make contributions into that fund has now been abolished it must be assumed that the categories of 'excessive payments' have been considerably reduced and will in time be eliminated. Penalties payable to state budgets (for instance, in respect of sub-standard goods) and other damages are not tax deductible.

Payroll Tax

The payroll tax, or the tax on the total amount of wages, is the equivalent of the employer's national insurance contribution in Britain and is the enterprise's contribution to the state social security fund. It is payable by most employers, including joint ventures and registered entrepreneurs. The tax is levied at the rate of 50 per cent of the total amount of wages, salaries and other remuneration paid during a year. This rate is reduced to 20 per cent for Czechoslovak-owned entities providing particular services as detailed in the appendix to Decree 193 of 1989. Where the company provides a mix of these and other services, the payroll is split according to the related division of employees providing the two different categories of services, and the appropriate rate is then applied. The computation of this tax must be agreed in advance with the relevant financial authority.

Wage tax and citizens' income tax

Wage tax

Employees in Czechoslovakia are subject to a monthly payroll deduction which their employer must pay over to the financial authorities each month. The tax is charged on gross pay but certain types of income, such as sickness benefits, child allowances and similar social security allowances, awards for innovations, scholarships, and some benefits in kind, such as agricultural workers' meals, are exempt. The rates of tax are progressive on monthly wages of more than Kčs2000, and tax is calculated by reference to coefficient factors which reflect the age and sex of the employee, and whether the employee is married and/or has children. The rates vary from 3.75 per cent to a maximum of 32 per cent of the monthly salary.

Citizens' income tax

The scope of the citizens' income tax includes all other income which is not otherwise taxable, including income derived from trades and professions, rental income and income from other property and rights. The costs of earning the income are deductible. The rates of tax are progressive: they vary between 15 per cent for incomes of up to Kčs60,000, and Kčs408,000 plus 55 per cent of any income in excess of Kčs1,080,000 (see Table 18.1).

Table 18.1 *Citizens' income tax rates*

Annual income (basis of assessment) Kčs	Tax payable Kčs	plus	%
1 – 60,000			15
60,001 – 180,000	9,000	over 60,000	25
180,001 – 540,000	39,000	over 180,000	35
540,001 – 1,080,000	165,000	over 540,000	45
1,080,001 –	408,000	over 1,080,000	55

Taxpayers are obliged to submit tax reports for the preceding calendar year to the financial authorities on the relevant form by 15 February. The tax is payable in quarterly instalments by the end of the month following the respective quarter of the calendar year. The final instalment is payable by 15 February of the following year.

The taxation of expatriates

Foreigners resident in Czechoslovakia and employed by a Czechoslovak company, eg a joint venture, will be subject to the same taxes as Czechoslovak citizens. Foreigners employed by a foreign company which has a permanent establishment, such as a representative office, in Czechoslovakia, are exempt from tax on the first 15 per cent of their Czechoslovak salary, and are liable to tax at 20 per cent on the remainder. Foreigners employed by a foreign company which has no permanent establishment in Czechoslovakia are not liable to Czechoslovak tax provided that they do not spend more than 183 days in any calendar year in Czechoslovakia.

Turnover tax

The turnover tax is still in operation but it is intended to replace it with a value added tax system from 1 January 1993. Turnover tax is an indirect tax designed to interact with the pricing structure, typical in a controlled economy. Various types of goods are subject to the tax and, until 1 January 1991, it was computed in a variety of ways leading to some 1800 different rates applying, the particular method used being appropriate to the category of goods involved. From 1 January 1991, the rates were reduced to four – 0 per cent, 12 per cent, 22 per cent and 32 per cent, with a small number of exceptions for certain luxury goods, including jewellery and cigarettes. In April 1991, these four rates were reduced to 0 per cent, 11 per cent, 20 per cent and 29 per cent.

Collection and administration of taxation

The Czechoslovak tax system is administered by the district and regional finance authorities under the authority of each Republic's Ministry of Finance.

Tax is required to be deducted at source by the Czechoslovak payer from wages, dividends, interest, royalties, income from literary and artistic activities and the profits paid to foreign taxpayers (ie, permanent establishments of foreign enterprises). Where the definitive liability of the taxpayer cannot be determined with any accuracy, the tax is collected by means of assessment rather than by withholding tax at source. Tax withheld by a Czechoslovak payer has to be accounted for to the Ministry of Finance within 15 days. The foreign recipient who has been subjected to excessive withholding is entitled to reclaim such overpaid tax within a period of three years following the end of the fiscal year in which the tax was withheld.

The accounts of a Czechoslovak enterprise, made up to the mandatory date of 31 December, are required to be filed with the Finance Administration by 15 February of the following year. The tax payable may be increased by 10 per cent where the taxpayer fails to file the required return within the prescribed period. Non-resident taxpayers commencing business in Czechoslovakia through a permanent establishment are required to notify the Finance Administration within 15 days of commencing activities. Termination of activities is required to be notified within 30 days and a tax return filed not later than the last day of the month following the termination of activities. Failure to file the relevant notifications could result in a fine of Kčs50,000.

FUTURE DEVELOPMENTS

It is intended to introduce a new tax system which will be suitable for the transition to a free market economy by 1 January 1993. New accounting concepts are being developed in line with Western practice for introduction in 1993 to enable this new tax system to function properly. However, a fully effective system of taxation will only appear once these generally accepted Western accounting practices become the norm in Czechoslovakia. VAT is also to be introduced in 1993.

Currently, enterprises are not allowed to set-off tax losses against future profits from the same business. It is expected that the new legislation will allow such losses to be carried forward for between three and five years. It is also expected that the new legislation will address the issue of transfer pricing.

19

The Environment

KPMG Peat Marwick McLintock and SJ Berwin & Co

ENVIRONMENTAL PRIORITIES

The Scope of Problems

'We are now trying to solve problems that were solved in Britain 50 years ago' was the comment from former Czech Republic Environment Minister, Bedrich Moldan (*Financial Times*, 21 November 1990). As with other Eastern European countries, environmental issues played a key role in the movement which led to the return of democracy in Czechoslovakia. Vaclav Havel, now President, was responsible for environmental issues in the dissident movement.

However, the advent of democracy has not solved environmental problems overnight. Simona Bouková, founding member of the environmental group Green Circle and now working in the Federal Environment Ministry said in 1990: 'the air, food and water is as poisonous as before. People give babies mineral water because tap water isn't safe even when it has been boiled' (*Guardian Environment*, 19 January 1990).

Life expectancy has declined rather than improved over the last ten years, and is now up to seven years lower than the average in the EC. Infant mortality and pollution-related cancers are reported to be soaring. Nearly one-third of the population are thought to live in badly affected environments. The Worldwatch Institute in Washington has estimated that Czechoslovakia is losing around 5–7 per cent of GNP annually to environmental degradation.

The country faces a wide range of pollution and waste disposal problems arising from a system which stressed high energy-consuming heavy industry despite limited natural and energy resources other than mainly poor quality coal, and where investment into environmental management was limited.

Air pollution

The main cause of air pollution in Czechoslovakia is the extensive use of coal, the country's only significant energy resource (60 per cent of primary energy). Per capita energy use in Czechoslovakia is considerably higher than in other industrial countries. The quality of the coal varies, but lower grade coal with high ash and sulphur contents is increasingly burnt in the country's power plants. Few power plants have adequate pollution equipment and emissions are high, especially in the 'black triangle' area where Czechoslovakia, Poland and Germany meet and where a large proportion of the country's electricity is generated.

Sulphur dioxide concentrations in some areas exceed acceptable daily means for over 30 per cent of the time, with extremely high concentrations occurring during adverse weather conditions. Sulphur deposit levels are among the worst in Europe. Together with uncontrolled nitrogen oxide emissions, these have caused some of the severest forest damage in Europe, with over 70 per cent of conifers suffering defoliation.

So far, little action has been taken to overcome these problems. Although Czechoslovakia has ratified the United Nations agreement on reducing sulphur emissions by 30 per cent, no commercial desulphurisation plants have been built (although one is under contract and there are some test plants). The country's resources of other energy sources, such as natural gas and renewables, are limited and safety problems have halted progress on the planned build-up of nuclear power capacity.

Water pollution

It has been claimed that 70 per cent of Czechoslovakia's rivers are heavily polluted and that over 50 per cent of drinking water is affected by industrial and agricultural effluent. At one point last year, residents in the city of Brno were warned not to drink the water without first boiling it. The main reason for this high level of contamination is the lack of effluent treatment facilities. Only 35 per cent of sewage is currently treated, and legislation requiring effluent treatment by industry is widely ignored.

Additional problems have arisen from accidental leaks and discharges. The extensive open-cast mining in parts of the country has disrupted water run-off and led to contamination with heavy metals. The decaying infrastructure of the country means that leaks from pipelines are increasing.

The country's main rivers, the Ultava, Elbe, Oder and Danube, are heavily polluted. This is fast becoming an international environmental issue. When Hungarian 'greens' forced work on a massive dam complex on the Danube at Nagymaros to be stopped, the Czechoslovak government demanded compensation. It is still unclear whether work on the Czechoslovak part of the dam complex, at Gabcikoyo, will be completed.

Waste and soil contamination

Like other Eastern European countries, Czechoslovakia has experienced problems with waste disposal and, in particular, control over the disposal of hazardous wastes. It has been estimated that 75 per cent of hazardous waste within the country is stored in dangerous conditions. Major waste disposal problems are also associated with the massive open-cast brown coal mine sites, especially in northern Bohemia.

Damage to the soil is also a significant problem. More than half of the agricultural soil in Czechoslovakia is claimed to be seriously eroded through mismanagement by the large collective farms that dominate the country's agriculture. There are also significant problems of soil contamination through poor waste disposal practices and, in mining areas, heavy metal contamination.

THE LEGAL STRUCTURE

The scope of Czechoslovakia's environmental problems is not due to lack of environmental protection laws. There are more than 50 of these relating to such matters as air and water pollution, forestry and noise. The problem has been lack of enforcement, due to the piecemeal way in which the laws have been adopted, the lack of effective monitoring and, above all, the lack of an integrated environment policy and the will (and means) to enforce it.

The attitude of the Czechoslovak government changed fundamentally after the 1989 revolution. In the words of its memorandum to the Group of 24 in February 1990: 'One of our principal priorities is to rectify the current state of devastation in our environment. In this area we have to pay back the debt we owe not only to the present and future generations of our citizens but also to Europe as a whole'.

As a first step towards creating the new climate, the government has embarked on a comprehensive programme of law reform.

The authorities responsible

Responsibility for the environment is divided between:

- the federal Committee for the Environment;

- the Ministry of the Environment of the Czech Republic; and

- the Slovak Commission for the Environment.

The federal Committee has responsibility for initiating policies and legislation on all major environmental questions as well as direct responsibility for legislation on waste management and nature conservation.

Within the Republics, responsibilities for various aspects of the environment are differently distributed. The Czech Republic gives wider powers to its Environment Ministry but separate aspects are divided between this Ministry and various other authorities. As regards water, for example, water quality is the responsibility of the Environment Ministry; the Ministry of Agriculture is responsible for providing water supply and sewage facilities; and the water-related buildings, plant and equipment are owned and operated by the municipalities. Conversely, in the Slovak Republic, the responsibility for water quality is divided between the Slovak Commission for the Environment and the Ministry of Forestry and Water Management, so that only some aspects of water quality control come within the Environment Commission's powers.

Future reforms

Czechoslovakia's law reform programme for the environment is outlined in the first section of *Programme A*, a policy document on the protection of the environment adopted by a resolution of the federal government.

A primary aim will be to bring Czechoslovakia's environment laws into conformity with EC standards. The basic principles are to be laid down in a framework law, the proposal for which is under discussion at the time of writing. This impressive document, which could be described as Czechoslovakia's 'environmental constitution', reflects the latest thinking: the debt to the EC approach and to the World Commission report, *Our Common Future*, are acknowledged. Sustainable development is the central concept.

The draft framework law provides that existing laws are to be brought into line with its principles, or new laws adopted, within fixed deadlines to be specified by government regulation. Under

Programme A, laws are being prepared, at federal and Republic level, in the following specific areas:

- nature protection (amendment);

- air pollution;

- protection of water resources;

- protection of soil, agricultural and forest land;

- forest management;

- conservation of mineral resources;

- wild and domestic animals;

- land use (urban planning and environmental impact assessments);

- waste management;

- 'green labelling', protection against toxic and dangerous materials;

- nuclear safety and protection against radiation (amendment);

- technical breakdowns and natural disasters; and

- state administration on environmental matters (responsibilities of central organs at federal and Republic level).

The law on waste management was adopted by the federal assembly on 22 May 1991 and will come into force on 1 August.

The draft framework law: some key features

Although the draft framework law is likely to be amended in detail before it is enacted, the draft in its original form reflects the government's basic approach to the protection of the environment. Even though not final, it therefore repays examination.

Basic principles

The basic principles of the draft law are:

- the principle of sustainable development;

- the principle of prevention;

- the principle of circumspection;

■ the control of pollution at source, applying the 'emission and imission' principle.

Sustainable development is 'development in which society consumes only such a quantity that there is maintained for present and future generations the possibility of satisfying their basic biological and cultural requirements and the opportunity and time to find their own way of life in accordance with the state of the environment and natural resources; it also includes the preservation of the great variety of nature and the protection of the natural functions of ecosystems'.

The draft law reinforces the principle of prevention, with that of circumspection. This has two aspects:

1. The need for environmental impact assessments before any change in the use of land and natural resources.

2. A duty for the authorities to take preventive action if there appears to be a threat of serious environmental damage, even if this has not been established with complete scientific certainty.

The control of pollution at source and the emission and imission principle involve:

■ Fixing limit values for emissions contaminating the atmosphere, water and soil.

■ Raising these limits where necessary to take account of local conditions 'so that people are not threatened, their welfare is not disturbed, so that other living organisms and the ecosystems in which they occur are not threatened, buildings are not damaged, the fertility of the soil is not disturbed, nor the quality of the water and the purity of the atmosphere'.

Ecological damage

Ecological damage is 'the loss or weakening of the natural functions of ecosystems or their components'. The draft law states that repair and renewal of ecosystems are, where possible, to take priority over monetary compensation (although one does not preclude the other).

The use of financial and fiscal measures

Experience in Czechoslovakia and elsewhere shows that centralised regulatory control offers only weak protection to the environment. All too often, businesses would rather pay fines and continue to break the law if there is sufficient financial incentive. In accordance with contemporary (and EC) thinking, the framework law calls for financial and fiscal measures which will create an economic climate in which market forces will dictate good environmental practice. The differential tax on unleaded petrol is an example of the success of the UK's approach.

The financial and fiscal measures remain to be formulated and little can be expected until Czechoslovakia has completed the fundamental reform of its tax system scheduled for 1992. The government's *Programme A* envisages a combination of incentives and penalties. These include special taxes on products with unsatisfactory ecological properties during manufacture, consumption, use, recycling or discharge into the environment; credits, grants and appropriations to encourage caring for the environment; taxes and fees for the exploitation of natural resources, such as water; fees and fines for the disturbance of the environment; and import, export and customs regulations to reinforce environmental protection. These taxes and penalties will be used to establish funds to further environmental protection, both at federal and Republic level.

Environmental interest groups
The draft framework law declares the right of 'every being' to 'an environment which creates the conditions for all-round physical and mental development'. Based on this right, individual citizens or environmental interest groups would be able to take court proceedings to enforce environmental protection laws.

Environmental impact assessments
Environmental impact assessments are already required under the existing laws in relation to water, soil and air. The draft framework law provides for regulations to introduce strict new rules for comprehensive environmental impact assessments for every new or imported technology, product or substance. These will include monitoring after the product enters the waste stream.

Packaging and waste
All products, including their packaging, which are not completely consumed in use will have to carry information on how to dispose of the non-consumable parts.

Enforcement powers
Deadlines will be set within which existing land use, products and technologies must conform to the new laws. These deadlines will be

set by special regulations and if not met, the offending activity will be limited or stopped.

Interestingly, it is proposed that, even where no law is being broken, the authorities will have power to stop activities posing a serious pollution threat.

GUIDANCE FOR INVESTORS

Key sectors

Environment-related goods and services represent a major investment opportunity in Czechoslovakia. It has been estimated that nearly $24 billion will be required to clean up environmental degradation over the next 15 years.

The most important sector for investment in Czechoslovakia, in environmental terms, is the energy sector. The mining and use of coal for power generation with inadequate control measures is a major source of the country's pollution problems. Czechoslovakia has only limited resources of oil and natural gas with which to substitute coal, and the government has concluded that the prospects for renewable energy are limited in the short term. Indeed, plans to boost hydropower output through the Gabcikoyo/Nagymaros dam complex have provoked strong objections from environmentalists because of the impact on wetland habitats.

The main response to this dilemma to date has been to increase investment in nuclear power: however, the Soviet technology used in existing plants and those under construction has given rise to serious safety concerns. So far, little attempt has been made to address the question of poor energy efficiency and hence high levels of energy consumption compared to similar industrial economies. Key components of investment in the energy sector in Czechoslovakia therefore include:

- diagnostic, safety and control systems for nuclear power plants;
- desulphurisation and denitrification equipment for coal-fired power plants; and
- energy conservation equipment and services.

The chemicals sector in Czechoslovakia reflects the country's dependence on imported oil. It focuses more on higher value-added specialty chemicals than on basic petrochemicals, with synthetic fibres and rubber additives being particularly important.

Considerable investment will be needed to upgrade the chemicals industry to meet developing environmental standards, particularly in relation to waste disposal and waste water treatment, and to improve energy efficiency.

Other sectors requiring investment in Western technology include:

- pollution monitoring equipment for air, water and soil pollution;

- modernisation of buildings, especially with regard to energy use;

- non-asbestos sealing and friction materials;

- equipment for pipeline repairs and lining to reduce polluting leaks; and

- waste treatment equipment, especially for hazardous wastes (a German firm has recently won a major contract for a hazardous waste incinerator to be located at a chemical factory east of Prague).

Who to talk to and steps to take

In developing contacts within Czechoslovakia, it is important to remember the high degree of autonomy of the two republics. Not only are there separate environment ministries, many industrial organisations are also doubled up. For example there are two chemical management organisations, Chempetrol in the Czech Republic and Slovnaft in the Slovak Republic. Awareness of environmental problems and policies to deal with them may vary between the republics. A wide range of environmental groups has also developed in recent years; again, most tend to operate within only one of the republics. More recently an umbrella group, Green Circle, has been established to co-ordinate their activities and aid contact between them.

The importance of the energy sector in environmental issues is reflected in the existence of an Energy Efficiency Centre in Prague. The aim of the Centre is to promote policy and technology development in energy efficiency and to form a link between Western firms with energy-efficient technology and potential joint venture partners. A co-operative agreement has also been signed between the Czechoslovak government, the US Agency for International Development and the New York-based World Environment

Centre to assist government and industry with environmental management.

While Czechoslovakia was not included in the EC's initial PHARE programme, assistance from the EC is likely to be forthcoming in the future. Assistance with environmental investment in Czechoslovakia is also likely to be high on the list for consideration by the European Bank for Reconstruction and Development, headquartered in London. In addition, a tentative offer has also been made by the EC for Czechoslovakia, along with other Eastern European countries, to benefit from the work of the planned European Environment Agency in environmental assessment and monitoring.

There is a considerable need within Czechoslovakia for additional investment in technologies to improve environment management and to clean up the effects of past mismanagement. Firms exhibiting at trade fairs in Czechoslovakia have reported a very good response to a range of environmental products and services. A UK firm specialising in pipeline repairs was 'swamped' with inquiries at a 1990 exhibition in Brno. This and other firms have emphasised that Czechoslovakia is not a market for operators trying to make a quick sale; there is a need for service follow-up and long-term thinking.

For all investors in Eastern Europe, the European Commission has drafted 'guiding principles' on good environmental practice. These are not compulsory, but are likely to be widely applied, not least by banks funding investment. The core principles are:

- Priority must be given to the environment and local needs when planning investment.

- Environmental evaluations of proposed investments should be carried out in co-operation with public regulatory bodies.

- Environmental impact assessments should be carried out.

- The best available techniques should be used to minimise adverse environmental effects.

- Continual monitoring of the effects of operations on the environment should be carried out.

- Management and personnel must be aware of and involved in the company's environmental strategy.

- Data from environmental audits should be shared with the relevant regulatory bodies.

- Companies should report publicly on their environmental performance.

■ Companies should work with the relevant authorities to help develop future measures to protect the environment.

These principles require a high degree of environmental awareness and sound environment management from all investors in Czechoslovakia. Companies with established environment management systems and practices are likely to gain a significant advantage in moving into Czechoslovakia.

Issues for the investor

Liability for damage caused by waste
The position is not yet clear as to who will take responsibility for damage caused by waste, where this results from an existing deposit, for example, in a landfill site. It remains to be seen whether strict liability will be imposed in these circumstances (on the lines of US and proposed EC legislation), or whether the present occupier of land will be liable for damage which results from the negligence of a previous state occupier. It is to be hoped that the state will clearly assume responsibility in such circumstances so that the interests of an incoming investor or joint venture partner will not be prejudiced.

Environmental standards for new investments
Even though all the new environmental laws are not yet in place, it will be in the interests of investors to apply the best available techniques to minimise adverse environmental effects and to aim for high standards, so as to avoid future disruption. The importance of a thorough environmental survey before acquiring, or entering into a joint venture involving a factory site or other significant land, will be self-evident; and where the survey reveals the existence of problems inherited from the past, both the clean-up costs and the possibility of future claims should be reflected in the price.

The administrative structure
Programme A includes the reform of administration at the level of both federal and Republic government organs. It is to be hoped that this will be extended to a thorough overhaul of the central and local administrative system through which environmental powers are enforced. The ambitious nature of the new Czechoslovak environmental law requires a determined attack on its government structure at all levels to make it fully effective.

20

Technology and Communications

KPMG Peat Marwick McLintock

In Czechoslovakia, and the rest of Eastern Europe, nearly all businesses operate with severely restricted IT services and facilities. A UK firm setting up in Czechoslovakia could overcome some of these problems with hard currency. Computer hardware or software, for example, can be bought from local suppliers or imported, although export and import restrictions can sometimes make this difficult. But the limitations or lack of telecommunications infrastructure and customer-focused technology services are harder to solve.

This chapter provides an overview of the political factors that have affected the development of technology in Czechoslovakia. It then looks at five technology areas, each crucial to doing modern business, namely:

- telecommunications;

- the workforce's IT skills;

- computer hardware and manufacturing technology;

- software; and

- maintenance and support services.

Each section aims to place the current situation in context and outline what is available to the UK company setting up or doing business in Czechoslovakia today.

THE TECHNOLOGICAL HERITAGE

Before World War II, Czechoslovakia had a thriving economy with particular strengths in engineering. Its scientific community was world class. That position has been eroded ever since by a combination of political, investment and industrial policies – or lack of them.

For any industry to develop, there must be a demand for its products and services. Indeed, if demand is strong enough, it can force the pace of development. In the UK and other Western countries, sectors such as banking, insurance, travel and retail have increasingly used IT as a competitive weapon. This has created a spiralling demand for more advanced and more commercially advantageous technology. In Czechoslovakia – and Eastern Europe in general – these industries remain weak and face little competition. They have made few demands for new technology. This is one reason that the commercial technology sector has developed so slowly.

In telecommunications, another barrier to progress was the state's desire to suppress and control communications and the free flow of information. It is worth noting that the government-controlled radio and television networks in most Eastern European countries are well-provided with advanced satellite and other broadcast systems, while the public telephone networks are stretched beyond capacity. Most of the manufacturing sector has been starved of computer integrated manufacturing and computer aided design systems. One reason is shortage of hard currency. Another is that central planning meant there was little incentive to invest in new technology to improve productivity, increase output and cut costs.

As well as internal restrictions, there was one major externally imposed barrier to technological progress. Through the Co-ordinating Committee on Multilateral Export Controls (CoCom), the Nato countries and Japan restricted exports of advanced Western technology to Eastern Europe on military and political grounds. These controls were eased in June 1990.

There is now wide recognition in Eastern Europe that technology has enabled the West to forge ahead in terms of industrial productivity and efficiency. Technology is seen as one of the keys to catching up and prospering in the free markets of the world which they are now entering.

TELECOMMUNICATIONS

Reliable voice and data communications are a critical and basic requirement for modern business, and without them IT cannot be used effectively. The basic telephone network suffers from three major shortcomings: penetration, capacity and quality. There are only around 25 telephones for every 100 people – less than one-third of the ratio in Western Europe. This network is so over-stretched that acquiring new telephone lines is a challenge that even hard currency struggles to overcome. In many areas a new line cannot be supplied unless an existing user is disconnected. Nearly all telephone exchanges are still analogue and electromechanical. The few attempts at modernisation have focused on international traffic, so these calls are often easier to make and provide better quality lines.

Data communications are an even bigger problem for the business user. Line quality is simply not good enough and the error rate is too high. This makes it difficult to use facsimile and almost impossible to communicate between computers via the public network. Telex remains one of the most popular business communication tools in Czechoslovakia today. Value added network services are almost non-existent and cannot really develop until the basic network improves.

So when will things improve? The Ministry of Telecommunications aims to implement a completely automated digital network nationwide by 1996. It also intends to have telephones in 70 per cent of homes by the end of the decade. Some services such as cable television and maintenance of private exchanges are likely to become wholly owned by foreign companies. But the government's preference is to encourage joint ventures that will transfer technology and know-how to Czechoslovakia's own manufacturers. These will cover areas such as payphones, directory services and basic equipment manufacture. The first major initiative in this category is a joint venture between the national PTT, US West and Bell Atlantic. This group aims to launch a cellular network in three main cities by 1992 and achieve national coverage soon after 1993.

So telecommunications should improve significantly during the next few years. It may be worth noting that some Western suppliers are considering setting up facilities-managed telecommunications services. This may provide the best short-term solution.

PEOPLE – THE HIDDEN IT RESOURCE

Although PC penetration in Czechoslovakia is lower than in some other Eastern European countries, it can still offer Western businesses a large pool of highly skilled computer professionals. Programming skills are particularly high, although CoCom restrictions mean that most are more familiar with assembly languages than more advanced software. One of the largest software contracting firms has a permanent staff of 60 and a network of 4000 programmers for hire.

From the UK business viewpoint, the importance of this highly skilled section of the work-force is two-fold. They are obviously a valuable resource for some companies setting up in Czechoslovakia. Secondly, because they are technically aware and technology-hungry, they create a strong demand for consumer and business technology.

TECHNOLOGY: COMPUTER HARDWARE AND MANUFACTURING

In the past, Eastern European countries often copied Western products, particularly in the computing sector. For example, most mainframe and minicomputers were based on IBM or DEC machines. This approach had its benefits, such as reduced development costs and machines that can run Western software. It also means that Eastern Europe has kept to international technology standards. Domestically produced computers, fibre optics, local and wide area networks and communications switching equipment are all compatible with Western hardware and software. For UK business people, this can obviously reduce hardware sourcing, operational and maintenance problems. The disadvantage is that Czechoslovakia and other Eastern European countries have all suffered from a combination of the quickening pace of technological change and difficulties with acquiring the latest hardware to copy.

Many computers are manufactured locally by companies such as Tesla Electronics and ZVT. In the PC market Tesla is in fierce competition with Agrokombinát Slušovice. This quasi-capitalist enterprise developed from a collective farm that decided to manufacture PCs and write software. From initial annual production of 40 PCs in 1982, Slušovice grew to achieve a 1989 output of 20,000.

Buying Western computers is becoming easier. During the last year several major Western computer manufacturers and distributors have set up operations or signed deals in Czechoslovakia, and the government has reduced customs duties on PCs and other IT products. The Western firms enjoy a significant marketing advantage compared with domestic manufacturers. Consumers generally prefer Western goods and brands even when home-produced products are competitive in terms of quality, price and performance.

Computer integrated manufacturing, computer aided design, production control and automation are not unheard of in Czechoslovakia. The country just needs more of these technologies – most manufacturing plants are hopelessly out of date. Eastern Europe in general does have under-exploited strengths in systems theory and in the development of algorithms and software. These skills, combined with the right technology, may enable countries such as Czechoslovakia to use advanced manufacturing techniques to catch up quickly. A good example is a furniture maker in the town of Rousinov. It has bought the latest German machines and is now turning out high volumes of furniture of a quality that allows it to export to the West.

However, for this new technology to be used to its full potential, other changes are needed as well. Management has little experience of mass production and even less knowledge of how to operate in a free market where listening and responding to customer needs is essential to success. They need help to acquire these skills.

SOFTWARE

In Czechoslovakia, as in most of Eastern Europe, software piracy is rife. But the government is now taking steps to encourage the use of legitimate software. It recognises software as an industry requiring little capital investment where Czechoslovakia could use its programming skills and lower labour costs to compete successfully with the West. As a first step the government's own departments are being encouraged to buy more legitimate software. New copyright laws have also been passed, although these have yet to be stringently enforced.

In the past there was very little attempt at developing software solutions to common business needs. Teams of programmers would work to develop similar software in different and isolated state enterprises. Despite this and the lawless software environment, there are some success stories. With a workforce of ten, Software602 sells Czechoslovakia's leading word-processing package called Text602. This is not a copy of a Western product but an original package including original commands and a spell checker. Over 8000 copies have been sold and, doubtless, there are many more illegal copies.

MAINTENANCE AND SUPPORT SERVICES

Under the previous regime, all maintenance services were provided by two state-owned monopoly distributors – Kancerlářské Stroje supplying and serving domestic producers, and a foreign trade organisation, Kovo, handling imported goods. The negative side is that they also have an image of poor service, slow response and heavy bureaucracy. IBM is currently negotiating agreements with both these large outlets.

Now that markets are becoming more liberal, many new companies are being spun-off from the large state-owned enterprises as they find that there is nothing to hold them together. This creates a problem for the state-owned organisations as they are being left with the less profitable, less marketable and less entrepreneurial employees. The one advantage they do still retain over the younger firms is their larger customer base and resources. But the UK business person will probably find that the small private sector companies are the most reliable suppliers of services or products.

21

Transport

KPMG Peat Marwick McLintock

Czechoslovakia is situated in the centre of Europe and is a long narrow country, about 800km (500m) from west to east, and comprises the regions of Bohemia, Moravia and Slovakia. Prague, the capital, is the only city which can be reached directly from the UK by air. No visa is required to enter Czechoslovakia from the UK.

FREIGHT TRANSPORT

Most UK freight forwarders will be able to arrange for freight transport to and from Czechoslovakia. Lloyds Loading List publishes a weekly guide which indicates companies specialising in transport services to Czechoslovakia.

LEP Group Plc is a specialist international distribution company with its headquarters in the UK. In September 1990 it entered a joint venture in Czechoslovakia to form LEP International CSFR – 70 per cent owned by the UK partner. This company has six offices throughout Czechoslovakia and its services include seafreight, air cargo, rail transportation, road haulage, container services and logistics and distribution. LEP International CSFR's main Czechoslovak competitors are Cechofracht Prague, Topsped, Drused, Spedservis and Ten Express. Foreign competitors include Hapag-Lloyd (German), Schenker (German), Hasped and Weltz.

Road haulage permits between the UK and Czechoslovakia will not be required from January 1992. The UK is the first country to agree with Czechoslovakia to abolish these. Permits are required for other EC and EFTA countries. Most road haulage is undertaken using trucks of Western manufacture. Certain forms of specialist equipment are available including tankers and refrigerated trailers, although checks should be made with freight agents prior to booking. Premium rates apply to specialist equipment. Both regular trailers and drawbar trailers are used on the service. It should be noted that most international transport charges will be payable in either US dollars or Deutschemarks.

Air cargo services are provided through both British Airways and CSA. In addition to these carriers, airfreight can be carried using most major national airlines. However the costs for this service are variable depending on demand and whether the hold capacities on the aircraft are limited. Normal airfreight restrictions will apply.

Container movements into or out of Czechoslovakia are normally undertaken by road. Container pools are established in Prague but the type and quality of equipment is limited. Problems can be expected in obtaining the appropriate road trailers for containers within the country.

The hiring of trucks and vans is not very well developed. Trucks are normally hired with a driver from either the main state trucking companies or smaller entrepreneurs. In both cases the vehicle will be basic and minimum per day charges are applied.

The new Rhine-Main-Danube canal link, when completed, is expected to contribute greatly to the future of Bratislava port. The port has recently seen major expansion, and a new container terminal is being built in which Czechoslovakia's Danube Shipping Company has a 69 per cent interest and Vienna port subsidiaries WeinCont and ReMain have the remainder. The port now has three bridge cranes and a large area of stowage. In 1990 it handled 1500 ships and over 15,000 rail wagons. Czechoslovak officials say the new container terminal could more than double freight handling. Bulk cargo is also expected to rise.

COURIER SERVICES TO CZECHOSLOVAKIA

TNT, DHL and United Parcels all offer express parcel, document and freight services to Czechoslovakia. United Parcels offer a business-to-business service only, but their rates are generally cheaper than the other courier companies. TNT and DHL offer a next day service, but this is not guaranteed as delivery is dependent on the documents or parcels clearing customs. Prices vary between £14 and £45 per half kilo. Any local office of the above companies in the UK will be able to deal with enquiries and make arrangements for transport to Czechoslovakia, and all have offices in Prague.

TRAVEL TO AND FROM CZECHOSLOVAKIA

Air travel

Prague airport is called Ruzyne and is situated 18km (11m) from the city centre; other international airports include Bratislava and Poprad. There are extensive international air services to and from Prague, but the only direct flights from the UK are from Heathrow.

Flights to/from Czechoslovakia
The current (winter 1990–91) timetable (see Table 21.1) shows two direct flights each way between Prague and Heathrow on weekdays, operated either by British Airways or CSA, the Czechoslovak national airline. The flying time is generally around two hours.

Table 21.1 *Aircraft timetable*			
	Departs	*Arrives*	*Notes*
From Heathrow	11.15	14.10	
	13.55/14.00	16.45/16.50	Later on Friday
From Prague	11.50	12.50	
	15.05	16.05	

Prague airport
There is a range of shops situated at the airport, including a post office and a duty-free shop which offers a limited selection of goods. Perfume and confectionery are priced in US dollars, but cigarettes can be bought in any currency. There is a bank available where foreign currency can be exchanged for korunas (only a minimal amount of local currency – approximately 50p – can be brought into or taken out of Czechoslavakia). It is important to retain exchange slips as banks usually require proof of where currency was previously exchanged. Porters are on hand at the airport and luggage trolleys are available free of charge. There is no hotel situated at the airport.

Getting to and from the airport
CSA provide a half-hourly bus service linking the airport with the CSA town terminal, Vltava, which runs until 7.00pm, with a journey time of approximately 30 minutes. This will cost Kčs6 (12p) but is free for domestic air passengers. A municipal bus service (no. 119) is available from 4.30am to 11.30pm and a one-way ticket costs Kčs4

(8p). Tickets are available from any newstand or from the driver. It is sometimes necessary to pay an extra charge for luggage. This service connects with the underground network at Dejvicka metro station. Another airport bus, operated by ČSA and Čedok, serves several principal hotels in Prague and runs four times a day. Taxis are available at the airport and the average cost to the centre of Prague is Kčs150 (£3).

Car hire arrangements can be made either in the UK, at Ruzyne airport or at offices throughout Czechoslovakia. Pragocar, Avis, Hertz and Budget have desks at the airport. Most credit cards are accepted and no deposit is required if payment is made in this way. Current (Spring 1991) hire charges for a medium-sized manual car (eg an Opel Vectra) average £30 per day, or between £165 and £200 per week. These rates include oil and maintenance (but not petrol) and public liability insurance. It should be noted that reservations will only be confirmed for car groups, not for individual types of car. Driving licences issued in any European country are valid in Czechoslovakia and the normal European conditions for car hire apply.

Rail services to Czechoslovakia

All international rail services connect with Prague and most of these go to Hlavni nadrazi station. Service is good on the Ostend-Prague line, via Paris, Strasbourg, Stuttgart and Nuremberg. The most direct service from the UK runs at 11.30am daily departing Victoria station and arriving in Prague the next day at 5.18pm via Paris. This service costs £259 first class return and £182 standard class return (not including the price of a couchette from Paris).

TRANSPORT WITHIN CZECHOSLOVAKIA

Air travel

Domestic air services are operated by ČSA and the airports served from Prague are Bratislava Ostrava, Sliač, and Pieštany. Poprad and Košice in the east of the country are reached by changing at Bratislava. A single ticket from Prague to Bratislava costs Kčs1400 (£28) and from Prague to Poprad Kčs1900 (£38). These must be paid for in foreign currency. It is advisable to book a seat one week in advance during the summer months but there should be no need to do so in the winter.

Domestic rail travel

Rail travel within Czechoslovakia is cheap, with connections to most major towns and cities. All trains are operated by CSD, the Czechoslovak state railway. There are two types of train - *osobni* which is of an ordinary speed, and *rychlik* which is a fast train (for which there is a surcharge of Kčs16. First class fares are 50 per cent higher than second class, though first class is not available on all trains (particularly small, local ones). A *rychlik* train from Prague to Bratislava costs Kčs140 first class and takes some six hours. Sleepers are only available on trains travelling over 300km and a first class compartment costs Kčs80 per person sleeping two. These compartments must be booked through Čedok, the Czechoslovak travel agency, and not at stations. All other tickets are bookable at stations and a seat reservation (generally advisable, and compulsory on some trains) costs Kčs4. There is a restaurant car or buffet on all fast trains. The telephone numbers for train information in Prague are 264930 or 2364441.

Public transport

The underground metro system in Prague extends for over 30km and is fast, cheap (Kčs4 per journey) and efficient. There are three lines - A, B and C - and trains run from 5.00am until midnight. Metro stations are marked by an 'M' symbol. Before travelling, a ticket should be bought from a machine in the entrance hall and this will enable the traveller to cover any distance including transfer to other lines. Maps are posted at the stations and also inside the trains. An announcement is made on the train at each stop.

In Prague the main bus station is Florenc, where there is also a metro station for line C. Bus services are operated by CSAD and are generally good, except that, as they are organised on a district basis, services between districts can be sparse or in some cases non-existent. There is also a comprehensive tram network throughout the city and into the outskirts, which, on some routes, operates through the night. A bus or tram ticket would normally cost around Kčs4 and should be purchased before boarding the bus at a PNS kiosk.

Most other towns and cities throughout Czechoslovakia are also served by local buses and trams which run throughout the day and into the night. Tickets normally cost Kčs4 and should be purchased in a PNS kiosk or at stations and punched when entering the vehicle in a validating machine. For long distance bus journeys tickets can

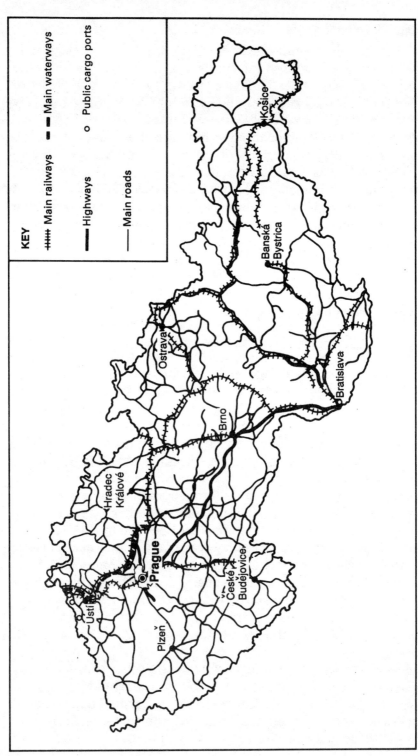

Map 21.1 *Infrastructure in Czechoslovakia*

usually be bought from the driver but on some routes reservations should be made. Express buses from Prague to Bratislava cost Kčs115 and take 4 hours 40 minutes.

Taxis are available at the many taxi ranks (often situated outside hotels) or can be booked by telephone on 203941 or 202951. Some taxis are metered but the drivers may charge extra for luggage. A 10 per cent tip is customary.

The road network

General European rules apply when travelling by car in Czechoslovakia and it is important always to carry an international driving licence, insurance documents and an international technical certificate (issued with the number plate). The following speed limits apply:

- Motorways - 110kph (69mph);

- Normal maximum - 90kph (56mph);

- Built-up areas - 60kph from 5.00am–11.00pm (37mph);

- Motorcycles - 80kph (50mph).

Emergency telephone numbers throughout Czechoslovakia are:

- Emergency breakdown - 154;

- Police - 158;

- Ambulance - 155;

- Fire - 150.

Most roads in Czechoslovakia have good surfaces, and traffic signs correspond with international usage. Roads marked with 'E' are important links with European motor routes.

There are five motorways constructed to date, three of which begin at Prague. More sections are gradually being opened and there will eventually be ten motorways. The longest continuous motorway stretches from Prague to Bratislava (327km). Motorways are marked with the letter 'D'.

Petrol in Czechoslovakia is supplied by a network of over 1000 filling stations, most of which are open on Saturdays and more than 600 on Sundays. The price of petrol is approximately Kčs10 per litre and diesel Kčs6. Cash can be paid for petrol but vouchers are needed for diesel; these can be obtained from regional and district branches of the Czechoslovak State Bank.

22

The Labour Market

KPMG Peat Marwick McLintock

The labour market will play a key part in the economic reform programme. For the programme to succeed, the labour market will have to function differently than under the previous regime where wages were set administratively. No wage differentials arising from differences in supply and demand across sectors and skills were allowed. In addition, the structure of the housing market has hampered labour mobility and there has been no tradition of job changing or retraining. The beginnings of the reform have already led to unemployment and skill shortages. The government's policies on unemployment, benefits, wage bargaining, trade unions and training will be of key importance during the transitional period in which there is likely to be high structural unemployment.

PROFILE OF THE CURRENT LABOUR MARKET

Working population

Until very recently, the Czechoslovak labour market was characterised by acute shortages, in particular, of skilled labour. The allocation of labour was administratively determined and unemployment was virtually unknown. However, this phenomenon was mainly due to the high degree of over-employment which prevailed in most of the state enterprises. Labour, typically, was hoarded to act as a buffer for unexpected output demands which largely occurred as a result of government directives. Labour was used as an alternative to capital to meet such demands as it was cheaper than investing in plant and machinery. However, now that the economy has embarked on the transition to a market economy, unemployment is expected to become a major problem. Indeed, current thinking is that unemployment will increase to 0.5 million by the end of 1991.

Over half (56.8 per cent) of the population is of working age (15-59 for men and 15-54 for women) although about one-quarter of people of pensionable age are in paid employment, accounting for almost 8 per cent of total employment. Female labour force participation is high at 75 per cent and women constitute 46 per cent of the economically active. The labour force is well-educated but does not necessarily have the specific skills that will be required during and after the transition to a market economy. In particular, managerial skills are thought to be weak as the legacy of 40 years of central control. Despite this, by Eastern European standards, the quality of labour in Czechoslovakia is regarded as relatively high.

There has been a recent addition of 100,000 to the labour force as a result of redundancies made in the Communist Party apparatus, a reduction in the length of military service to 18 months and a reduction in the number of civilians being called up. These new members of the labour force have gone into unemployment. The size of the labour force is expected to increase each year by around 60,000 as the population reaching working age increases.

Table 22.1 contains the latest available data which summarise some of the main characteristics of the working population. Approximately 4.6 per cent of those able to work are in education

Table 22.1 *Working population*

Characteristics of the labour force	1988
Population of working age	8,882,691
Workers of retirement age	741,433
Workers abroad	-936
Foreign workers	33,400
Total	9,656,588
Workers in national economy as sole or main employment	7,544,658
Women on maternity leave	358,436
Students and schoolchildren of working age	445,205
Apprentices of working age	295,248
Population of working age unfit for work	267,003
Others (including self-employed of working age)	746,038
Total	9,656,588

Source: *Statisticka Rocenka*

some 3.0 per cent are apprentices and almost 2.8 per cent of the labour force is classified as unfit for work. Only a fraction (0.34 per cent) of the labour force is of foreign origin.

Distribution between sectors

During the last 20 years there has been a marked change in the structure of employment. The share of agriculture declined from 17 per cent to 10 per cent but was offset by an increase in the tertiary sector. Shares of employment in industry (37–38 per cent) and construction (8–9 per cent) remained constant. In industry, the greatest proportion of workers are found in the engineering sector. Fuel and power, metallurgy, electrochemicals, metal working and textiles are also major industrial employers. While the industrial composition of employment between the two Czechoslovak republics moved closer during the decade 1978–88, there is still a fairly marked difference between them, as indicated in Table 22.2. It can be seen that the Czech Republic has a relatively higher proportion of industrial employment and a relatively lower proportion of employment in agriculture, forestry and water.

The industrial composition of the labour market will change as the economy is restructured. Already, it is apparent that the rates of change are likely to differ between the Czech and Slovak Republics. By mid-March 1991, the Slovak construction industry's output was decreasing and around half of the industry's employees were threatened with unemployment, according to the Slovak Minister of Construction. Unemployment is now twice as high in Slovakia than

Table 22.2 *Federal structure of employment by main sectors, 1988*

	Czech Republic %	Slovak Republic %	CSFR %
Agriculture, forestry and water	11.4	15.0	12.5
Industry	38.9	33.7	37.3
Construction	8.2	10.4	8.9
Transport and communications	6.5	6.7	6.5
Science, education, culture, services and welfare	18.7	19.2	18.9
Others	16.3	15.3	15.9
Total	100.0	100.0	100.0

Source: *Statisticka Rocenka*

in the Czech Republic. Other industrial sectors that are forecast to contract include chemicals, light industry, wood-working, machine-tools and electricals. Arms production is set to fall to 27-37 per cent of its 1987 value. This, in combination with Slovakia's reliance on chemicals, will give rise to severe job losses in that Republic. Furthermore, Slovak enterprises tended to focus exports on the Comecon market. Following the disintegration of that market, almost all Slovak industry is threatened with job losses. However, Slovakia is thought to be the key area for the development of tourism so that in the longer term there are likely to be many job opportunities in that industry.

The number of state and co-operative employees fell by 490,000 in 1990 and the number of private businessmen grew rapidly to 488,400 by the end of the year.

Basic education indicators

In Czechoslovakia, school attendance is obligatory for ten years. The education system is based on the German model and pupils study the same curriculum until 15. Up to the age of 16, pupils attend *Zakladni Skoly* ('base' school) at which they are educated to the equivalent of British GCSE level. Following this, pupils attend secondary school: either *Gymnazia* for academic studies or *Stredni odborné skoly* (trade school) for vocational studies. The studying lasts 4-5 years after which pupils are qualified to the UK 'A' level or OND equivalent (*Maturitni Zkouska Maturita*). After *Gymnazia*, pupils may attend higher education. There is a relatively good (by UK standards) pupil-teacher ratio in secondary schools – 15:1, whereas in the UK the DES guidelines stipulate a pupil-teacher ratio of 30:1. However, at 3.8 per cent of GNP, expenditure on education is relatively low.

In 1988, there were 556 *Gymnazia* schools and 36 higher education (*Vysoké Skoly*) establishments. Approximately 1.09 per cent of the population was in higher education in 1987, as compared with 0.94 per cent in Hungary, 0.89 per cent in Poland and 1.63 per cent in the UK. The institutions of higher education include five traditional universities, four technical universities and specialised institutions with university status. The Ministries for Education (both Czech and Slovak) determine annual quotas. Qualifications include: *Absolvent Vysoké Skoly* – equivalent to a UK BA; PhDr – between a UK Masters and a PhD; Candidate of Science – compares to a British PhD; and a Dr Sc – this generally compares with a DLitt/

Table 22.3 *Subjects taken in higher education 1989–90*			
	CSFR	*CR*	*SR*
Natural sciences	6,058	4,031	2,027
Technical subjects	69,314	41,831	27,483
Agricultural, forestry and			
veterinary science	15,749	10,656	5,093
Medical/pharmaceutical subjects	15,471	10,937	4,534
Social sciences	63,852	43,331	20,521
Arts	3,103	2,194	909
Total	173,547	112,980	60,567

Source: *Statistická Rocenka*

DSc. Table 22.3 contains a summary of the distribution of higher education students across subjects.

Private schools are now allowed and, to date (April 1991), nine are known to have opened. The Ministry of Education is reforming the state system by changing the school curriculum and preparing revised textbooks but it is expected to be two years before they are available in schools. Russian is no longer compulsory in all schools. University courses are to be extended in length and to focus on progressive scientific disciplines. Vocational courses are also to be increased in length. At the end of March 1991, Czechoslovakia ratified three of the Council of Europe education conventions: length of university courses, academic recognition of university degrees and equivalence of diplomas giving access to university establishments.

Skills, strengths and weaknesses

The main strength of the Czechoslovak labour market is that it is highly educated. In addition, there are good engineering, computing and other technical skills. However, owing to the regime which operated over the past 40 years, under which there was over-employment and no tradition of changing jobs or retraining, there is a shortage of many skills. Most workers have had no exposure to a market economy and there is a lack of entrepreneurial skills which is perceived to be more pronounced in the Czech Republic than in Slovakia.

Due to previous over-manning and misallocation of labour, at the start of 1990 the government listed vacancies of more than 300,000. At this stage of the transition, data available are somewhat piecemeal, but notable skill shortages include engineering workers (lathe-workers, milling handoperators, welders and foundry men). Of current (February 1991) vacancies in the Czech Republic, more than 84 per cent are for manual workers. In general, there is an acute mis-match between job vacancies and the characteristics of the unemployed.

In the professions, there is a shortage of economists, lawyers, design engineers and accountants. In general there is a lack of banking, financial and accounting expertise. Highly qualified workers are still in demand yet high school and university graduates find it extremely difficult to obtain a job.

Trade unions and wage bargaining

On 28 January 1991, the government, trade unions and employers signed a General Agreement relating to employment, wages and social benefits. The agreement is based on Czechoslovak regulations in conjunction with the recommendations of the International Labour Organisations. The agreement laid down stipulations for the process of collective bargaining and an outline of the government's active manpower policy. By mid-March 1991, the government accepted indexation of wages for the first time, stating that wage growth was to be 9 per cent for the first 4 months of the year (an upwards revision of the originally proposed 5 per cent). The minimum wage, Kčs2000 per month in March 1991, should be increased to keep pace with cost-of-living rises. However, on 5 April 1991, the government broke its commitment to link wages to inflation on the grounds that it could not afford it. The trade union movement has protested and stated that it will fight the government.

The governing body of the recently formed Czechoslovak Confederation of Trade Unions is the National Trade Union Centre in Prague. There are approximately 90 trade unions in Czechoslovakia of which 61 are members of the National Trade Union Centre. Unions are organised by industry and by profession. The union membership rate is high at 97 per cent of the working population. Prior to the start of the reforms, the unions used to 'tow the Party line' but, now that they are free, there has been some public activity. For example, the signing of the General Agreement was held up until the government agreed to raise the minimum wage level to Kčs2000. However, the unions are viewed as being moderate rather than militant. It is expected that their activity will increase as unemployment worsens. Strikes are legal only if they are approved by more than half the workforce and only during the negotiation of a collective agreement. All other strikes are illegal. The state influences recommendations for the rate of nominal wage increases. Collective wage bargaining is to be practised at top level, at branch and sectoral level and at enterprise level. Nominal wage increase recommendations in combination with productivity increases will generate real wage changes. Wages, by Western standards, are low. In March 1991, average wages were around Kčs3500 (approximately £70) per month. Despite the liberalisation/restructuring programme to date, wage differentials are still very narrow: an unskilled worker earns around Kčs2500 per month and a professional Kčs4000 per month. Hence there are still very limited work incentives in operation. In 1990, real wages fell by 5.6 per cent and during the first two months the cost of living increased by almost 32 per cent yet the government recommendation was for a wages increase of only 9 per cent.

Unemployment and social security benefits

Included in its active manpower policy, the government has given individuals who qualify the right to use job centres, access to requalification programmes and unemployment benefit. Unemployment benefits amount to 60 per cent of previous earnings for the first 6 months, followed by 50 per cent for the next 6 months, subject to a maximum of Kčs2400 per month. After one year of receiving benefits, individuals are entitled to the minimum income support which, set at the poverty threshold, is Kčs2000 per month. School leavers receive Kčs1200 per month. The government has planned to spend Kčs15 billion on job creation in 1991. On 1 February 1991, the Czech Ministry of Labour and Social Affairs passed an ordinance allowing the unemployed to become private businessmen. They receive average benefits for 12 months and can receive further subsidy if they employ others who are unemployed.

The unemployment rate for 1990 rose to 1 per cent. Of those unemployed, almost 50 per cent are blue collar workers, 11.2 per cent from university and 32 per cent from secondary schools. There are, however, three times as many vacancies as there are blue collar workers, but for other categories, job seekers outnumber vacancies by a quarter. Just over half of the unemployed are female and 75 per cent are aged under 41. There were 152,000 unemployed in February 1991 – 2 per cent of the labour force.

Unemployment is forecast to increase further during 1991 to 7 per cent–8 per cent of the labour market. There is a marked difference in unemployment rates in the two republics: unemployment at 3 per cent in Slovakia is twice the rate in the Czech Republic. Of the 58,400 job vacancies in January 1991, only 9700 were in Slovakia. The most pronounced falls in Slovak employment were in the electronics and electrical engineering industries.

Training

Training provided at educational establishments was described earlier in this chapter. Many of the vocational training schools are located within large state enterprises and are being privatised. However, owing to lack of finance, many are becoming extinct. They are currently the responsibility of the Ministry of Education, Youth and Physical Training which is faced with great problems. At the time of writing the future of the training schools is uncertain as there is no legislation to provide, say, subsidies for the schools through the tax system. The Ministry hopes that legislation will be passed some time during this year.

The Ministry of Labour and Social Welfare is responsible for retraining and training of the unemployed. As part of the General Agreement signed by the government, employers and unions, the government and employers have agreed to secure the establishment and financing of state and in-business employment programmes, requalification programmes and, if required, requalification centres. Special institutions, with legal status, are to be set up specifically to ensure employment opportunities for those leaving school and university and those who leave state administration posts. Training, especially in banking and finance, is to be organised and funded by overseas aid.

Despite these proposals, according to a recent report requalification programmes are still very rare. For example, the Czech Ministry of Labour and Social Affairs is said to be organising some regional requalification courses and preparing others. In principle the relevant bodies are working on the schemes and have interested Western consultants and firms as well as attracting grants under the EC Tempus and PHARE programmes. A total of 25 per cent from both Republics' employment funds are earmarked for programmes of job creation, small business establishment, public benefit works and requalification programmes.

One example of a training initiative is the signing of an agreement between the Czech Ministry of Labour and Social Affairs and the

Nuremberg-based Institute for Labour, under which Czechs have three-month job opportunities in Germany. This has resulted in discussion at federal level of possible 6, 12 and 18-month opportunities. Other examples include IBM setting up a training centre at a Slovak university where trainers are to be trained on a regional basis, the EC granting funds for training Czechoslovak interpreters, and the creation of an advisory and retraining network for unemployed women in Slovakia financed by the Dutch government. Other training has occurred as a result of joint ventures where, typically, the foreign firm sends Czechoslovak employees abroad for training.

Hence, training is taking place very much on an *ad hoc* basis. As the economic reforms continue, it is expected that a more co-ordinated approach to training will be developed in Czechoslovakia as has occurred in Poland and Hungary which are more advanced in their reform programmes.

Other recruitment issues

Great efforts are being made to dampen the impact of the transition on the labour market, in particular with respect to developing the recruitment infrastructure. Legislation grants individuals free use of job centres in addition to unemployment benefit and access to requalification. Job centres are being set up with a backing of Kčs990 million. They are mainly sited in old industrial centres where redundancies on a large scale are anticipated. The first job centres were opened in July 1990. There are 76 planned for Czech districts and 37 opened in Slovakia in October. In addition, jobs for high school and university graduates are advertised in newly established tax offices, the public prosecutor's office and job centres. Start, the Dutch temporary employment agency, signed an agreement with the Czechoslovak government in April 1991. Under the deal, in addition to opening an agency in Bratislava, the organisation will assist in the training of staff from existing and new employment agencies.

23

Management and the Professions

KPMG Peat Marwick McLintock

LEVEL OF MANAGEMENT SKILLS

The centrally planned economy had a significant impact on the level of management skills, making managers far less proactive and entrepreneurial. As implementers of a production process fuelled by centralised demand, they were cushioned from the need to improve efficiency and quality, from demands to innovate, to improve profit, or to sell their services. Indeed, as politically indoctrinated appointees with a job for life, these managers were concerned to avoid risk and maintain the status quo at all costs.

This led to a downgrading of those aspects of business concerned with accounting and finance. Marketing, sales and audit functions are now almost unknown, as are most aspects of international trading. Where professional functions survive, such as lawyers or accountants, there is little experience of commercial aspects, and those under state control have suffered an erosion of quality.

However, perhaps more than most other Eastern European countries, Czechoslovakia has maintained a high standard of knowledge through its educational system which will provide a bedrock for future changes. The system tends to teach industry-specific skills which will make it difficult to transfer knowledge in the future, but the country has a strong tradition of skilled heavy engineering and has continued to impart a knowledge of production techniques and quality control, although a lack of components or materials, of new equipment, and of incentives to improve design have hampered the application of these techniques. There are a large number of scientists and technologists, and IT skills are adequately represented, although they have been developed in isolation from the need to develop commercial products and applications.

While the banks have retained access to Western techniques and information, little knowledge of financial management, taxation and international banking systems has transferred to industrial enterprises. However, qualified accountants have tended to progress to the highly skilled role of forecasters, statisticians and planners in the centralised economy, and these skills should transfer readily to the free market.

MANAGEMENT ETHOS

The style in which enterprises are managed has to be considered in terms of the effects of the commercial and political upheavals of recent months on the individual. This is a culture in which top managers are highly educated, but until recently politically indoctrinated and appointed. Some of the initiatives of privatisation are actively undermined by the old guard, by inertia, resistance, and use of loopholes to hamper the process and to maintain the position of these managers. The perception of the old guard is also tainted by the knowledge of the widespread corruption and black-marketeering of the communist regime.

Such managers have, however, valuable experience of 'the way things are done here' – the day-to-day frustrations of working with enterprises with heavy bureaucracy, ageing equipment, a lack of ability to pay for goods, and low quality of components and materials. Much of business is done via personal contacts, and managers have a valuable role to play in keeping day-to-day operations functioning during the transition process.

In dealing with the West, particularly in joint ventures, differences in style become obvious. Czechs and Slovaks are suspicious of Western motives in doing business with Czechoslovakia, and envious of Western living standards and wages. Czechoslovak priorities in developing joint ventures differ from those in the West; Czechoslovaks may be perceived by the West as naive in business, but see the West as overly demanding in the pace they set for change.

The education process continues to produce younger managers of a high standard, and will fuel the necessary injection of commercial knowledge at all levels of management. The Slovaks, in particular, are said to possess an entrepreneurial spirit which will spur small privatised enterprises in the new economy.

While those from a Western culture can have little perception of the shift in behaviour and attitudes required of Czechoslovak managers, it is equally true that the Czechoslovaks are speaking of the urgent need for training in areas such as marketing and finance, with no real concept of what these imply. But at least as far as joint ventures are concerned, they will be able to learn quickly from their Western counterparts.

More problematic are the larger enterprises with no Western partners who will undergo larger privatisation. With perhaps the most radical need for change, their managers have least immediate access to Western training and few, if any, criteria for judging the quality of training available through the commercial and state institutions. The danger is that many individuals will resist change and seek to retain familiar management structures and existing staff, since they are unable to identify alternatives.

Managers face a wholly unfamiliar environment of tough decision making and proactive business development, coupled with an enormous task of learning as new accounting and finance methods, legal and tax reforms and market liberalisation policies take effect. Business conditions will shift markedly in a very short timescale as competitive conditions begin to bite. Managers will find that demand for their products changes rapidly, and that higher standards of quality and delivery are demanded – the company that cannot modify its output within a realistic timescale will founder.

The stringent timetable set by the government for privatisation and liberalisation of the economy does not appear to recognise the time needed to prepare managers adequately to take on their new role; it may be that events early in the privatisation process will dictate the approach to the larger privatisation.

MANAGEMENT TRAINING

In the vast majority of businesses, a desperate need for training and development to help individuals to operate in a market economy will be combined with unprecedented levels of stress and uncertainty during the radical restructuring of the businesses. It is essential that individuals are helped through this process to develop the quality of management skills necessary to sustain the business.

However, management development institutions are themselves facing upheaval. Those in the public sector are tainted with their past involvement in political education and are viewed with suspicion. Not only do they have to begin to generate fee income to survive, but these institutions must bring their teaching staff up to speed in the areas where training is required. Initially this will be solely by book-learning, but these staff must also gain direct experience of the market economy. Another consideration is that the training skills of these staff may not match those required for management training to Western standards. Both the Institutes of Management, in Prague and in Bratislava, and the 40 or so research and training institutes attached to various ministries face a change of role in order to survive. The IOM in Bratislava is likely to focus on aspects of public administration, while the future of the IOM in Prague is under discussion. The specialised institutes must depend wholly on fee income to survive; companies will not be compelled to use them and some will undoubtedly founder.

Co-operative colleges will also struggle to find a role as well as undergoing internal restructuring from centrally controlled institutions to organisations controlled by small groups of individuals. They may fuel small business training. Other avenues for training will be provided by existing technical consultancies which aim to expand their scope to include management training. Undoubtedly large companies, and particularly joint ventures, will race ahead in training to Western standards; they have the resources to train internally and have access to Western experience and knowledge.

There is a plethora of new training agencies growing up to feed increasing demand, and it is difficult to assess their potential calibre. Of these, the industry associations may prove the most successful. They have been formed by management in particular industry sectors and, while lacking experience as trainers, have extensive knowledge and contacts on which to build. Sources of information and training standards may be provided by the management associations: the Czech and Slovak Management Associations and the Management Consultants Association. These look likely to expand vastly their training capacity, again supported by their knowledge and contacts. It is essential that some degree of regulation and levels of training standards are set, and these associations may take a role in monitoring and providing advice.

The City University in Bratislava has set up a project to develop distance learning; it is unclear whether this ambitious lead will be followed by the other universities. Prime management training sources are the Bratislava and Prague Schools of Economics, Charles University, Comenius University, and the technical universities. The current focus is on long-term training, but the pace of change is likely to force a shift to shorter courses for current managers, as well as a restructuring of longer courses to focus on techniques to support the market economy.

THE LOCAL PROFESSIONS

Lawyers

The legal profession has recently been denationalised, allowing lawyers to become independent entities and economically private entrepreneurs. The previous service offered by state-controlled legal offices could not be perceived as wholly independent and left the client in a weak position.

While the new legislation works to improve the quality of legal services, there are still only a limited number of lawyers with little or no specialisation. Most have experience slanted towards property, criminal, and administrative law. The legislation has left unresolved a number of issues, particularly the types of co-operation that can exist between attorneys. However, the rapid advance of changes in all aspects of commercial law, combined with the roll-out of the privatisation programme and the increasing desire to set up joint ventures, means that the legal professional is in demand as never before.

Engineers

Before the World War II regime, Czechoslovakia was a dynamic and vigorous industrial nation with a tradition of top-calibre engineering. More than 40 years of protracted neglect and inefficiency have severely damaged industry; however, the engineering work-force has benefited from maintaining educational standards and is highly skilled.

While possessing knowledge of traditional engineering, modern production techniques and quality control, engineers have suffered from a lack of access to Western computer technology, a lack of expertise in environmental issues, and from severe stresses on the manufacturing process caused by lack of new equipment, components and materials.

Accountants

Accounting was previously regulated by the Federal Ministry of Finance, which set out accounting principles and regulations. Under the centrally planned economy the accountancy system was unified for state organisations and central ministries, and specified the nature of information and accounting. The accounting system revolved around state-controlled funds and was administered by some 6000 qualified staff, 4000 of whom are in the Czech lands and 2000 in Slovakia. About 35 per cent of these are university graduates and 65 per cent possessors of secondary school diplomas. These practitioners are supported by on-the-job training.

Since the use of accounting information was removed from the day-to-day operation of each enterprise, and was seen as fuelling the needs of the state plan or local authority budget, accounting and accountants assumed a low status. Particularly in comparison with other statistical activities such as planning or producing national statistics, accountants and bookkeepers are badly paid and low on the social scale. The audit function is very limited, even in the public sector.

In order to reach the higher levels of accounting, a degree from the universities of Prague or Bratislava in economics with an accounting major is required. However, most of the highly qualified entrants to accounting progress into planning or central statistics. This leaves a large number of lesser qualified staff with lower career ambitions: it is significant that more than 80 per cent of accountants and bookkeepers are women.

Accountants will have to bear the brunt of the Czechoslovak government's proposals for reform in tax legislation, commercial accounting, and the move to international accounting standards. The timetable for privatisation will set the timetable for developing new accounting and auditing skills. In addition, the speed of change to the public and private sectors will dictate the pace of training in managing state and local authority income.

Two embryonic professional bodies have been established: the Union of Czechoslovak Accountants (UCA) and the Association of Accountants and Auditors of Slovakia (AAAS). These are at present voluntary bodies. Both these and the academic institutes will need to reorient to provide restructured diploma, degree and professional training courses.

24

Grants and Aid

National Westminster Bank

Aid for Central and Eastern Europe has to date been aimed predominantly at those countries which are perceived to be engaged in thorough political and economic reforms. The main criteria employed to determine whether a country receives aid have been the extent to which it has implemented a democratic political system and a free market economy. In this context the first two candidates for aid have generally been Poland and Hungary followed by Czechoslovakia, Bulgaria and Yugoslavia.

When the momentum for reform in Czechoslovakia became unstoppable in 1989, it opened up the potential for a wide range of economic and educational assistance. In this chapter we examine the various channels through which grants and aid are becoming available to Czechoslovakia.

THE UK GOVERNMENT KNOW-HOW FUND

The central objective of the Know-How Fund is to help with advice and expertise in assisting designated countries in Central and Eastern Europe to move towards a democratic political system and a free market economy. The first fund was set up for Poland in June 1989 and was valued at £25 million, subsequently doubled to £50 million. The extension of the fund to the rest of the area was announced in January 1990 but funds are only being allocated once each country demonstrates that it is fully committed to reform. A fund for Czechoslovakia was announced during President Vaclav Havel's visit to Britain in March 1990.

A Joint Assistance Unit was established within the Foreign and Commonwealth Office in November 1989 to manage the Know-How

Fund. It has access to a wide range of expert and professional advice which it uses to assess proposals submitted to it.

As far as Czechoslovakia is concerned the initial priorities will be in privatisation and financial services, management training and public administration. There will also be assistance with employment services, the generation of small business and adult retraining. Close co-operation with the Department of Employment is envisaged. Training and advice in the environmental sector will be given as this is perceived as another priority for Czechoslovakia. A small proportion of the Know-How Fund covers projects in the political area in the broadest sense. To date the main expenditure in this field has been in the training of journalists and of broadcasters on courses organised by the BBC World Service.

In administering the fund to date, the approach of the Joint Assistance Unit has been to designate a priority sector and to follow this up with a project identification mission. An outline set of project proposals is then developed which they are prepared to finance. If there is a positive reaction from the Czechoslovak authorities to these proposals, the Joint Assistance Unit seeks to match them on a competitive tender basis with the various sources of expertise available in the UK.

OVERSEAS PROJECTS FUND

The Overseas Projects Fund (OPF), administered by the Projects and Export Policy Division of the Department of Trade and Industry, is available to assist UK companies with the cost of pursuing major projects overseas (except in EC countries). The Fund can help meet the costs of feasibility studies, consultancies and other pre-contractual activities with the objective of increasing the number of contracts UK companies can pursue and win. Where a contract is won with its help, OPF assistance is repayable together with a 15 per cent premium.

Major overseas projects with a potential UK content of goods and services of £50 million or more are eligible for OPF assistance. They will usually involve a package or turnkey approach with elements of consultancy, design, engineering, construction, supply, operation and training. Assistance will not be available where contracts are solely for the supply of hardware, technology, ships, aircraft or defence equipment.

Exceptionally, projects with a UK content of £10–£50 million may be eligible where there are reasonable prospects of securing business worth at least £50 million overall in related or subsequent contracts, or where the project is of special significance (eg in terms of market or product development).

OPF can assist with the costs of pre-contractual studies where a client is unable to finance a feasibility study or other consultancy and where there would be advantage in offering a free or reduced cost consultancy so as to improve the prospects of winning the implementation contract. The balance of costs will typically be met by the contractor or supplier pursuing the project.

The assistance offered will take account of the nature, duration and potential benefits of the project and in particular the expected value of the UK content of the contract in question. The appropriate assistance will be assessed on the basis of the individual circumstances of the project, but normally the applicant will be expected to meet the bulk of the costs – at least 50 per cent.

THE EUROPEAN BANK FOR RECONSTRUCTION AND DEVELOPMENT (EBRD)

EBRD, which officially opened for business on 15 April 1991, has been established to assist in the transition of various Central and Eastern European countries from command to market-related economies. In doing this EBRD will seek to promote entrepreneurial initiative in these countries provided they demonstrate a commitment towards applying principles of multi-party democracy, the rule of law, respect for human rights and market economics. On 20 May 1990 a total of ECU10 billion (£7 billion) was pledged to the formation of EBRD by 38 countries spanning 6 continents, together with 2 European institutions. EBRD has a unique mandate and its structure reflects this in aspiring to be an unprecedented blend of merchant bank and development bank.

Unlike any other international financial institution, EBRD is committed to providing at least 60 per cent of its loans and investment to private sector borrowers. No other organisation makes political reform, in the shape of transition towards a multi-party democracy, a condition of its support. EBRD is also unique in that within its constitution is a commitment to promote environmentally sound and sustainable government.

A further stipulation provides that, over a five-year period, at least 60 per cent of the EBRD's exposure in any one country has to be to the private sector. This stipulation followed pressure from the US, the UK and Japan to maximise the EBRD's private sector role in order to avoid lending support to moribund, state, socialist structures. The remaining 40 per cent can be used to finance the public sector but this is primarily limited to projects which will help to build the necessary infrastructure to make the market economy work rather than the kind of wide-ranging programme aid available from other organisations such as the World Bank.

Jacques Attali, the president of the bank, has let it be known that the needs of the countries of Central and Eastern Europe could amount to as much as ECU1000 billion (£700 billion). The EBRD could become a significant source of project and investment finance in a region already anticipating a high upturn in World Bank lending. The plethora of funds which are, theoretically, shortly to be available from various multilateral agencies should go some way to meeting the needs of the region, although it is educative to bear in mind that the EBRD's capital base is equivalent to less than half the cost of cleaning up the Polish power industry alone.

Consultancy services should lead the way rather than big ticket project finance. It has been estimated by the London-based Overseas Development Institute that EBRD could lend up to $2.4 billion a year – however it is unlikely that this level of lending will be reached for some years.

The major shareholdings in EBRD are broken down as follows:

1.	USA	10 per cent
2.	UK	8.52 per cent
3.	Germany	8.52 per cent
4.	France	8.52 per cent
5.	Italy	8.52 per cent
6.	EC	3 per cent
7.	EIB	3 per cent

The Central/East European members have the following shareholdings:

1.	USSR	6 per cent
2.	Hungary	1.55 per cent
3.	Czechoslovakia	1.28 per cent
4.	Yugoslavia	1.28 per cent
5.	Bulgaria	0.79 per cent
6.	Poland	0.79 per cent
7.	Romania	0.48 per cent

EUROPEAN COMMUNITY FUNDS:
THE PHARE PROGRAMME

The initiative of Western countries to institute an assistance programme for Central and Eastern European countries striving to make the transition to a free market economy was taken at the summit meeting of the Group of Seven in July 1989 in Paris. The seven most industrialised countries then opened this proposition to the 24 members of the OECD (subsequently designated as 'G-24') who accepted it and charged the European Commission with co-ordinating bilateral aid to assist with the reorganisation of the economies of Poland and Hungary, and subsequently Czechoslovakia.

In August 1989 priorities were established by the G-24 and working groups were created to follow up specific aspects of bilateral assistance. An action plan was then presented under which the European Commission undertook to finance cooperation programmes giving priority to meeting immediate, short-term needs and seed projects. The action plan covered four priority fields – agriculture, industry and investment, environment and training. A total of ECU300 million (£220 million) was earmarked in the 1990 Community budget for this purpose.

The amount specifically set aside for Czechoslovakia in 1990 was ECU35 million (£25.7 million) but this was because the Czechoslovak PHARE programme only got under way in the middle of the year. In 1991 the amount will be in the region of ECU100 million (£73.5 million). At the Czechoslovak federal Ministry of Economy, working groups have been set up for various projects according to the following priorities:

1. restructuring and privatisation;

2. small and medium-scale businesses;

3. development of the banking and financial systems;

4. ecology;

5. power industry;

6. health service; and

7. education.

In the field of education the PHARE programme has enabled Czechoslovak experts to attend courses at various universities and companies abroad. As far as Czechoslovakia's access to EC scientific and research programmes is concerned, the opportunities for co-operation and participation are still limited. One possibility yet to be explored is that of involvement in research on a sub-contracting basis whereby a Czechoslovak institute may become a sub-contractor for partners who are participating financially in a scientific research project.

It is anticipated that the EC Business Co-operation Network, formed by banks, credit institutions and chambers of commerce, will shortly open a centre in Czechoslovakia which will enable interested parties to obtain information about legislation and technical standards in EC countries.

INTERNATIONAL FINANCE CORPORATION (IFC)

Czechoslovakia became a member of the IFC in September 1990. IFC has established an office in Prague and its initial work programme has focused on advisory services to the government on the privatisation programme, to companies considering joint ventures and to authorities seeking to develop the Czechoslovak financial system. It anticipates a wide variety of investments in the industrial and financial sectors as the reform process moves forward.

IFC is the world's largest source of direct project financing for private investment in developing countries. Its purpose is to promote the economic development of its member countries by supporting the private sector. Of the 139 IFC member countries, over 115 are developing nations. In recent years it has approved annually some 90–100 projects in 40 countries, with total project costs exceeding $9 billion a year.

IFC is affiliated to the World Bank, but operates with a separate staff and funding. It supplements the activities of the World Bank by providing to private business equity and loans without government guarantees in whatever form and combination are best suited to a project. The corporation serves as the catalyst for a project by encouraging other sources of finance – from inside and outside the host country – to provide loans or equity along with the local sponsors. Since IFC accepts no government guarantees, it shares the full risk with its partners.

What IFC does

IFC can invest in all types of projects in Central Europe, both large and small. It only finances ventures that have realistic prospects of being profitable and that will benefit the economy of the host country. When appropriate, it supports joint ventures between private enterprises and government entities. In any project, local investors should be able to participate, either at the outset or later. IFC will only invest in a venture when appropriate arrangements exist for the repatriation of its investment capital and related earnings.

IFC can offer most types of financial instruments in whatever combination is necessary and feasible to ensure that a project is soundly funded from the outset. Its loan and equity investments in Central Europe for its own account are usually limited to no more than 25 per cent of project cost for greenfield projects: 50 per cent in cases of expansion.

While the Corporation typically invests in ventures costing at least $10 million, its funding is also available for smaller projects through credit lines and agency arrangements. The largest amount it will invest for its own account is around $100 million. When needed, it can also raise substantial funds in addition to its own investment.

Equity investments

IFC can invest up to 25 per cent of the share capital for a venture. Once an investment has matured, IFC typically seeks to divest by selling its equity to local private sector investors. In some countries, IFC shareholdings are treated as domestic or neutral capital for nationality ownership purposes.

The Corporation does not itself assume management responsibilities in companies; it expects its investment partners to provide management. IFC is generally not represented on the boards of companies, but it will do so when there is a need or when its stake is substantial.

As a rule IFC prefers to make both an equity investment and a loan, but when appropriate it will provide just one or the other.

Loans

Both fixed rate or variable rate loans in US dollars are offered, although other arrangements can be made according to the needs of a project. IFC does not provide subsidised finance; interest rates and fees are determined on a commercial basis.

The terms and grace period of loans are designed to accommodate the cash flow needs of each venture. Their overall term usually runs from seven to twelve years. Loan repayments can be structured to match the needs of projects involving relatively long construction periods and slow build-up of capacity utilisation.

The Corporation has developed a special participation mechanism to facilitate the syndication of its project loans among commercial banks. It signs a single loan agreement with the borrower, but the loan has two portions – one for the account of IFC and the other funded by participant banks. The terms of the two portions may differ as regards periods, currencies and interest rates. Commercial bank funds mobilised in this way by IFC now exceed $600 million a year.

Other types of financial mobilisation by IFC include underwritings, partial guarantees and backstop arrangements for both public offerings and private placements of securities issued by companies in developing countries.

Advice and technical assistance

Based on its long experience of development through the private sector, IFC provides governments and companies with an unusual range of advisory services. It has its own in-house technical, legal, and financial staff, who come from some 80 countries. IFC can also draw on the World Bank's wide experience, as well as on its own working relationships with financial institutions and development agencies.

Through its Foreign Investment Advisory Service (FIAS), IFC also assists governments of Central Europe in creating the framework of policies and institutions necessary to attract and regulate foreign direct investment. FIAS has studied and made recommendations on a number of issues affecting foreign investors in Poland, Hungary and Yugoslavia.

THE EUROPEAN INVESTMENT BANK

The European Investment Bank (EIB) is an autonomous institution within the EC structure, established to finance capital investment projects that promote the balanced development of the Community. Set up in 1958 by the Treaty of Rome as part of the decision to establish the European Economic Community, the EIB operates as a bank, raising the bulk of its financial resources on capital markets to fund projects meeting Community priority objectives.

The EIB is owned by the member states of the EC who all

subscribe to its capital. As a major international borrower, which has always been awarded a first class 'AAA' credit rating by the leading rating agencies, the Bank mobilises large volumes of funds at fine terms. It on-lends the proceeds of its borrowing to finance projects on a non-profit basis at cost plus 0.15 per cent to cover administrative expenses.

The volume of the EIB's operations has grown steadily and it is today the largest financing institution of its kind in the world, along with the World Bank (International Bank for Reconstruction and Development). While the bulk of EIB's loans are within the EC, the Bank has been called on (because of its expertise in project financing) to participate in the implementation of the Community's development co-operation policy.

The EIB's board of governors, having already authorised lending up to ECU1 billion (£700 million) for capital investment projects in Poland and Hungary, has been invited by the EC to extend lending to Czechoslovakia, as well as to Bulgaria and Romania. The total amount sanctioned for lending to these three countries is ECU700 million (£490 million) which will not necessarily be evenly split; the distribution of the funds will depend on where appropriate projects are identified.

Types of project

EIB loans are project-linked, orientated to the financing of the fixed asset components of an investment. The Bank finances viable public and private sector projects in infrastructure, industry, agro-industry, agriculture, energy, tourism and services of benefit to those sectors.

In Czechoslovakia the Bank aims to support capital investment in priority sectors and gives particular emphasis to infrastructure projects which play key roles in encouraging exports and restructuring the industrial sector (eg energy, telecommunications and transport), the environment and industrial projects, especially those involving joint ventures with EC enterprises. Investment projects in social infrastructure such as health, general education and welfare are not eligible for EIB finance.

For larger-scale projects the EIB makes individual loans available either directly to a project promoter, or indirectly through a government or banking intermediary. The state and any private or public company (whether or not including the participation of foreign investors) have access to EIB finance on equal terms.

There are no formalities involved in approaching the EIB for financing. In all cases requests for finance must be for specific projects and subsequently must have the agreement of the authorities of the country concerned.

A complementary source of finance

The EIB is a complementary source of funds and, within the framework of an appropriate financing plan, can provide loans which will not exceed 50 per cent of the cost of a project. In practice, banks and other credit institutions (public and private) often co-operate with the EIB in drawing up the overall financing package for major projects and in acting as intermediaries for indirect loans.

The EIB also co-operates and co-finances investment with other project financing institutions, particularly with those of EC member states and the World Bank group, as well as with commercial banks. The EIB will subscribe 3 per cent of the EBRD's capital and nominate a member of the new bank's board of directors. The EIB was requested to play a role in the establishment of EBRD by providing appropriate assistance during its constitution and start-up phase.

The EIB uses its 'global loans scheme' to provide long-term finance to reach smaller-sized investment. Under the scheme, the EIB arranges finance for an intermediary finance institution, operating on a national or regional basis, which on-lends the funds in a number of sub-loans for selected projects agreed by the Bank.

Global loans bring together the financial resources of the EIB, and the operational experience, contacts, local knowledge, and awareness of national development priorities of local financial institutions in the selection, assessment and monitoring of small-sized investment. EIB global loan finance is designed for investment with a total cost not exceeding ECU15–20 million (£10.5–£14 million). It is directed as follows:

1. Small and medium-sized projects with particular emphasis on export potential and international competitiveness in industry, agro-industry, agriculture, fishing, tourism and services related to the productive sector.

2. Small and medium-sized schemes in energy production and energy saving, infrastructure works (which are usually promoted by local authorities, or other public and semi-public bodies) and industrial and infrastructure projects protecting or improving the environment.

Part III

The Options for British Business

25

Strategic Planning
KPMG Peat Marwick McLintock

Czechoslovakia was one of the most successful industrial economies in Europe between World Wars I and II. Although Soviet-style
state planning has undermined much of this achievement, Czechoslovakia still has considerable potential as a market-driven economy.

There is no lack of will on the part of the government to create a
market economy. The difficulty is over how its objectives may be
attained. In common with the other Eastern European countries,
life for the Western businessman can be frustrating, especially with
the added complications of a federal system and unpromising short-
term economic prospects. Both inflation and unemployment have
risen steeply, and the transformation into a Western-style economy
is proving a painful and slow process. Investment in Czechoslovakia,
therefore, has to be seen in a long-term context, but opportunities
are unquestionably available.

A Western businessman considering investment in Czechoslovakia should make regular visits, get to know the country and develop
contacts in the business community first. It will take time and a
considerable amount of effort to evaluate the market-place as
statistics are poor and there is little market research information
available. The British Embassy can conduct small surveys and make
introductions, but setting up in Czechoslovakia is a time-consuming
and drawn out process and investors must be prepared for this.

FORMULATING A STRATEGY

In many ways the basic approach to strategic planning for a British
company looking to invest in Czechoslovakia is no different to the
approach that would be required for entering a new market in other

countries, including other East European ones. Obviously the specific factors that need to be considered will not be the same and it is important to ensure that all relevant details are taken into account. However, the overall framework would not need to change a great deal from that which a company would use for its investment or location decisions elsewhere.

It is essential to take a considered approach to Czechoslovakia, that is driven by both a company's long-term goals and clearly stated objectives in Eastern Europe. Crucial decisions which need to be taken include:

- the desired level of financial commitment;

- the period over which a positive cash contribution is expected or acceptable;

- target return on investment;

- the scale of managerial resources available to develop the business;

- the degree of risk and uncertainty which is acceptable to the investor; and

- investment location.

There are numerous examples of investors underestimating the risks associated with Eastern Europe and the time and resources required to establish a successful operation. The long-term potential of Czechoslovakia is undoubtedly there but in the short term significant and, in some cases, unpredictable obstacles remain.

Once the decision has been taken to look more closely at the possibility of investing in Eastern Europe, a more detailed strategic planning exercise will need to be carried out. Figure 25.1 illustrates the sort of framework that might be adopted. Following the setting of objectives it will be necessary to determine which business activities to develop and which product and country markets to target. The main activity options would be to establish a sales only operation or to carry out production, which could be targeted on existing Western markets, the Czechoslovak market, other Eastern European markets, or some combination of these. The choice of activity will be determined both by the long-term objectives of the company and by the current and expected future market conditions.

For example, it would make sense for a company that is using

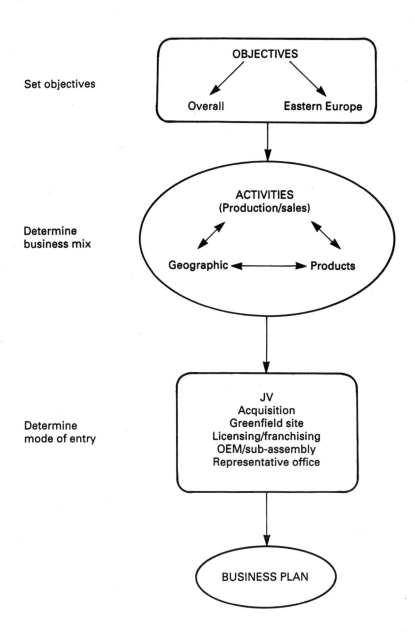

Set objectives

Determine
business mix

Determine
mode of entry

Figure 25.1 *An approach to strategic planning in Czechoslovakia*

Czechoslovakia as a production base for other Eastern European markets to develop a solid domestic sales base as well. Alternatively, a firm that originally intended only to sell in Czechoslovakia may identify a joint venture partner with strong sales contacts in the Soviet Union that would make a larger scale of operation more attractive. Or a manufacturer looking to set up production may conclude, after a more detailed examination of market conditions, that given their uncertainty and volatility it would be more prudent to establish a trading venture and move into manufacturing at a later date.

In Czechoslovakia it is also important to consider the regional implications of the federal structure. If planning to serve the market in the Slovak Republic, for example, it may be necessary to set up in Bratislava rather than in Prague. As with the choice of business activity, the decision on what products to make and/or sell will be influenced by such parameters as:

- the relative competitive advantage that the company's products are likely to have in the market;

- projected returns on investment for the various products;

- the strategic positioning of the company in the chosen markets; and

- the evolving economic and market conditions in Czechoslovakia.

Another important element of the planning process comprises the choice of country in which to invest. As indicated earlier, the decision to invest in Czechoslovakia rather than in another country should not be a foregone conclusion. Even if a company is initially predisposed to a Czechoslovak investment as a result of press reports, the experience of business contacts or other information, at least one or two other potential investment locations should be evaluated for comparison.

An approach that many have found useful is to start off with a set of broad country comparisons. These should involve the evaluation of broad indicators collected, as far as possible, on a comparable basis. Selection and weighting of these indicators depends to a certain extent on the company's own profile and preferences. In general the types of indicators that would be most relevant would include those set out in Table 25.1.

This information is available from various sources, although the issue of comparability is important. This is particularly the case for

Table 25.1 *Country indicators*	
Indicator	*Examples*
Political	Regional issues Government stability
Economic	GDP and growth Consumer expenditure/retail sales
Regulatory	Openness to foreign investors Currency convertibility Repatriation of profits Property rights Tax incentives
Market potential/wealth	Population and growth Penetration of consumer durables (cars, telephones, TVs) GDP per head
Costs	Labour Building rental Finance
Infrastructure	Internal transport International links Telecommunications Development of media/business services
Other	Political/economic stability Component and raw material suppliers Financial incentives Industrial relations Access to other markets

Eastern Europe, including Czechoslovakia, where data is often more scarce and less reliable than in the West. However, the situation is improving. Chapter 5 of this book provides an indication of likely sources of information and its reliability.

It may well be the case that this initial examination would be enough to identify Czechoslovakia clearly as the prime target. If not, it would at least enable the investor to narrow down the range of possibilities. More detailed analysis would then need to be carried out before a final decision can be made.

MODE OF ENTRY

The next phase of the strategic planning process concerns the selection of the mode of entry into Czechoslovakia. Again, this will to some extent be determined by the structure and aims of the investor. The information on the economic, regulatory and market background will also be important. A wide range of entry options are available, some specific to Eastern Europe, others in more widespread use.

Joint ventures

In Czechoslovakia, and indeed elsewhere in Eastern Europe, joint ventures (JVs) are a favoured option. Recent legislation has been designed to attract foreign involvement in Czechoslovak enterprises and this route has proved particularly popular with companies seeking to establish a production or servicing base in the region. The JV option is particularly relevant where a more active involvement by the Western partner, rather than a passive financial investment, is potentially the most rewarding. The privatisation process has meant a large pool of potential JV partners in Czechoslovakia and the government has introduced tax incentives to encourage foreign participation in JVs. The difficulties arising from constantly changing regulations and general uncertainty over the future has served to make the JV the most favoured form of Western investment in Czechoslovakia.

Under the Large Privatisation Act of February 1991, some 3000 enterprises will be required to prepare a privatisation project. Foreign participation will be a major element in the large privatisations and where foreign investment is anticipated the enterprise will need to specify which foreign companies are interested in investing with the organisation. The privatisation project will also have to specify, among other details, the value of company assets and a specific timetable for privatisation. This will mean many more opportunities for Western investors. The Czechoslovak government is keen to encourage Western investment and there will be no restrictions on the extent or the form of such investment (although approval will be required for JVs or acquisitions from the Ministry of Privatisation or the ministry that had previously been responsible for the enterprise concerned).

Even joint ventures have their difficulties, however. Although there are now no restrictions on foreign equity, there remain ambiguities over important issues such as repatriation of profits and property ownership. In addition there is the problem of managerial control. The lack of entrepreneurial culture among senior managers makes it important for a Western investor to retain managerial control in a JV (see, for example, the Berox case study in

Part IV) even if only a minority shareholding is held. A good, well-motivated local deputy is also important in order to help cope with the bureaucracy and the constantly changing regulatory environment.

The Agency for Foreign Investment and Assistance in the Ministry for Economic Policy and Development maintains a database of potential Czechoslovak partners in JVs, each with a profile including information on financial figures, capacity and numbers employed. However, while this information may be useful, it is unlikely to reflect the true situation. The assets of a potential JV partner need to be valued and have audited accounts according to Western standards and an investor will need professional advice in order to help choose his partner. A good local lawyer will also be necessary in order to register a company as a Czechoslovak entity.

Acquisitions and other options

An alternative to joint ventures is outright acquisition, which may be attractive under certain circumstances. In particular, the higher degree of control permitted by full ownership could be a deciding factor. With JVs, difficulties can arise when there is a divergence in the business objectives of the two sides. The large privatisation programme should make outright purchase of Czechoslovak companies easier than it has been in the past.

The success of a JV or acquisition depends to a certain extent on there being appropriate Czechoslovak partners already in existence, but where this is not the case – for example where an industry has not yet been established or if a highly specialised facility is required – the main option is to carry out a new investment on a greenfield site. In Czechoslovakia this option has been rare, mainly due to continued economic uncertainty as well as legislative difficulties.

Another form of Western involvement in Czechoslovakia is through licensing. This has happened especially where Czechoslovak firms wish to access Western designs or technology while Western firms were prevented or put off from a more substantive involvement by the legislative and other barriers in force at the time. The main visible benefits of this kind of arrangement would tend to accrue to the Czechoslovak licensee, which gains access to Western products and/or technology. However, licensing would be one way for Western companies to test the water in Czechoslovakia without risking substantial resources. In particular, a licensing deal could be used to evaluate the capabilities of a potential joint venture partner.

The risk, however, is that if a company waits too long the most attractive partners will be snapped up by the competition.

If interest is mainly in production for sale on Western markets, contracting Czechoslovak firms as original equipment manufacturers or sub-assemblers could be attractive options. The market for such work has become increasingly globalised. However, there are several reasons why Czechoslovakia could be competitive *vis-à-vis* the more traditional South East Asian suppliers. These include the proximity to Western European markets, particulary important where transport costs or timeliness of delivery are significant factors, and the low cost, relatively highly skilled labour force. Again, the letting of sub-assembly contracts could be used to evaluate a potential partner prior to a full joint venture.

For marketing a Western product the establishment of a representative office is usually the first step. In such cases, however, it becomes particularly important to establish good local contacts. Franchising is an option that is currently more established in the West than in Eastern Europe especially in the retail and fast-food trade.

Other possible modes of entry include dealerships and agency arrangements. These will become more popular over the medium term as Western goods and services become more established in the market. However, the cost of setting up a nationwide dealer network can be considerable, while there are few existing Czechoslovak equivalents that might be accessed. The need to maintain effective control over the local agency or dealership is also an important factor.

THE BUSINESS PLAN

The final phase of the strategic planning exercise would be the preparation of the business plan. Depending on the mode of entry, this would include:

- a detailed analysis of market potential;

- an assessment of the competition;

- the identification and evaluation of potential joint venture partners or acquisition targets (with many opportunities provided by the privatisation programme); and

- detailed financial projections.

These are standard elements in any business plan but the practicalities of drafting the plan will reflect the unique business conditions evolving in Czechoslovakia. Much of the work will need to be based on detailed analysis and it may be necessary to commission research. This could be from locally based firms or from Western consultants, which have now built up considerable experience, contacts and in some cases local offices in Czechoslovakia.

The broad approach to strategic planning outlined over the preceding pages is not intended to be either comprehensive or foolproof. However, our experience indicates that this can be an extremely flexible way forward. It is particularly applicable to markets which are hedged with a considerable degree of uncertainty.

The pace of change in Czechoslovakia, both in the economy and in the regulatory framework, means that no matter how well an investment is researched it is likely to bear a higher risk than its equivalent in, for example, the UK. On the other hand the longer-term rewards may be significant and market entry will be much more costly once the economy has been transformed and profits are being made.

26

Marketing

Saatchi & Saatchi Advertising Worldwide

As Czechoslovakia moves from a planned market economy, it must be understood that although socialist rules no longer apply, the rules of capitalism have not yet been fully implemented.

Prices of most goods and commodities have risen sharply since the beginning of 1991, in many cases more than doubling. Import monopolies are slowly being dismantled and domestic producers are reappearing, but it is not yet possible, with any degree of consistency, to consider sophisticated marketing programmes.

In a society where the population has had little real sense of material values, considerable stress is placed on the value of negotiating joint ventures, thus deflecting discussion away from other commercial questions. Owners or managers, having no experience or any solid basis of comparison, frequently grossly overestimate the value of their assets. One is therefore not dealing with normal economic forces and the marketing process has still to find a meaningful foundation. Those countries, such as Austria or Germany, who have consistently traded with Czechoslovakia over a number of years, understand these complexities. 'Marketing' and 'advertising' are not familiar practices and cannot be simply applied to otherwise underdeveloped commercial situations. There are, of course, exceptions – the key is to appreciate them.

The impact upon the marketing and, more specifically, the advertising process is that in this period of reform many companies have come to recognise the importance of an organised marketing strategy. To be successful in the medium and long term, commercially oriented companies must push harder to create the standards required to operate and be successful in a free and open market. There are short-term frustrations in attempting to organise cohesive marketing and advertising activities, but patience, sensitivity and commitment will pay off in the long term.

CONSUMER MARKETS

The average net monthly income in Czechoslovakia is about US$100. Despite this, however, in real terms a large number of people have a car, fully furnished accommodation equipped with most household appliances (TV, refrigerator, washing machine, and so on) and many families in the major cities have a weekend country house or cottage. Average income is a rather meaningless statistic because state-controlled prices for most consumer items were ridiculously low by Western standards. They also tell one little in a society where the salary of a surgeon was the same as a skilled factory assembly line worker.

It used to be, and to a large extent still is, an accepted fact that consumers must search for products, never vice-versa. In the process of moving to a market economy, the Czech consumer will endure a lot more pain before the process gets better. This situation could continue for a number of years, depending on the success of the planned reforms. It is a very difficult process in the short term as the market balances short-term pain against long-term gain. Marketeers must be very sensitive and patient.

Grocery prices, having remained more or less static in recent years, have started to rise rapidly. Until recently, prices were heavily subsidised by the state, particularly energy, housing and public transportation prices. Consumer durable goods are – as elsewhere – relatively expensive, particularly in comparison to food items.

The average Czech disposes of his income as follows: food 35 per cent; rent 15 per cent; consumer goods 10 per cent; clothes 10 per cent and others 30 per cent. About 40 per cent of the working population have a secondary and supplementary source of income which provides at least another 70 per cent (sometimes even 100 per cent) on the average income level of US$100. Many people who previously had the opportunity to create secondary and unofficial sources of income, are today putting the same energy into working for themselves and creating their own full-time business opportunities – a sign of the new entrepreneurial work ethic.

Following deregulation of all prices (although on food items upper limits are controlled) inflation has taken hold. In US dollar terms, some examples of price rises include: 0.25kg of butter, a 35 per cent rise to $0.60; one litre of gasoline 'Super', a 100 per cent rise to $0.59; a Skoda Favorit car, an 80 per cent rise to $4750; transportation, a 300 per cent rise to $0.13 per trip; and gas, a 300 per cent rise (US$1 = Kčs30.55 – April 1991).

Generally there is a far wider choice of food in comparison to other consumer goods, but the supply of fresh fruit and vegetables remains poor, especially out of season. Because little or no emphasis is placed on health care or nourishment – large amounts of sugar, fats and oils are consumed and vitamins are practically non-existent – there is no real consumer demand for fresh products. Also, the growing choice and variety has brought exorbitant prices – 1kg of imported Spanish plums cost nearly US$3.00 in June 1991.

Home produced consumer durables are being replaced by the wider choice of imported brands. Locally produced products are out of date technically and aesthetically, while imported brands offer up-to-date performance and features. However, the initial surge of interest in imported products such as microwave ovens and cooking pots has diminished as sufficient volume of stock and variety of choice become more universally available. The wider range of products is ensured thanks to a number of private entrepreneurial importers/dealers, but it should be noted that they are not, as yet, importing in sufficient quantity to be able to pass on any price advantages to the consumer.

Market research

Market research is extremely underdeveloped because it was almost non-existent up to 1989. The Ministry of Commerce and Tourism was the only state institution that provided statistical information. Market research for anything other than state reasons was, of course, absurd when consumers queued for hours or even days for certain goods such as furniture, cars and other durable items.

Today, several private companies do conduct research in certain sectors; in many cases, the employees or managers of these companies still have working relationships with state institutions. Thus, piracy of databases can and does occur, often for private gain by state employees. The opportunity for organised qualitative and quantitative market research is enormous and is already recognised as a vital ingredient in the marketing mix. Considerable activity and development in this area is expected throughout 1991–92, but it will depend on investment and organisation based on established Western practice.

Labelling, health and safety and the environment

Dull and unimaginative labels and/or poor quality packaging still exist. For example, packs of washing detergent often cannot be opened; yoghurt carton covers cannot be torn off; plastic milk containers can easily be punctured; 'sell by' or 'consume by' dates are often illegible. However, some products are now becoming more appealing simply through well-designed, effective packaging, especially in the case of small grocery items. Environment-friendly packaging is almost unheard of in Czechoslovakia, but will certainly have greater importance in the future as people become more aware of the country's environmental problems. The first major evidence of this has been the public outcry and resistance to plastic bottles made by a co-operative farm called Slusovice.

Greater regard is paid to safety, especially of products powered by electronic motors. But even these are not on a par with Western standards. There have been some cases of milk and fish contamination by PCB but, perhaps unfortunately, without any serious consequences which might have forced the authorities to make producers improve standards. Labelling of imported goods is always distinguishable from home-made products without even reading the name – simply as a result of the higher standards of packaging and label presentation.

Pricing

The benefits of price liberalisation are often stressed without regard to volume or turnover, the consumer's relationship to the goods or the store. This is seen especially in grocery items. Thus a foreign trader can sell southern fruit from a lorry in Prague for half the price of a local greengrocer. This highlights the situation caused by present price policies.

Nowadays pricing is very important, certainly more important than it was in 1990. It affects not only the consumer but frequently also the wholesaler who is not able to convey sufficient stock either because of bad cash flow or even insolvency. Another problem is the way retail surcharges are calculated on imported goods. They are derived not from the basic price of the goods but from the total sum of products prices and additional import tax.

Retail and distribution

The former state-controlled retail and distribution network is slowly being dismantled, as are other monopolistic arrangements in the import/export sector. However, no viable alternative system has so far replaced it. Unfortunately, the process of small-scale privatisation will only prolong the transition to a logical, nationally organised system of distribution and marketing. This is because the small-scale privatisations and the complex restitution process mean that purchasers have to accept, at minimum, a two-year franchise on the business (not necessarily the premises) and are obliged to buy the existing stock as well as obsolete fixtures and fittings. Other problems arise simply from the lack of buying experience, the difficulties of irregular supply, and the negative impact of the previous lack of investment.

MEDIA

In general, all media (TV, press, radio, outdoor and cinema) are now available for advertising, but the market is still in a state of transition.

Since early 1991, the government has been reviewing TV, press and radio legislation and this will have a significant impact on the development of the media scene. Among the recent problems, for example, is that up to Spring 1991 there were two different scales of TV advertising rates - higher for foreign advertisers, lower for local advertisers. The situation is now being regularised, although foreign advertisers still seem to have to pay in hard currency. Thus, the definition of what is a foreign product is a vital issue. Is Coca-Cola, made under licence in Czechoslovakia, a foreign or domestic product?

Television

There are approximately 4.5 million TV households reaching 95 per cent of the population (57 per cent with colour sets).

At present, there are TV studios in Prague, Bratislava, Brno, Ostrava, Kosice and Banska Bystrica. They broadcast on four channels: FI, the federal channel; CTV, the Czech regional channel; ST, the Slovak regional channel; and OK3, an international satellite channel with programmes from, among others, La Sept, MTV, BBC, Screensport and Vremja. In general, all programmes beamed by Astra 1 and Astra 2 satellites are received in Czechoslovakia. There is, at present, practically no cable TV in the country, with only slow growth expected in the future.

Advertisements are still broadcast in blocks, although changes are expected in 1991–92 to possibly allow them to be broadcast within programmes. The authorities are interested in sponsorship and barter deals. No tobacco, spirits, drugs or firearms advertising is allowed.

Print

There are around 8 important national daily newspapers in Czechoslovakia (each with a circulation of approximately 250,000), 10 regional and 3 evening papers and over 500 magazines. A recently introduced tax (11 per cent, reduced from 22 per cent) on all publications will force many to close down. There is a considerable shortage of good quality paper and the majority of publications are poorly reproduced. A number of Western magazines such as *Burda* and *Neue Mode* are now printed in Czechoslovakia (both in the Czech and Slovak languages) to Western standards. *Playboy* is also now available. Many more are expected in the foreseeable future, although a note of caution should be sounded – some Western publishers rushed into the market in early 1990, overestimating the reception that their publications would receive: they closed down and withdrew soon after simply because of lack of research and overconfidence concerning consumer demand.

Radio

Radio in Czechoslovakia is going through major changes. Up until the end of February 1991, only six state-run stations were broadcasting (two nationals, two Czech and two Slovak). Independent radio has just been legalised and already 35 applications for licences have been received by the government. The first independent station began broadcasting in the Prague area earlier this year. It is called *Nezavisle Radio* and hopes to reach the whole of the Czech Republic within the coming months. *Nezavisle* broadcasts non-stop and attracts a youth audience by playing mostly pop/underground music. Both the BBC World Service and Radio Free Europe are now available on Czech frequencies.

Advertising spots are in Czech and Slovak on *Ceskoslovensko*, and the *Interprogram* station will also accept spots in English, French or German. There is no fixed schedule for advertising. Timing should be agreed with the Czech Radio department of advertising. Their intention is to allow more and more advertising with various programmes.

Outdoor

Relatively unknown until two years ago, well-constructed and well-positioned poster sites are now being erected in major cities and on principal thoroughfares throughout Czechoslovakia. The standard of outdoor advertising has generally been raised by the intervention of companies from Belgium, the UK, France and Austria in joint ventures with local Czechoslovak companies. The average rate for a poster site (June 1991) is $300 per month per site.

Cinema

Advertising in cinemas is only allowed in one block following the newsreel, usually featuring messages on static slides. In 1988, there were 2800 cinemas with 70 million admissions.

ADVERTISING

Advertising, as we accept it in the West, is a relatively new phenomenon in Czechoslovakia. In the past, it was recognised more as a device associated with state-controlled propaganda, so today's more sophisticated mass media creative messages have an impact over and above the norm.

The former state-owned 'advertising agencies' – as is the case with many other state enterprises – are trying to transform themselves into private companies or, even better, to link up with the leading world-wide advertising networks. Several new Czechoslovak agencies have emerged from former creative studios and production organisations, and are establishing relationships with international networks. For such relationships to work, these agencies need to co-operate with people who have proven experience in the film, communications or creative industries. Scores of small local agencies have also emerged which, in spite of much raw talent and enthusiasm, really cannot aspire to professional Western standards although they *can* offer *basic* production services.

Czechoslovakia has world-class creative talent and experience, particularly in the field of exhibitions, film production, illustration and graphics. The creative potential of local personnel is high and can significantly contribute not only to the growing domestic market but also to the advertising industry world-wide.

A vital consideration for the development of Western agencies is the need for training and know-how to be transferred into the local advertising community. Already, the most ambitious agencies are providing on-the-job training by moving trained professionals in to work alongside local personnel as well as sending local personnel for prolonged training to their companies in other Western European countries or in the USA. The international advertising community and its principals must be prepared to limit their expectations to the circumstances of new and continually changing market conditions. The primary objective for advertising agencies is to create opportunities to help their clients accomplish market entry as quickly and as easily as possible.

In 1988, the breakdown of advertising expenditure was estimated as follows: fairs/exhibitions, 40 per cent; TV, radio and cinema, 30 per cent; company documentaries and information videos, 15 per cent; and leaflets, catalogues, brochures, 15 per cent. It will be interesting to see how these proportions change in the coming years as Western media such as TV becomes more available and better organised.

DIRECT MAIL

Direct marketing is still non-existent in Czechoslovakia. The reason is simple: statistical databases have not yet been established to target commercial messages to precisely defined groups of consumers. Statistics do exist within the appropriate ministries, but they are not available for commercial use. Generally, the best approach will be for companies to develop their own databases from scratch.

27

Export and Import
KPMG Peat Marwick McLintock

It is important that Czechoslovakia's current trading situation is not looked at in isolation, but that it is seen in a regional context and set against the background of developments in Central and Eastern Europe as a whole. The break-up of Comecon and the demise of the transferable rouble will have a profound impact on the orientation of Czechoslovakia's foreign trade. The country has been negotiating for associate membership of the EC and it is certain that the former Comecon area's share of Czechoslovakia's foreign trade will continue to decline in the immediate future.

Within Czechoslovakia itself, the legislation that is opening the way for a move to a free market economy, and particularly the price liberalisation and devaluation of the koruna, has affected the Czechoslovaks' ability to pay for imports and made foreigners looking to purchase Czechoslovak goods with hard currency particularly welcome. These factors have an important effect on those wanting to trade with Czechoslovakia, and should be kept in mind.

This chapter outlines the foreign trade situation existing before the 'Velvet Revolution', and then details the measures designed to bring about a liberalisation of foreign trade, before highlighting the current situation and suggesting ways for British businessmen to approach the Czechoslovak market.

THE SITUATION PRE-LIBERALISATION

As with other Eastern European countries, foreign trade in Czechoslovakia used to be a monopoly of the Ministry of Foreign Trade in Prague, operating through the Foreign Trade Organisations

(FTOs). Particular FTOs were themselves monopolies responsible for the exporting and importing of a range of products in a designated market sector. The FTOs formed an integral part of the centrally controlled economy for planning purposes, and a British businessman wanting to export to, or import from, Czechoslovakia had to go through the FTOs, only having any contact with his customers or suppliers as a result of arrangements made by the FTO. This centralised approach meant that Czechoslovak foreign trade expertise and contacts only existed in the FTOs. At the same time, because of their quasi-governmental status, sales to the FTOs were seen as being guaranteed as their debts were seldom defaulted on.

FOREIGN TRADE LIBERALISATION

The liberalising legislation

The liberalisation of foreign trade was one of the key elements of the federal government's policy to bring about a free market economy in Czechoslovakia. Foreign trade liberalisation began in 1988 with the passing of Act No 102. In May 1990, the Act on Economic Relations with Foreign Countries (113/1990) was passed, which ended the monopolistic role of the FTOs, and allowed certain Czechoslovak enterprises to trade directly with foreign counterparts. The need for a Czechoslovak to obtain a foreign trade licence or special permission from the Ministry of Foreign Trade to act as an importer/exporter was abolished in January 1991. Now, everybody who is registered as an 'economic person' can engage in foreign trade in the same business in which he is registered to act internally. The other side of these developments is that British importers/exporters can now choose who will act as their agents and can deal directly with their customers or suppliers.

There are still some restrictions in force, and Decree 256 of 1990 explicitly states all the cases when a foreign trade licence is necessary. These include oil, natural gas and weapons and ammunition. The list of Czechoslovak goods requiring an export licence is much longer, covering certain metals, minerals, pharmaceutical products, and some agricultural products. The Federal Ministry of Foreign Trade administers the foreign trade licence system and deals with applications for licences. The legal aspects are covered under Decree No 266 of 1990 from the Ministry. A licence application must include details about the enterprise, its type of business, and its existing and potential foreign trade activities. The Ministry must decide whether to grant a licence within 15 days of receiving the application.

Other aspects and issues

This section mainly concerns those wanting to export goods into Czechoslovakia.

Import surcharges on consumer goods

On 17 December 1990 under Act No. 569 of 1990, and with backing from the IMF, an import surcharge of 20 per cent was introduced, which covers the import of consumer goods into Czechoslovakia. The surcharge is based on the purchase cost of the goods in the UK, exclusive of VAT, which is used to calculate the customs duty. It is the importer's responsibility to settle the import surcharge within the appropriate time period. The surcharge does not apply to goods sold for hard currency in the Tuzex stores.

The surcharge is designed as a short-term measure to protect the Czechoslovak balance of trade, and is due to be phased out by the end of 1991 and more quickly if the economic situation permits. Effective from 1 May 1991, the rate was reduced to 18 per cent and, as from 1 June 1991, was further reduced to 15 per cent. Full details of the items on which the surcharge is payable are available from the Federal Ministry of Foreign Trade.

GATT and tariffs

Czechoslovakia is a member of GATT. The majority of its tariff rates are internationally tied to GATT treaties. Customs duties are generally lower than those for the surrounding countries, with the average tariff rate being just below 5 per cent.

The Co-ordinating Committee for Multilateral Export Control (CoCom)

Following the political changes in Eastern Europe during 1989, CoCom carried out a major exercise in the Spring of 1990. Working groups were set up in the three priority sectors of computers, telecommunications, and machine tools, which had been identified as the most critical to the economic regeneration of the Eastern and Central European countries. As a result of this exercise, a significant number of CoCom restrictions on the export of goods to Czechoslovakia have been lifted, and some Czechoslovak goods have been written into the CoCom restricted lists. A British exporter should contact the CoCom licensing unit who will be able to advise about any export restrictions that are in force.

THE CURRENT SITUATION

FTOs and agents

The trading situation now offers more opportunities for the British exporter. As a result of the legislative changes, the FTOs, which used to be the centralised points of contact, have not been abolished but they are no longer monopolies organised according to product types and may trade any commodity. Many are moving towards becoming general trading service companies. It is unlikely that all of them will transfer successfully into the private sector. Although the legislative developments are having a fundamental impact on the role of the FTOs, they still represent an important source of accumulated expertise, though this is decreasing with the growth of the private sector.

Advice about the best way of approaching the Czechoslovak market differs. Some businessmen advise that it is preferable to have direct contact with the customer or supplier, thus avoiding the need to pay any commission to trading service companies or agents. However, these companies are only now becoming involved in foreign trade, and, in most cases, have still to acquire the necessary experience and contacts. This situation is changing, but former FTOs or other agents should not be ignored at the moment . Good agents, covering both the Czech and the Slovak Republics, are seen by some businessmen as the key to a successful trading operation in Czechoslovakia.

Difficulty of credit assessment

In addition to the central role of the FTOs under the old trading system, a central banking role in foreign trade was played by *Ceskoslovenska Obchodni Banka* (CSOB), the foreign trade bank. This central bank position of CSOB has ended, and, when combined with the endings of the FTO monopoly, has affected the mechanics of foreign trade.

Most private sector companies have no trading 'track record' as yet, so caution should be exercised when establishing payment terms. Their accounts, as detailed in Chapter 37, are of little if any value in their standard Czechoslovak format. The Czechoslovak Chamber of Commerce, among others, is introducing services making credit evaluation more easy, but it will be some time before exporters can obtain meaningful financial statements of private sector companies. Exporters should proceed with caution in assessing a customer's creditworthiness. Liquidity and solvency problems are being experienced by a number of Czechoslovak companies and exporters are advised to use irrevocable confirmed letters of credit (ICLC).

British banks are reappraising their approach to the Czechoslovak market as they are being asked to guarantee letters of credit drawn on new banks or banks with which they have had few contacts in the past. This can cause delays, and exporters are advised to ask their banks for a list of banks which are acceptable to them.

Planning

The fundamental importance of thorough and detailed preparation and planning before a visit to Czechoslovakia, and the importance of careful research when in Czechoslovakia were mentioned repeatedly in conversations with business people involved in that market. It is also brought out by the case studies. There is little point in flying out on the off-chance that some interesting opportunities might appear during a visit. Such an approach is unlikely to be successful or cost-effective. Prior research and the establishing of precise objectives will make the time spent on the ground that much more effective.

By the time a visit is made to Czechoslovakia, sufficient information and details of contacts should have been gleaned to allow a well-structured and full programme of not less than seven days, covering all the major industrial centres.

The importance of communicating clearly with business contacts cannot be understated. Jargon and terminology used as second-nature by Western businessmen will not always be fully understood by the Czechoslovaks. A Western businessman's thinking is conditioned by a number of preconceptions that are so central to 'doing business' that their role is often overlooked. The legacy of 40 years of central planning control and rigid adherence to 'the plan' is such that the Czechoslovaks do not have these preconceptions. Unless care is taken at the start of negotiations to ensure that terms are defined, and the ground rules are fully understood by both sides, misunderstandings are likely to occur. Patience and persistence are prerequisites for success.

The opportunities for selling goods to, or buying goods from Czechoslovakia have been dramatically increased by the liberalisation of foreign trade. The relative importance of particular factors or issues will vary according to the products which are being traded. In addition to the need for planning, patience, and persistence, the importance of clear and unambiguous communications with Czechoslovaks and of realising that personal visits are essential, there are a number of other points that should be borne in mind.

When buying from Czechoslovakia

The overriding message is the need to be imaginative. A detailed consideration of the items that you are looking to buy, including the source of any components and the production process, should enable the buyer to determine the most cost-effective method of acquiring the goods. Advice has highlighted that certain points should be borne in mind. First, when in Czechoslovakia:

- The need to move away from Prague, and cover the whole of Czechoslovakia including Bratislava, Brno and Pilsen.

- The need to define the payment terms – whether the price is ex works or free border.

- The need to study both the method of transport and the route so as to minimise cost.

- The need for an agent or agents who speak English as well as Czech or Slovak, have access to communications (fax or telex) and are mobile.

And for this country:

- The need to ensure that the goods meet the relevant standards set down in EC and UK regulations.

- The need for a country of origin certificate, endorsed by the Chamber of Commerce in a format which is acceptable to UK Customs and Excise.

- The need to carry out detailed research into the relevant documentation to avoid paying unnecessary import duty.

When selling to Czechoslovakia

Again, advice has highlighted certain points that should be borne in mind. In this country:

- The need for detailed research prior to a visit.

- The need to talk to banks in this country in order to obtain details of approved counterparty and guarantor banks in Czechoslovakia.

■ The need to consider CoCom and other restrictions.

And in Czechoslovakia:

■ The need to move away from Prague to cover the whole of Czechoslovakia.

■ The need to spend at least a week on the ground on your first visit.

■ The recommendation to visit the Commercial Section of the Embassy in Prague.

■ The need for an agent or agents.

■ The difficulty of assessing the creditworthiness of customers – particularly in the light of liquidity and solvency problems.

■ The recommendation to use ICLCs as the method of payment.

28

Trade and Project Finance
National Westminster Bank

UK companies considering entering into a trading relationship of any kind with a Czechoslovak entity should be aware of all the available sources of finance. Most businessmen will be familiar with the concept of a documentary credit but will perhaps know rather less about more esoteric products such as factoring or leasing. An awareness of these financing techniques will enable companies to decide which means of funding is the most appropriate in their particular case.

While this chapter provides a basic insight into various methods of trade and project financing, expert guidance should be sought as to how to best proceed.

DOCUMENTARY CREDITS

Where an established trading relationship with a customer does not exist, the safest means of ensuring payment is to open a documentary credit, commonly called a letter of credit or l/c. Most exporters to developing countries rely on documentary credits to ensure they receive payment for their goods. Around 50 per cent of all shipments to Czechoslovakia are on l/c terms and four out of ten of those are confirmed.

An l/c is effectively a written undertaking given by a bank on behalf of the importer to pay the exporter an amount of money within a specified time, provided the seller presents the appropriate documents strictly in accordance with the l/c. As soon as the importer's bank receives documentation proving that goods have been shipped according to the contract, it will pay the exporter, normally through a bank in the exporter's country. Since the issue of the l/c can obligate the importer's bank to make a payment at some future time, the bank will include financial liability in its risk assessment of the importer, so it cannot therefore be assumed that a bank will be willing to issue an l/c.

There are several variations on l/cs. The first choice is between a revocable and an irrevocable l/c. As a revocable l/c can be cancelled or amended by the issuing bank, it gives little security to the exporter and is therefore seldom used. The second choice is whether it is confirmed or not. Although an l/c may allow the bank in the importer's country to make payment, there may be problems that stop the money getting through. In this case, the exporter can ask for the credit to be confirmed by a bank in his own country, so that it will pay up regardless of whether the money has been received from the issuing bank. As this constitutes a form of insurance it costs money. However, where the exporter considers the risk high, the use of an irrevocable confirmed letter of credit is a sensible option.

As banks rely on the documentation, and do not involve themselves in the actual goods or underlying contract, they must be certain that the documentation is correct, and may refuse to pay simply because of a spelling mistake in the paperwork. It is the responsibility of the exporter to ensure there are no mistakes, and this has been made easier by the steady simplification of documents by bodies like the Simplification of International Trade Procedures Board (SITPRO). Increasingly, computers are being used to prepare paperwork, and the most sophisticated l/c users can handle most of the documentation without touching 'hard copy'.

To ensure that standard l/c procedures are followed throughout the world, the International Chamber of Commerce has produced detailed guidelines called *Uniform Customs and Practice for Documentary Credits*. This is the key text for everyone involved in l/cs and only a handful of countries are not signatories to it.

Example of a confirmed irrevocable l/c

The Quickdry Machines Company of Bristol wins an order to supply 5,000 hairdryers to company X in Czechoslovakia. Quickdry has not supplied X before because it is a new company without an established trading record. For this reason, Quickdry requires X to have its bank issue an irrevocable confirmed documentary credit. Quickdry and X draw up a contract of sale: its main points cover the price (and whether that includes insurance and freight costs), shipping period, what the goods are, method of payment (ie a documentary credit payable in sterling at sight and confirmed in London), how the goods are to be shipped, the documents required and the name of the seller's bank.

X then applies to its bank (the issuing bank) to issue a documentary credit. This will include certain details of the contract of sale, and an instruction to the bank to telex or mail full details to the seller through the exporter's bank (the advising bank), asking it to add its confirmation to the credit. If the issuing bank is willing to undertake the obligation on X's behalf and is satisfied with the details of the credit, it passes them on to the advising bank, which in turn advises the credit (with its confirmation) to Quickdry. Quickdry should study this carefully, to check that it reflects the contents of the contract of sale. It must also make sure that it can comply with the credit requirements.

If Quickdry decides that it cannot get the hairdryers to Czechoslovakia in one go, it immediately asks X to delete the 'partshipment prohibited' clause. This amendment will only become effective when it has been passed to Quickdry by the advising bank.

Having shipped its hairdryers, Quickdry presents the documents specified to the advising bank. It sends a covering letter, which lists the documents enclosed, the documentary credit reference, and says how it wants to be paid. If the advising bank is happy with the documents – in this case, a sight draft (a demand for payment under the term of the credit, signed by the seller), invoices, insurance certificate and a complete set of bills of lading – it will pay up immediately.

Specimen documentary credit

National Westminster Bank PLC
International Trade and Banking Services
Documentary Credits Department
National Westminster Tower
25 Old Broad Street
London EC2N 1HQ

Direct Line 01-920
Switchboard 01-920 5555
Telex 885361 NWBLDN G

Quickdry Machines Co Ltd
High Road
Bristol

Dear Sirs

We have been requested by Traders Bank of Czechoslovakia to advise the issue of their irrevocable Credit Number 01/765 in your favour for account company X, Prague, Czechoslovakia for £100,000 (say one hundred thousand Pounds Sterling).

Available by your drafts on us at ....
sight accompanied by the following documents namely:

1. Signed Invoices in triplicate certifying goods are in accordance with Contract No. 1234 dated 24 October 1991 between X and Quickdry Machines Co Ltd.

2. Marine and War Risk Insurance Certificate covering 'all risks' warehouse to warehouse, for 10 per cent above the CIF value, evidencing that claims are payable in Czechoslovakia.

3. Complete set 3/3 Shipping Company's clean 'on board' ocean Bills of Lading made out to order of the shippers and endorsed to order of 'Traders Bank of Prague', marked 'Freight Paid' and 'Notify X c/o EC Line'.

Covering: Hairdryers CIF Prague, Czechoslovakia

Transported from UK Port to Prague

Partshipment prohibited   Transhipment prohibited

Documents must be presented for payment within 15 days from the date of shipment.

We are requested to add our confirmation to this Credit and we hereby undertake to pay you the face amount of your drafts drawn within its terms provided such drafts bear the number and date of the Credit and that the Letter of Credit and all amendments thereto are attached.

The Credit is subject to Uniform Customs and Practice for Documentary Credits (1983 Revision), International Chamber of Commerce Publication No. 400.

Draft drawn under this | X | Payment)not later
Credit must be presented | | Negotiation) than
to us for
                 | | Acceptance)14.12.1991
and marked Drawn under C
Traders Bank of Czechoslovakia dated
1 November 1991

Discounting

Had Quickdry agreed to give company X credit, the sight draft would have been replaced by a draft drawn on the advising/confirming bank, demanding payment at a future date ('at 90 days sight', for example). Instead of paying immediately, the bank returns the draft annotated with its acceptance by which it undertakes to pay 90 days hence. This credit is called an acceptance (or sometimes a term or usance) credit.

Quickdry could discount the draft, meaning it would get paid immediately, with 90 days' interest at the finest rate deducted. Most banks will discount their own acceptances at up to 180 days, and sometimes longer. In the EC, it is common practice for documentary credits to be issued deferring payment, but without calling for the seller to draw a draft: this is known as a deferred payment credit. The advising bank will provide a letter to the exporter saying that the issuing bank agrees to pay in 90 days. This does not of itself provide a discount facility. However, if the credit is confirmed, a letter from the advising bank undertaking to pay on the due date may be sufficient to enable the exporter to obtain an advance.

ECGD - SUPPORTED FINANCE SCHEMES

Various forms of support for Czechoslovakia are available from the British government through its Export Credits Guarantee Department (ECGD). In contrast to various other Central and Eastern European countries, Czechoslovakia currently enjoys full cover from ECGD.

The financial guarantee schemes promoted by ECGD can be summarised as supplier credit, buyer credit and lines of credit. All three schemes relate to support for the export of capital goods and services. The maximum terms of support are 85 per cent of eligible contract value, financed through the banking sector in the United Kingdom, in any acceptable free market currency, at a fixed interest rate throughout the term of the loan. Credit periods vary from two to eight-and-a-half years depending on the size of contract, and run from delivery, installation or the estimated commissioning date of the contract depending on the extent of the exporter's contractual obligations. Eligible value can be loosely described as the value of contract having no more than 40 per cent EC content or other foreign content with a value no more than 15 per cent of contract value. If, however, a mix of EC country and other foreign content were under consideration, ECGD should be approached at the earliest stage for an indication of the level of support.

Supplier credit relates to contracts where finance is required through deferred payments under the contract. Finance in this instance is provided on a non-recourse basis to the exporter, and would normally be considered as without recourse after the bills of exchange, which evidence the debt, have been accepted by the buyer's bank in Czechoslovakia.

Buyer credit relates to finance for projects which are normally valued in excess of £1 million and payments are regulated through a loan agreement signed with a borrower, normally a bank. The supply contract is negotiated on cash terms and would provide for 15 per cent of the contract value to be paid by the buyer and the remaining 85 per cent financed through the loan agreement.

Lines of credit have been used quite substantially over many years. The mechanism is simple, with access to finance provided through a pre-agreed application process. In essence, if a line of credit is in place then exporters are relieved of the need to negotiate individual financing arrangements for their contracts. They can go to the market, armed with specific financial information, and direct their clients to people familiar with the terms and operation of the line of credit in their own bank for advice and assistance on the procedures which are necessary to take advantage of the fixed interest rate lending facilities which are offered.

LIMITED RECOURSE FINANCE

Large projects often require specialist financing, arranged by either the project sponsor or by the contractor in support of a bid. The wide variety of options might include capital issues, export credits, bilateral and multilateral aid and limited recourse finance.

Limited recourse finance, also known as project finance, has been available for several years, but the concept is not always fully understood. Broadly speaking, it can be defined as 'finance for a project wholly or partly on the credit of the project itself, with the revenue from the completed project being the sole or primary source of repayment'.

Numerous sectors lend themselves to this form of finance, especially infrastructure (toll roads, bridges and tunnels), power generation, industrial processing and leisure (such as theme parks and satellite television). Over the past few years, especially in the UK and now in Europe as a whole, there has been a surge in these kinds of projects. Private sector companies have been expanding into areas previously the sole preserve of governments.

The general concept of pure project finance transacted with Western countries is probably little known in Czechoslovakia as it relates very much to the financial risk being legally tied to the product which will be produced and will eventually form the source of repayment. Czechoslovakia has however entered into a number of pure project finance contracts with certain Middle East countries notably Iraq where their experience has been less than satisfactory. Syria and Libya are other examples.

Projects which require finance in excess of £10 million may be supported through the International Finance Corporation, as long as the buyer is in the private sector, or projects of a lower value will be supportable through a line of finance which the IFC is currently discussing with one of the commercial banks in Czechoslovakia.

The borrower's objectives

With limited recourse finance, the borrowing companies limit their obligations to the lenders by restricting the lenders' interest and repayment rights to the assets and revenues of the project. In other words, the lenders have 'limited recourse' to the companies behind the project; but the lenders have full recourse to the single purpose company and the project. Another advantage of this form of finance for borrowing companies is that it may minimise guarantees and contingent liabilities in its consolidated accounts.

Generally, borrowing companies will have one or more of the following objectives:

- To transfer some of the project risk to the lenders.

- To match repayments to the project revenues.

- To maximise the amount which can be raised against project assets.

- To reduce the impact of financing on their balance sheets, thereby maintaining flexibility for further borrowing and making it easier to ensure compliance with any existing loan agreements.

- To isolate the security and to avoid cross-default provisions.

The role of the Banks

Over the years major international banks have become more willing to assume limited recourse risks as they have grown more familiar with them. Large project financing is frequently managed by a lead bank which will syndicate the loan among other banks in order to spread the risk. The key point for contractors to remember is to involve the banks from the outset. The banks must be allowed to assess the eligibility and viability of a project. There is no point in signing contracts without first being sure of getting the necessary finance.

FORFAITING

Despite its strange name, forfaiting is a simple concept: without recourse discounting. You receive a series of promissory notes or accepted bills of exchange from the buyer and sell them immediately for cash to a forfaiter. The forfaiter takes the risk (the forfaiter forfeits the right to come back to you if the buyer does not pay) and you get the money.

The origins of forfaiting lie in the 1950s when exporters in West Germany wanted to sell to the countries of Central and Eastern Europe. The basic goods were capital equipment and the regular credit terms were five years. West German companies accepted promissory notes or bills of exchange, payable every six months, and guaranteed by a bank in the importing country. The exporter then sold the notes to a forfaiter, who would calculate the present value of the notes and give the discounted cash sum to the exporter. The technique suited the German way of business. The credit was effectively fixed rate, the company bore no credit risk and the cash balances were steadily built up.

This sort of forfaiting is usually called the 'classic a' forfait or 'ten-by-six' (ten equal promissory notes payable at six-month intervals over the five-year credit term). But the development of forfaiting, due largely to the arrival of London banks and specialist forfaiting houses in the market, has meant that almost anything can now be financed through the market: 90-day terms for consumer goods, say, or military equipment over a few years, up to huge 13-year projects. Short-term forfaiting often substitutes deferred payment letters of credit for promissory notes. Cigarettes, plumbing equipment, even footballers, have been forfaited over the last few years. Generally, forfaiting covers deals worth more than £50,000, although smaller, repeat business could also be covered.

How does forfaiting work?

First, speak to a forfaiter as soon as you think there is a chance of closing the deal. All the major banks have forfaiting units or subsidiaries and there are also some independent houses that are very active in the business. Getting some preliminary advice from them will help you when it comes to negotiating the sales finance. If the deal looks certain, ask the forfaiter for a commitment. He will charge a fee for this but you will have the certainty that the price he quotes will be the actual price for the deal. The fee will be expressed annually (around 0.5 or 0.75 per cent) or on a monthly basis (about 0.1 per cent).

The forfaiter will guide you on how much to charge your

customer. The total will equal the sales price plus interest charges over the credit period, plus an amount that reflects the risk that the money will not be paid when the notes mature. As the promissory notes (or bills of exchange) are usually guaranteed by a first-class bank in the importer's country, this margin in effect represents the risk of national upheaval. The net result is, though, that you can tell your customer exactly what interest charge you are passing on: the finance is, by definition, fixed rate.

When the sales contract is signed and a delivery date agreed, the forfaiter can move ahead with the technical details of the transaction. He needs evidence of debt; in the case of a ten-by-six, ten promissory notes maturing at six-month intervals for the next five years. The paper will also include a guarantee from a bank in the buyer's country. This may be a separate piece of paper, guaranteeing that the buyer's obligation will be assumed by the bank, or an aval which is simply written on the document.

The actual details of the sale are completely independent of the financing because forfaiting provides finance without any recourse to the exporter. But usually, the evidence of debt will be presented at about the same time as the delivery of goods. The forfaiter buys the notes or bills for cash and will then hold them for presentation as they become due or, if he wants, sell them to an investing institution or another forfaiter in the secondary market.

It is worth noting that forfait rates are usually expressed as discount rates, rather than interest rates. This is because the amount that the exporter receives is calculated by discounting interest and risk margin from the total amount the importer pays.

A great advantage of forfaiting is that it makes any sale abroad just as easy as a domestic cash sale. The exporter may want £80,000 for a shipment to a customer who wishes to pay in a foreign currency over five years. The forfaiter will handle all the calculations and pay cash in sterling on delivery of the promissory notes. The exporter can be safe in the knowledge that, financially, an unknown company hundreds of miles away is no longer its customer – a High Street bank, with assets of billions of pounds is responsible for payment.

FACTORING

Factoring provides a source of working capital which can be used by a company instead of an overdraft or a loan to bridge the gap between invoicing and receiving payment. It is used for both domestic and international trade. A factoring house (which is usually owned by a bank) will buy a company's trade debts and make finance available immediately, thus providing the company with working capital. The factor also provides useful services such as credit checking all the company's sales ledger and taking responsibility for collecting debts from the company's customers. Some factors provide bad debt protection on approved debts, others do not. Factoring is therefore a form of instant finance and bad debt protection, which saves the supplier the trouble of pursuing his buyers for payment.

These benefits are particularly attractive to small and growing companies which frequently find themselves suffering from cash flow problems. A common feature of rapid growth is that as sales increase, the cash necessary to finance those sales can dry up, and over-trading can result.

Overdrafts are almost always the business's first method of raising finance but they are, technically, repayable on demand. In addition, security is often required, sometimes involving the business owner putting the family home at risk. Factoring is a useful alternative because the finance it provides, being geared to sales, automatically matches the rate at which the company grows. As the sales increase in value, so does the amount pre-paid by the factor.

Generally speaking, factoring companies will only take on firms that have an annual turnover of at least £100,000 with a projected growth to, say, a minimum of £200,000 within a year or so. Companies with a smaller turnover than this would not generate enough business to make it worthwhile for the factor.

There are three types of factoring: non-recourse, where the factor provides bad debt protection (favoured by the larger companies where there is an element of credit risk among their customers); recourse, where the factor has recourse to the client for bad debts (used mainly by smaller companies); and invoice discounting, which is basically factoring without the service element (used mainly by companies with sales in excess of £1 million, which have a well-organised and efficient sales accounting and credit control function).

With invoice discounting, the company simply gets a pre-payment on its invoices, less a discount, from the factor but does not use any of the ancillary services. The advantages of invoice discounting are that it is cheaper than factoring and it is confidential, since the company maintains direct contact with its customers. However, companies discounting usually have to bear the cost of any bad debts.

From the factor's point of view, invoice discounting is riskier, because the factor has to rely on the company to collect payment instead of on its own staff. For this reason, it is generally not available to companies with turnovers of less than £1 million a year. Finance advanced is charged at overdraft rates, and there is an administrative fee for the service of between 0.2 per cent and 0.7 per cent of sales.

LEASING

Leasing is no longer confined to one country, but extends across frontiers and this particularly applies to what is known as big ticket leasing, involving purchases of ships, tankers, aircraft, oil refineries and large plant and machinery.

Yet the problem is that leasing is not the same product in all countries. In the UK a financial lease is one where the lessor owns the assets and recovers over the lease period the costs of the assets, the finance charges and the profit. At the end of the period the asset is sold to a third party.

Leasing is a financial instrument which is in favour in Czechoslovakia. The use of leasing has grown quite substantially over the past 12 months but a warning note should be sounded in terms of cost. Many companies have expressed concern over the financial cost of some leasing transactions which have been taken through certain Western European leasing companies. Here again ECGD is capable of providing support to leasing transactions.

Companies wishing to lease equipment in Czechoslovakia can do so without seeking a credit facility from their bank provided they have sufficient koruna in their account to meet the initial rentals. This may be less relevant in view of the understandable caution which banks are adopting to buyers who cannot produce financial information or demonstrate a track record.

29

Countertrade

National Westminster Bank

Countertrade has emerged since the early-1970s as a significant medium of world trade. Estimates vary as to its extent but it is generally thought to account for between 10 per cent and 15 per cent of world trade. For every countertrade deal made public there are at least three or four that remain secret. Consequently, a useful guide to the growth of countertrade is the increasing number of countries which have regulations for countertrading. In 1972 there were 15 such countries; in 1979 this figure stood at 27; in 1983 there were 88 countries; and, by the end of 1986, approximately 100.

TYPES OF TRANSACTION

Countertrade is an umbrella term for a whole range of commercial mechanisms for reciprocal trade. These mechanisms include counterpurchase, barter, buy-back, offset, switch trading and evidence accounts. The common characteristic of countertrade arrangements is that export sales to a particular market are made conditional upon undertakings to accept imports from that market. For example, a British exporter may sell machinery to country X on condition that he accepts agricultural products from X in payment.

Simple barter deals like this are unusual, and most countertrade deals are much more complex. All British exporters should be aware of the potential demands for, and the intricacies of, countertrade since it has, over recent years, become a feature of trade with more than half the countries in the world. Even at its simplest, countertrade can be a difficult, expensive and uncertain mode of trading. It is fraught with pitfalls. With careful and imaginative planning, exporters have been able to turn this undesirable necessity to their advantage, although, in an ideal market it would not arise.

The principal reasons for a country to require countertrade terms are:

1. To acquire vital imports in the absence of foreign exchange of credit.

2. To develop new exports or new export markets by transferring all or part of the marketing to a foreign supplier.

3. To receive new technology, increase the manufacturing base, create employment and conserve scarce foreign exchange reserves.

4. To balance trade, for political and economic reasons, through the use of bilateral trading arrangements.

As a form of international trade, countertrade is undoubtedly one of the least desirable ways of doing business but many exporters have come to believe it is better than doing no business at all. Countertrade is more difficult for small and medium-sized exporters to contemplate as they are less able to devote the necessary resources to bear the additional costs involved.

CZECHOSLOVAKIA'S ATTITUDE TO COUNTERTRADE

It has not been the policy of the Czechoslovak government to insist on countertrade but, traditionally, lack of hard currency made it the preferred option. Due to their former monopoly position in Czechoslovakia's foreign trade system the various Foreign Trade Organisations (FTOs) were able to insist on countertrade transactions. Difficulties would often arise when it was discovered, often late in the day, that Czechoslovak goods of the type and quality envisaged would not be available for export within the time limits outlined in the countertrade deal.

To a great extent, whether a countertrade requirement was included in a transaction would depend on the relative bargaining strengths of the two sides. The import of goods perceived to be less than absolutely essential or unlikely to increase Czechoslovakia's hard currency earnings could be likely to have heavier countertrade obligations attached. The crucial thing was to identify at the outset which Czechoslovak products would be available for export.

Countertrade is now becoming less of a means through which

business can be transacted for two specific reasons. First the introduction of internal convertibility of the koruna. Second, the fact that central purchasing and selling agencies are disappearing brings with it a very restricted product range of individual companies with which to trade.

However, offset and buy-back, two other particular areas within the countertrade arena, are expected to continue and quite possibly grow. When it is recognised that Czechoslovakia's current priority is for quick turn-around projects and those which have potential for export earnings, it is conceivable that an element of two-way trade is foremost in their minds. What better way to build the industrial base than to seek help from those who are selling equipment to Czechoslovak buyers, in finding markets for the quality products which will materialise. To a certain extent the countertrade aspirations of Czechoslovakia could well be satisfied through the formation of joint venture companies.

FORMS OF COUNTERTRADE

Barter

Barter is also referred to as compensation trading or payment in kind. Barter is the direct exchange of goods for goods. The exporter agrees to accept payment in the form of goods from the importing country which can be used in the business. The scope of a barter agreement can range from taking a few Czechoslovak fork-lift trucks for use in a UK warehouse to regular and substantial supplies of raw materials such as industrial chemicals. Barter arrangements may be formal or informal and some agreements can call for partial payment in goods with the balance in hard currency. In a formal arrangement, a single contract covers both flows and no cash is involved under the primary agreement. Pure barter deals are uncommon and are suitable only for the more versatile exporting companies which must have an appropriate corporate philosophy and internal organisation to accommodate such business.

Many problems can arise under a barter arrangement which are attributable mainly to the valuation of goods in relation to each other. These problems include variations in the quality of the exchange merchandise, quantities involved in each shipment and the achievement of the agreed percentage of barter trade. In addition, the price of exchange goods may differ substantially from prices on the world market and the inherent cost to the exporter can rise unexpectedly. Exporters and importers will often require evidence accounts to be maintained in order that performance of the barter arrangement can be evidenced by a neutral party such as a commercial bank.

Counterpurchase

This is the most common form of countertrade in which the exporter undertakes to purchase goods or services from the importer to a given percentage of the value of the sales contract. This can range from 5 per cent to well over 100 per cent depending on circumstances and the objectives of the importing country concerned. A major feature of counterpurchase is that two separate contracts should be signed and linked on an informal basis. One contract should cover the sale by the exporter while the other represents the counterpurchase obligation to be fulfilled over a period of time (see Figure 29.1). It is important for the exporter to ensure that the counterpurchase obligation is freely transferable to a third party (usually a trading house) willing to take responsibility for taking and disposing of the exchange goods.

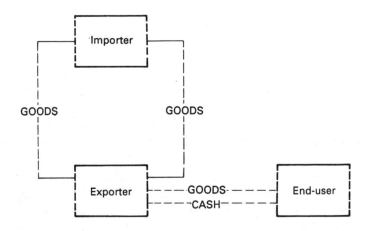

Figure 29.1 *A counterpurchase transaction*

A counterpurchase arrangement can vary from a general declaration of intent or best efforts to a binding contract specifying the goods and services to be supplied in exchange, the markets in which they may be sold and penalties for non-performance or if conditions are not met. The goods offered are usually quite unrelated to those being exported and often involve commodities or basic raw materials and unfinished products.

Advance purchase

This is a variation of counterpurchase, the major purpose of which is to secure payment in advance for the exporter's goods and thereby eliminate the risk of non-payment. The exchange goods are taken and disposed of in advance of any export shipments and the hard currency funds so generated are placed in an escrow account to meet future payments under an export contract. Advance purchase is a technique being used increasingly in dealing with heavily indebted countries. This technique can provide hard currency for the importer without payment risk or lengthy and bureaucratic central bank foreign exchange procedures in the importing country.

Buy-back

Buy-back is a type of countertrade where the suppliers of capital plant or equipment agree to full or part payment in the form of goods produced from the original export or investment. For example, an exporter of equipment for a chemical works may be paid from part of the resulting output of the plant (see Figure 29.2).

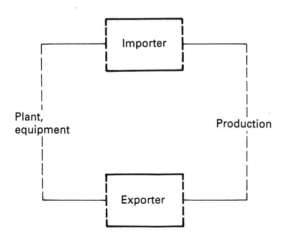

Figure 29.2 *Buy-back*

Buy-back percentages of the original sale can vary substantially (eg from 30 per cent to 100 per cent or more) and arrangements tend to be much longer term and for much larger amounts than counterpurchase or simple barter transactions. Some countries favour long-term buy-back arrangements as part of their industrial co-operation policies.

Offset

This is a condition imposed on the export of certain products, particularly those embodying advanced technology, for the exporter to incorporate specified materials, components or sub-assemblies procured from within the importing country. This has long been an established feature of trade in defence systems, aircraft and military equipment but is spreading rapidly to many other sectors, especially where the importing country is seeking to develop its own industrial capabilities.

The long-term objectives of the importing country are to increase local input, create new markets, reduce unemployment and share in advanced technology.

A different form of offset can arise in some large contracts or projects for which the importing country may demand successful bidders to establish local production facilities and other means of long-term industrial cooperation. Offset obligations are usually directly related to the production or services being purchased and will most likely involve co-production, licensed production, overseas investment, technology transfer, joint venture and research and development. Many major exporters faced with offset requirements will separate out normal contract requirements for training and technical assistance to form part of such obligations.

The requirements for offset in individual contracts will vary according to the needs and desires of the procuring country. In turn, opportunities for undertaking offset are likely to be limited by the level and sophistication of the industrial base and the country's comparative economic or geographical advantages.

There are various other forms of countertrade which are less relevant for exporters interested in the Czechoslovak market. These would include bilateral clearing accounts, special trade agreements and switch trading. For further information a specialist counter-trader should be contacted.

30

Credit Insurance
National Westminster Bank

Credit insurance is more than simply a way of protecting receivables. It can play a crucial role in providing finance for growth. If you show your bank manager that you have credit protection and that any new business your sales force can generate will also be covered, you stand a much better chance of getting the finance you need. From your bank's point of view, you will be a better risk. Insurance may enable you to raise money at finer rates from your bank, although you must remember that the premium is part of the overall financing cost.

While you can deal directly with underwriters, it often makes sense to talk first to a broker, who will advise you which company will suit you best.

The leading insurer for UK exporters is the Export Credit Guarantee Department (ECGD). The short-term department, called the Insurance Services Group, is based in Cardiff and is in the process of being privatised by the government. Without cover from the government the group may well have to charge higher premiums or, otherwise, sacrifice its rate of return. The main advantage of using ECGD at present is that bankers are familiar with its documentation, and the spread of its regional offices can also be helpful.

ECGD's main competitor is TI; the size of its export business is small, relative to ECGD, but growing. If you already use domestic credit insurance, it might be worth asking for details of TI's export schemes.

How does credit insurance work?

Colourshoot makes up slide transparencies into educational filmstrips. It has a turnover of around £1 million. Most of its business goes to government departments or advertising agencies in Britain. With customers like these, Colourshoot does not bother with credit insurance. The company has a good credit control department for its few smaller customers and the security of payment of the major part of the business keeps the bank happy.

Suddenly, Colourshoot gets an enquiry from a Czechoslovak company for an order that could double turnover. But, to fulfil the order, Colourshoot will have to increase its capacity immediately – a capital investment of some £50,000 – and increase its staff. The customer appears to be creditworthy but Colourshoot's bank is wary, and is unwilling to lend for expansion unless the firm takes out credit insurance. The bank's trade finance unit is able to introduce a broker and, before selecting any particular cover, Colourshoot is advised to review its plans for doing business in Czechoslovakia. If business is likely to increase, the identity of the new customer may make a difference to the sort of policy that should be chosen.

Both ECGD and the private underwriters provide individual contract or whole turnover cover, or something in between. Individual contract cover is just the first choice; ECGD, in particular, has a vast range of schemes. Cover can, for example, be arranged from the date of contract or from the date of despatch. It can also cover contracts denominated in foreign currencies. The policy will normally cover 90 per cent of commercial risk – that is, non-payment by the buyer – and 95 per cent of political risk. If, for example, a run on a currency were to cause a government to impose exchange controls, the buyer may be willing to pay in local currency but be unable to remit it abroad; in this case, 95 per cent of the money would still be paid by ECGD.

ECGD-SUPPORTED FINANCE SCHEMES

In addition to its range of insurance policies, ECGD provides guarantees to banks to enable exporters to obtain export finance for goods and services at competitive and sometimes favourable interest rates. ECGD also offers banks credit insurance guarantees; alternatively, it provides separate bank guarantees, which give direct security to banks for their export financing.

With the bank guarantee schemes, if the exporter's customer defaults under the 'without recourse' loan made available to support the transaction, the bank can claim from ECGD the full amount guaranteed, so the bank bears no risk. ECGD may, however, then seek to cover that amount from the exporter, but only in circumstances where it can be proved that the default occurred as a result of non-performance by the exporter. ECGD-supported finance comes in various forms, such as short-term and medium-term supplier finance and medium-term buyer credit (see Chapter 28).

Unfair calling cover

ECGD can offer insurance to exporters against unfair calling of bonds raised with or without direct ECGD support. This cover is available for contracts (except external trade contracts) on cash or credit terms insured under a normal ECGD guarantee which includes a pre-credit risk cover, provided the form of the bond is acceptable to ECGD and the buying country is considered suitable for this form of cover.

The insurance takes the form of an addendum or endorsement to the basic guarantee. ECGD agrees to reimburse the exporter for 100 per cent of any loss due to the calling of a bond if it is shown subsequently that the exporter was not in default in his performance of the contract, or if any failure on his part is due to specified events outside his control. Under comprehensive guarantees (goods insured on short terms and extended terms), which include pre-credit risk cover, this cover is available only for contracts with public buyers and does not apply to tender bonds. For short-term business, cover is given automatically for all such contracts by prior endorsement to the relevant basic guarantee. For extended terms contracts under these guarantees, bond cover is given for individual suitable contracts on application. For specific guarantees and buyer credit guarantees, all types of bonds qualify for cover by an addendum to the basic guarantee.

The Overseas Investment Insurance Scheme

This scheme is designed to insure an investment abroad against the political risks of expropriation, war and restrictions on remittances.

The commerical risks of the investment are not covered.

Risks insured include not only nationalisation or confiscation of the investment or of the property of the overseas enterprise, but also indirect forms of expropriation brought about by the host government with the intention of discriminating against the investor or the overseas enterprise. The expropriatory action must normally continue in force for at least one year before the fact of expropriation is established for the purpose of claims. In the case of equity investment the occurrence of expropriation establishes the right to claim, while in the case of a loan investment the right to claim arises only if the expropriation results in default.

Also covered are losses due to war in which the host government is a participant, or due to revolution or insurrection in the host country. The aim is to cover the investor not only against damage to, or removal of, all or part of the tangible property of the overseas enterprise, but also against the inability of the overseas enterprise to operate the project due to war.

In order to qualify, the overseas enterprise must have been physically unable to operate the project for a period of a year, or have been unable to operate it at a profit for a period of three consecutive years. For loan investment, again, there must be default arising from the occurrence of the risk before a claim can be established.

Insurance can be provided against the frustration for a period of six months of the investor's attempts to convert into sterling earnings not retained in the business, the proceeds of any disinvestment, or interest on, and repayment of loans. Cover is also given if the conversion is permitted but only at a rate of exchange which discriminates against the investor. The insurance does not cover restrictions in force when the investment is made or the guarantee executed, whichever is the later. Cover is available only for sums which the investor attempts to convert within six months of receiving them.

Eligible investors and enterprises

All companies carrying on business in the UK, and their overseas subsidiaries, are in principle 'eligible investors' for insurance purposes, provided that the investment is identifiable as British in the host country. This definition would normally exclude: (a) the UK branch of a company incorporated outside the UK; and (b) the UK subsidiary of a company incorporated outside the UK, which is being used by the foreign parent merely as a channel for the investment.

Cover can be considered where an eligible investor channels his investment through a non-UK intermediary which he (or other UK interests) controls directly or indirectly. In dealing with this method of making an investment, ECGD will take into consideration several factors which include where the intermediary is located, whether it is operational or otherwise, and whether the investment is regarded as British by the host government. Any cover given to the UK investor would reflect the extent of his interest in the intermediary. The premium payable to ECGD would be adjusted, where appropriate, to take account of any multiple exposure to risks due to the method of making the investment (eg double transfer risk).

As regards eligible enterprises, cover is in principle available for eligible investment in any legally constituted foreign enterprise (including an unincorporated branch of the investor or a partnership) carrying on business in any country outside the UK, the Channel Islands and the Isle of Man, in which the investor has a direct interest (ie he controls it, or has a management or trading interest in it).

Since the object of the scheme is to encourage lasting investment, the investor must intend to keep the capital in the overseas enterprise for at least three years. In the case of loans, a mean repayment period of not less than three years must be provided for in the loan agreement. An investor is, of course, free to dispose of his investment within three years if he wishes, but if he does so voluntarily ECGD accept no liability for loss due to inability to repatriate the proceeds.

Amount of insurance

In the case of equity investment, insurance will normally be offered in respect of:

- the sterling amount of the initial contribution;
- earnings retained in the enterprise up to 200 per cent of the investor's initial contribution of equity capital; and
- the remittance of distributed earnings.

The guarantee will specify a maximum insured amount (MIA) that will constitute ECGD's maximum liability for the payment of claims. The investor may, if he wishes, confine his MIA to the amount of the initial investment and this will provide cover on the initial contribution and remitted earnings only. If, however, he wishes to cover earnings up to a maximum of 300 per cent of the amount of the initial investment, the investor would need to agree his requirements with ECGD. To avoid the risk of being under-insured it is often to an investor's advantage to select an MIA of, or near, the maximum available rather than one that is too low.

PRIVATE MARKET INSURANCE

There are, in the commercial market, several alternative sources of insurance to government export credit agencies, including Lloyd's of London. These can be used to insure contracts or risks for which cover from a national scheme is not available. For example:

- The contract may not be eligible for cover because not enough of the goods or services to be supplied under it are sourced from the country of the national scheme.

- The contract may not be eligible for cover because the terms of payment do not conform to international agreements.

- The national scheme may be 'off cover' for the particular country.

- The national scheme may not cover the particular risk concerned (eg the buyer's failure to supply goods in a countertrade arrangement).

Risks insured

In the field of political risk insurance, the main types of coverage are grouped under the generic heading of 'contract frustration' and 'confiscation' insurance. Contract frustration includes the following risks:

1. contract repudiation;
2. export or import embargo;
3. exchange transfer embargo;
4. 'on demand' bonds and guarantees;
5. *force majeure* termination; and
6. barter and countertrade.

Confiscation, which is a short way of describing a cover which includes confiscation, seizure, appropriation, expropriation, requisition for title or use or wilful destruction by a host government, protects against the following risks:

1. confiscation of fixed or permanent investments;

2. confiscation of loan securities;

3. confiscation of mobile assets;

4. confiscation of aircraft under lease or purchase contracts; and

5. confiscation of contractors' plant.

The commercial market, unlike the government export credit agencies, is not required to observe national considerations. Cover can therefore be arranged irrespective of the nationality of the insured exporter or the origin of the goods or services. On the other hand, government export credit agencies may be prepared, in the national interest, to underwrite contracts where the risks are unacceptable to commercial insurers.

The commercial market can be selective about the contracts or even the risks which it underwrites. Thus, contracts involving the supply of high priority goods may be acceptable for insurance in countries where the risks would otherwise seem too high. Similarly, in countries where the exchange transfer embargo risk is considered too high, the commercial market may be prepared to underwrite other risks (eg countertrade risks).

Deprivation of collateral insurance

This is a new product which protects banks and financial institutions making loans to private companies where such loans are secured by mortgages, charges, debenture etc. on assets located in Central or Eastern Europe. Such loans may be made direct to those companies seeking to modernise their factories or, alternatively, to Western companies seeking to purchase newly privatised industries. In most instances, the principal collateral will be a mortgage over the companies' factory or premises.

Deprivation of collateral insurance recognises that the concepts of mortgage, collateral, insolvency, financial default, private property and secured loans are unfamiliar to these markets, and it protects the lending institution against the risk that it is unable, following a default under the loan, to exercise its legal rights under the mortgage.

31

Agencies, Distributorships and Franchises

SJ Berwin & Co

Access to new markets is often obtained indirectly, by selling goods and services into that market through an agent, distributor or licensee. This indirect form of establishment in a foreign territory has the advantage of providing a new market for goods and services and a source of income, with the minimum degree of financial outlay and limited management and sales involvement. The major difficulty, particularly at the present time, is trying to determine whether there is a market for particular goods or services in Czechoslovakia. There are few sectors in which one can determine consumer demand, how and in what way to seek access to that market, and the extent of that market. This makes it very difficult to calculate the level of necessary investment.

The second difficulty is identifying and finding an entity suitable to act as an agent or distributor, who is capable of representing, promoting and selling, delivering and protecting the goods or services in Czechoslovakia. Where the use of a name, intellectual property rights or know-how are concerned, this may involve the grant of a licence and, in other special situations, a franchise may be more appropriate.

This chapter concentrates on agency, distribution and franchise arrangements as a means of entry to and for the Czechoslovak market. Licences are dealt with in Chapter 32.

LEGAL REGULATIONS

There is very little direct law in Czechoslovakia dealing with agency, distribution or franchise relationships. The law is essentially permissive in that it allows parties a large degree of freedom of contract to determine the terms of their agreement and their respective rights and obligations. In Czechoslovakia, agency is regulated by the 1963 International Trade Code which contains provisions to regulate the relationship between agents and principals. However, these provisions appear to be biased in favour of the principal as a result, it seems, of the old system of foreign trade monopoly: Czechoslovak foreign trade organisations (FTOs) appointed agents outside Czechoslovakia and, therefore, in the absence of express agreements, the law aimed to support the .interests of the principal.

There is no law in Czechoslovakia dealing specifically with distributorship relationships. Therefore, there are no restrictions, limitations or requirements of authorisation for distributorship appointments, and the rights and obligations of the parties will depend on what they agree. Due to the monopoly on distribution that previously operated in Czechoslovakia, it was not possible for a foreign company to freely appoint a distributor. There was no real market for foreign goods and no purpose in appointing a distributor to hold a stock of goods for sale. In any event, special authority was needed to import foreign goods and foreign currency authority was also required.

Neither are there any laws regulating franchise agreements. A franchise is a mixture of a licence arrangement and a distribution agreement and basically consists of a contractual licence under which the franchisee is permitted to carry on business under a well-known trade name and system for marketing and producing goods or services, which belongs to the franchisor and under which the franchisor controls the way in which the franchisee does business and provides continuing advice and assistance to the franchisee. The businesses of the franchisor and franchisee are, however, separate.

Finally, the Act on Protection of Economic Competition, discussed in Chapter 16 on commercial law, may apply to an agency, distribution or franchise agreement. Advice should be taken as to whether the agreement needs to be registered and an exemption applied for under that Act.

AGENCY

To appoint an agent or representative is the easiest and least expensive method of entry into a new market. The appointment of an individual or company to represent a foreign company, to promote the sale of its goods and services, to follow up opportunities on its behalf, to collect information relating to the marketing of its products in that country, and to be the 'ears and eyes' of the foreign principal, is often the first step to entry into a new market-place. The law relating to agency has not changed since the 'Velvet Revolution', but the major difference now is that individuals and companies are free to enter into commercial transactions at will and there is a free choice of agents in Czechoslovakia although, in practice, identifying suitable agents may present a difficulty.

There are two categories of agent recognised by Czechoslovak law, namely brokers and commercial representatives.

Brokers

- A broker has a specific authority or operates on a case by case basis, and his activities consist mainly of introducing third parties to his principal for the purpose of concluding a contract. The broker may also have certain additional responsibilities in respect of supervision or administration of performance of the contract.

- A broker is required not only to assist his principal in concluding contracts with third parties but also to be active in the fulfilment of contracts.

- The broker is not entitled to accept or bind or otherwise commit the principal except when authorised by a power of attorney to do so.

- A broker is entitled to an agreed commission or, if not agreed, to an appropriate commission.

- Commission is normally payable only when the third party has fulfilled all of the obligations towards the principal under the contract.

- A brokerage agreement may be oral or in writing.

Commercial representatives

- This type of agent works systematically for the principal in a specific territory, in a specific commercial area and for a specific period of time.

■ The authority and power of the commercial representative is dependent on his agreement with the principal. Generally, the commercial representative is not empowered to conclude transactions in the name of, or on behalf of the principal, or to bind or commit the principal unless expressly authorised in writing.

■ Under a commercial representation agreement the agent is generally required to fulfil very detailed instructions on behalf of his principal if he is to earn his commission.

■ The contract appointing a commercial representative must be in writing.

While there is no employment relationship between principal and agent, it is quite normal for agents to be expected to assist and co-operate in the realisation of transactions. Agents are expected to keep the principal informed about market developments, to keep information about the principal and his business confidential, and to look after documentation, samples and other materials belonging to the principal.

Czechoslovak law expressly recognises exclusive and non-exclusive agencies and, unless a contract provides expressly for the appointment of an exclusive agent, the principal is free to employ other commercial representatives in the territory. However, if an exclusive agent is appointed, the principal may not choose other representatives for the agreed type of transaction in the territory, although he will still be entitled to conclude transactions in the territory without involving the agent, but will have to pay the agent a commission on such transactions.

The duration of appointment of an agent is a matter to be agreed between the parties. In the absence of an agreement as to the duration, the appointment of an agent is deemed to be for an unlimited period, but can be terminated by giving written notice of one month, except where the agency has lasted for more than a year where at least three months' written notice must be given.

At the time of writing, the law makes no provision for compensation on termination of an agency. However, the forthcoming Commercial Code will almost certainly do so. The present draft provides for compensation to be paid to an agent under a formula based on the commission earned in the last year of his appointment, multiplied by the number of years the agency lasted. The parties are allowed to agree a lower figure in the agency agreement but the principle of compensation has to remain. Agency agreements should, therefore, specify the compensation figure. Compensation can be excluded if it is agreed that English law will apply to the agreement (but it must be borne in mind that provision for compensating agents will shortly be introduced in accordance with the 1986 EC Directive on the Protection of Commercial Agents).

Agency contract check list

The essential terms to be covered in an agency agreement include the following:

- The subject matter of the agency (ie the specific goods and services).

- The territory of the agency, including the right to promote and conclude sale arrangements outside the territory.

- The exclusive or non-exclusive nature of the agency, including the agent's right to represent competitive products.

- The specific authority of the agent to bind and commit the principal.

- How and the extent to which the agent is to hold itself out or be held out as representing the principal.

- The terms of payment, including in respect of contracts concluded but not performed and part performance.

- The agent's remuneration terms, commission rates and fixed payments, including any right to continuing commissions after termination of the agency, and repayment of expenses.

- Duration and the grounds for termination of the agency and the notice to be given of termination.

DISTRIBUTORSHIP

A distribution arrangement generally involves goods being purchased from the manufacturer or supplier and imported into the territory and sold by the distributor, in its own name and at its own risk, to customers in that territory.

In many respects the relationship between a distributor and the manufacturer or supplier is at arm's length, as the distributor buys and sells on to the customer for its own account. However, there are areas where the respective obligations between the manufacturer or supplier and the distributor, and the distributor and the final purchaser of the goods, will be inter-related – for example, responsibility for defects, warranties, after-sales service and intellectual property.

There are no legal rules concerned specifically with distributorship arrangements and the specific contract terms will be a matter for negotiation. British companies are free to appoint private persons, newly established companies or existing enterprises to act as distributors for their products in Czechoslovakia. However, because in the past practically everything was distributed through the monopolised networks which are currently being dissolved, it is now very complicated to establish distribution arrangements, particularly as markets for products are unclear.

When negotiating commercial terms with the Czechoslovak distributor, the absence of capital and, therefore, the difficulty in investing in plant, in machinery, in the ability to provide an after-sales service and of course to purchase and hold a stock of the products, will have to be taken into account. The foreign manufacturer or supplier appointing a Czechoslovak distributor should be clear as to what he is actually seeking. Factors for consideration to be covered in the contractual terms include:

- Is it the intention to develop the market in Czechoslovakia only, or is the Czechoslovak distributor to be a base for Central and Eastern Europe generally?

- Is there already a market for the goods or services in Czechoslovakia or is the intention to develop a new market? This may be relevant in respect of support for the distributor and the level of sales relevant to the fixing of minimum purchase obligations.

- Are the goods and services to be sold or provided under a trade mark or name? If so, such trade mark or name must be registered to ensure protection.

- Is an after-sales maintenance and repairs service to be provided? If so, has the distributor the necessary infrastructure, skill, expertise and technical knowledge? If not, will the manufacturer or supplier provide the training, machine tools, manpower and support for this purpose?

- Are the goods and services appropriate for the Czechoslovak market or are adaptations necessary – to comply with local electrical standards? If so, whose responsibility will this be: manufacturer/supplier or distributor?

■ Are there any import restrictions for the goods to be distributed and, if so, who will be responsible for obtaining the necessary import licences?

■ What price is the Czechoslovak distributor to pay for the products and what are the payment terms? Is payment to be in advance of delivery or is credit to be given to enable the Czechoslovak distributor to purchase the goods, sell them within Czechoslovakia and then pay the manufacturer/ supplier?

■ Is the appointment to be exclusive or non-exclusive?

■ Are there to be minimum purchase and sale requirements? Will the distributor be required to hold minimum stocks?

■ How long is the contract to continue and what are the terms on which the distribution agreement may be terminated?

■ Which law will govern the agreement and what system will govern dispute settlements?

An important issue is to provide expressly in the contract that on termination the distributor will not be entitled to any compensation. This will avoid the situation where a distributor maintains that he has established a market within Czechoslovakia but does not satisfy the requirements and wishes of the manufacturer/supplier, and claims damages for his 'lost' investment. When the British manufacturer/supplier takes over the market it should not be obliged to compensate the Czechoslovak distributor for the market he has developed, other than as provided expressly in the contract.

Other obligations often imposed on distributors which may be relevant for distribution arrangements in Czechoslovakia include having to purchase from the manufacturer a minimum quantity of goods and to resell a minimum quantity in the territory; to pay the manufacturer in convertible currency for the goods; to hold a stock of goods, spare parts and accessories as appropriate; and to keep the manufacturer/supplier informed of market conditions, any competitive products, any counterfeit products, or any infringement of the patents, trade marks and other rights of the manufacturer/ supplier.

Areas of particular concern

All the contract terms will be a matter for negotiation but there are certain specific matters that will have to be considered in the light of circumstances in Czechoslovakia.

- Who is to be liable for damage incurred by users of the goods or third parties due to defects in the goods?

- Environmental concerns are of major and increasing importance. While it may be possible to sell goods that are not environmentally friendly in the market, this may be short term as Czechoslovakia will be implementing strict environmental controls in the coming years.

- The pricing of the goods for the Czechoslovak market place should reflect the problems in Czechoslovakia.

- In the present economic climate, it is likely to be very expensive and time-consuming to develop a network of customers for one's products. There will be few customers readily available to purchase products and the manufacturer/supplier will therefore need to carefully consider the question of demand for his product in Czechoslovakia.

- When negotiating commercial terms with the Czechoslovak distributor, the absence of capital, and therefore the distributor's difficulty investing in plant and machinery and its ability to provide an after-sales service, and of course to hold a stock of the products, will have to be taken into account.

FRANCHISING

There are, as stated earlier, no laws in Czechoslovakia regulating franchise agreements. Subject to the law on intellectual property rights, the parties are free and should set out as fully as possible the specific terms and conditions of the agreement reached between them. Many of the principles and general contract law concerns discussed in connection with agency, distribution and licence agreements are also relevant to franchise agreements.

The principal reason a prospective franchisor would consider franchising is to expand a tried and tested business formula. However, while there are considerable advantages for the franchisor in franchising, there are also inherent disadvantages. Among the advantages is the fact that a franchise is a means of expansion using the franchisee's capital; that a franchisee which has committed its own funds is likely to be highly motivated; and that a franchisee is likely to have valuable local knowledge. However, disadvantages include the lack of control the franchisor has over the franchisee; the franchisee may be satisfied with a certain level of income and under-perform or under-state its turnover in order to reduce royalties; and in involving third parties in the business, franchisors will inevitable have to divulge substantial know-how and information concerning their business. These are all issues which need to be agreed between the franchisor and franchisee and the appropriate rights, duties, obligations and protections must be set out in the contract.

A franchisor looking to grant a franchise in Czechoslovakia should decide as issues of principle whether:

- to develop the franchise within Czechoslovakia and have a whole series of outlets;

- to retain a share of the franchise business itself as a joint venture partner;

- to assist with the financing of the franchise through direct lending or through credit or raw materials purchased; and

- to repatriate profits in the short term.

The need to establish and maintain the basic standards of production, presentation and quality, essential to a successful franchise, are generally dealt with through staff who regularly visit the franchisee, by requiring the franchisee to purchase raw materials from the franchisor or its nominated suppliers, and by training and supervision. These are all issues which one should try to regulate through the contract terms because Czechoslovak law does not cover them. However, the infrastructure necessary to maintain standards may not be available at the present time. The difficulties of determining value and taking security over land or other property highlights the problems that are likely to be encountered when trying to seek finance for an independent Czechoslovak franchisee.

32

Licensing

SJ Berwin & Co

The licensing of intellectual property rights and know-how has a vital part to play in the rebirth of Czechoslovakia's market economy. This chapter is in four parts, dealing with:

- new opportunities for licensing in Czechoslovakia;
- the protection of intellectual property rights;
- specific rights; and
- licensing considerations.

NEW OPPORTUNITIES FOR LICENSING IN CZECHOSLOVAKIA

Czechoslovakia offers prospective licensors significant opportunities. Enterprises in the armaments industry, for example, with well-equipped factories and with highly skilled staff, are urgently seeking new products. Conversely, many foreign companies, particularly in the USA and Japan, are looking for a low cost manufacturing base in Europe and would prefer to begin by building a relationship with a licensee rather than by immediately taking the risk of a major investment in a joint venture.

Before the revolution, licences to state organisations could be super-profitable – the state enterprise had a guaranteed market for its products and, in some instances, a monopoly for the whole of Czechoslovakia. The emphasis has now changed. The new Act on Protection of Economic Competition ('the Competition Act') is designed to break up monopolies. Licensees no longer operating in a production-led economy have to compete and learn the techniques of marketing and business decision making based on consumer demand. The ability of the licensor to provide effective training in these areas may be crucial to commercial success.

Under the pre-revolution Foreign Trade Act, the state regulated all agreements with foreign companies for production co-operation, scientific and technical co-operation and intellectual property licences. The 1990 amendments to the Foreign Trade Act abolished state regulation in these areas. Foreign companies and Czechoslovak parties are, therefore, now entirely free to enter into licensing agreements. In particular:

- The parties can agree whatever terms they wish – there is no restriction on the contents of the agreement, except insofar as the Competition Act applies (see page 278).

- There is no limitation as to the amount or form of royalty (for example, whether it should be a lump sum to be paid by instalments or variable by reference to turnover). This is now a matter for negotiation.

- Royalties are freely convertible into hard currency and transferable outside Czechoslovakia, as part of the internal convertibility regime under the Foreign Exchange Act 1990.

THE PROTECTION OF INTELLECTUAL PROPERTY RIGHTS

Intellectual property is the term used to describe various intangible forms of valuable rights. Intellectual property rights include copyright, patents, trade marks, trade names, service marks, industrial designs and secret know-how. These rights can be among the most valuable assets a company owns because they create a form of monopoly – though know-how affords a much weaker protection as its value depends on the information being kept secret.

As intellectual property gives exclusive rights of use to the owner, the only way another party can use the rights is with the owner's permission (ie by a licence). A patent or industrial design licence avoids the time, delay and cost of research and development on the part of the licensee. 'Buying' the technology rights or know-how from the owner enables the licensee, in theory at least, to reach the same technological standard as the licensor and to try and develop its technology from that stage. Trade mark licences give the licensor a source of immediate additional income and the licensee the opportunity to increase sales due to the 'cachet' conferred by the mark.

Before granting a licence in a particular territory, the licensor will need to determine the protection for his intellectual property rights in that country. This depends both on the law in that country and on its membership of international treaty arrangements. Similar considerations also arise, in some respects, when taking a licence from a person claiming to be the owner of rights. Questions of particular concern include:

- Is the licensor/licensee authorised to give the undertakings contained in the licence? In particular, does the licensor own the rights?

- Are the relevant legal requirements such as registrations and approvals by competent authorities met?

- Is the licensee also the person who will exploit the rights in the territory?

- Are confidentiality undertakings and obligations enforceable?

- How can monopoly rights be protected if infringed?

- What law will govern the legal relationship under the licence agreement?

Local laws and international conventions

In every country the rights attached to intellectual property vary according to the local law and the country's international commitments. Czechoslovakia's legislation includes a new law on inventions – the Industrial Designs and Innovations (Rationalisation Proposals) No. 527/1990; the Trade Marks Act (No. 174/1988); the Copyright Act; and relevant provisions of the Economic Code as amended. The existing system will shortly be strengthened with the adoption of the Commercial Code. This important measure will provide a more solid basis for the law against unfair competition and the protection of know-how and trade names.

Czechoslovakia is a party to the main international conventions dealing with intellectual property, including:

- Paris Convention (International Union) 1883–1967.

- Madrid Agreement Concerning the International Registration of Marks (Madrid Union) 1891–1967.

■ Madrid Agreement for the Repression of False or Deceptive Indications of Source on Goods 1891–1967.

■ Nice Agreement Concerning the International Classification of Goods and Services for the Purposes of the Registration of Marks 1957–1977.

■ Lisbon Agreement for the Protection of Appellations of Origin and their International Registration (Lisbon Union) 1958–1967.

■ Convention Establishing the World Intellectual Property Organisation (WIPO Convention) 1967.

■ Locarno Agreement Establishing an International Classification for Industrial Designs (Locarno Union) 1968.

■ Strasbourg Agreement Concerning the International Patent Classification (IPC Union) 1971.

■ Comecon agreements: including the Agreement on the Legal Protection of Inventions, Industrial Designs, Utility Models and Trade Marks in the Framework of Economic Scientific and Technical Co-operation (Moscow Treaty) 1973, and other treaties with former socialist countries.

Registration of intellectual property rights

The federal Office for Inventions ('the Office') in Prague is the central regulatory body for patents, industrial designs, and trade and service marks ('industrial rights'). The Office maintains a Trade Marks' Register, a Patents' Register and an Industrial Designs Register, and is responsible for the registration of all registrable industrial rights, whether of domestic or foreign origin. It also publishes a regular Bulletin (*Vestnik Uradu*) ('the Bulletin'), with information including applications for, and grants of, patents and industrial designs and other significant decisions by the Office, as well as registrations, renewals and expirations of trade marks.

Proceedings regarding registration and related issues are a matter of administrative law. Appeals against the decisions of the Office, such as a decision to refuse a trade mark registration, may be made to the President of the Office. In most cases his decision is final. In a few instances, such as the withdrawal of a patent or compulsory licence, an application may be made to the civil courts for judicial review.

A foreign applicant must be represented either by a Czechoslovak advocate, by a 'commercial lawyer' (lawyers previously employed by state organisations) or by a patent agent. Czechoslovak citizens have only recently been allowed to practise as patent agents. Such individuals must be authorised by the Office to carry out activities similar to those of British patent agents, after requirements such as proof of qualifications and knowledge are met. It is important to check that a patent agent is licensed to practise.

In the case of trade marks, foreign applicants and owners of marks must be represented by an authorised organisation or by one of its members. Agencies where foreigners can seek representation include the Institute for Technical Development and Information (UTRIN), the Law and Patent Bureau No. 1 (*Advokatni poradna c.1*) and the Law and Patent Bureau No. 10 (*Advokatni poradna c.10*), all in Prague.

The means of protection available to a foreign proprietor

As Czechoslovakia is a country in the civil law tradition, it does not recognise 'judge-made' law. Decisions of the courts are not legally binding precedents for the future and owners of intellectual property can therefore look only to existing statute law and regulations as a basis for protection.

In the UK, actions for the infringement of industrial rights such as patents and trade marks are often met with a two-fold defence – first that the patent is not being infringed and, secondly, that it is in any event invalid. This 'belt and braces' approach is not possible in Czechoslovakia. Questions of the *validity* of these rights are dealt with under the administrative procedure of the federal Office for Inventions. Litigation by commercial bodies and state organisations about the *infringement* of these rights currently takes place within the system of state arbitration, originally designed for state organisations and extended to other business entities in 1990, and due to be replaced by Commercial Courts under legislation which is currently awaited.

The following remedies are available:

- an injunction to prohibit infringement;

- an order for the proprietor to be compensated for losses incurred, plus the amount by which the defendant has been unjustly enriched through the infringement;

- damages for 'intangible' losses such as damage to goodwill are available under the new laws regulating patents and industrial designs.

Where goods bearing infringing trade marks are being imported, the proprietor may request that the customs authorities refuse clearance for such goods.

SPECIFIC RIGHTS

Patents

The right to a patent belongs to the inventor or his legal successor. The inventor is the person who created the invention by his own creative activity. The invention must be new, the result of inventive activity and must be capable of industrial application. Definitions are equivalent to those in the UK Patents Act and the European Patent Convention. If there is more than one inventor they own the patent rights jointly and share the benefits in proportion to their contributions to the invention.

If an employee makes an invention in the course of his employment, the right to the invention passes to the employer, unless otherwise agreed in writing. The inventor must inform his employer about the invention and the employer must state whether it intends to apply for a patent. The inventor retains certain royalty rights. The extent of employees' rights can be an important issue in privatisation projects.

A patent becomes effective on the date on which it is published in the Bulletin and remains valid for 20 years from the date of application. The owner of a patent has the exclusive right to use, grant licences under or assign the invention. Licence agreements must be made in writing and become effective on the date they are recorded in the Register.

The Office may grant a compulsory licence where an important public interest is involved, or for reasons of non-use, within four years from the date of application or three years from the date of grant of the patent. Such licences can be granted to anyone who wishes to exploit the invention in Czechoslovakia, including foreign persons.

Industrial designs

An industrial design is a product's outward shape which is new and industrially applicable. The outward shape of a product is its plane or three-dimensional external condition consisting especially of its shape, contours, design, a particular arrangement of colours, or any combination of these features. The designer is the person who created the design by himself, unless he produced it in the course of his employment. The same regime which applies to employees' inventions also applies to employees' industrial designs.

Registration of an industrial design gives the proprietor the exclusive right to use, assign or license it. A licence or assignment must be in writing and must be registered in order to become effective. Registrations are valid for five years from the filing date and can be renewed for up to two successive five-year periods.

Improvements

Improvements are a special kind of intellectual property right peculiar to former socialist law systems. They consist of technical, production or working innovations made by employees, as well as their solutions to problems concerning safety and protection of health at work, or to environmental problems. Improvements are not subject to registration.

The innovator must offer his improvement to his employer. If the employer accepts it, an agreement is concluded which states the remuneration to be paid to the employee. The employer's right to use the improvement comes into existence on the date of the contract. If the employer is not interested in the innovation, the employee is free to dispose of it. These provisions may apply even to employees of a wholly foreign-owned subsidiary.

Trade marks and service marks

Trade marks and service marks are used to distinguish goods and services from a particular source from goods and services from other sources. In Czechoslovakia, a mark may be registered as a verbal, figurative, three-dimensional or combined sign, which is capable of distinguishing the goods or services of the manufacturer or supplier from those of others. Unlike the position in some other countries, audio signals such as 'tunes' cannot be registered.

An application may relate to more than one of the classes listed in the 'International Classification of Goods and Services', subject to an additional fee. After an application has been filed, it cannot be amended so as to extend the list of goods or services covered.

Registration is essential. It confers the exclusive right to use the trade or service mark. Czechoslovakia does not follow the UK's principle of 'first use', which gives the first user of a trade mark stronger rights than the person who obtains first registration. Failure to be the first to apply for registration may, therefore, be disastrous.

The Trade Marks Act 1988 was adopted under the conditions of *perestroika* and some of its provisions, designed for socialist organisations, are not appropriate for a free market economy. Thus, an application may be filed only by a person pursuing an 'authorised economic activity', and the goods or services for which the mark is to be registered must be within the scope of that activity. The applicant's field of activity is evidenced by a certificate attached to the application. Likewise, while assignments and licences are permitted, the Office has power to refuse registration if the field of activity of the assignee or licensee does not extend to the goods for which the mark is registered. It is expected that these provisions will be treated largely as a dead letter until the law is brought up to date.

These questions do not arise when a foreign company with a trade mark registration in its home country seeks to register the mark in Czechoslovakia. Here, a certificate of the home registration accompanied by a notarially certified translation will suffice.

The period of protection for a trade or service mark is ten years from the date of application. It can be renewed indefinitely for further ten year periods. If a mark is not used for five years without legitimate reasons, the registration can be cancelled. This applies to use on goods, packaging or commercial stationery and in advertising.

Copyright

Copyright protects original literary, scientific and artistic creations and vests in the author of the work. The copyright owner is free to control the way in which, and the time at which, the work is made available to the public and is entitled to remuneration for third party use of the work at any time. Protection continues for the duration of the author's life, plus 50 years.

A work which has been published first outside Czechoslovakia is protected in Czechoslovakia if the author is a citizen of Czechoslovakia, or if he or she is entitled to protection under an international convention or on the basis of reciprocity.

Copyright is not subject to registration. A copyright owner can apply for the same remedies which are open to patent and trade mark owners.

Under legislation adopted in 1990, computer software is a separate 'object of copyright protéction'. It is not treated as a 'literary work', as in the UK.

Know-how

Know-how is difficult to define and even more difficult to regulate. It is not in itself subject to registration. It gives the owner an exclusive right to information which he has developed and kept confidential.

There are no rules dealing with the licensing of know-how to Czechoslovak entities. The way in which this information is passed on and protected therefore depends, primarily, on the terms of the licence agreement between the foreign party and the Czechoslovak party. The draft of the Commercial Code available at the time of writing includes know-how (for which the term 'trade secrets' is used) in the scope of protection against unfair competition. A trade secret has the following characteristics:

■ The subject matter is information of a commercial, manufacturing or technological nature, which has actual or potential value, whether tangible or intangible.

■ It is not currently available in relevant trade circles.

■ The enterprise is concerned to keep it secret and takes precautions for this purpose.

If these characteristics are met, the entrepreneur has the exclusive right to the trade secret and the right is protected as long as all the above conditions continue to be fulfilled.

Unauthorised disclosure of trade secrets is treated as an act of unfair competition if the infringer is an employee of the owner or is otherwise in a confidential relationship (for example through a licence agreement) which allows access to the information. If there is no such relationship, unauthorised disclosure amounts to unfair competition only if the information was obtained unlawfully. The owner of a trade secret is entitled to the same remedies as for the infringement of a patent or trade mark – including an injunction, damages or a claim for unjust enrichment.

LICENSING CONSIDERATIONS

Every licence agreement should take account of the particular interests of the licensor and licensee, the subject matter of the licence, and the legal problems and uncertainties in the territory in which the licence is granted. The parties should specify, to the fullest extent possible, their respective rights and obligations and the effects of particular problems or occurrences.

Two special aspects should be considered. First, the draft Commercial Code contains some basic rules about the terms of licence agreements, most of which are assumptions which apply in default of agreement to the contrary. If these implied terms are not required, the parties must be sure to exclude them in the agreement. Secondly, very careful consideration must be given to the Competition Act referred to below (and discussed in Chapter 16 on commercial law).

Every effort should be made to avoid having commercial and intellectual property disputes decided by the inexperienced officials in the state arbitration bodies, or their successors who will be the judges in the Commercial Courts. The agreement should, therefore, include clauses stating which law is to govern the contract and for what particular issues, and an arbitration clause, conferring exclusive jurisdiction on a foreign arbitration tribunal, such as the International Chamber of Commerce in Vienna or Stockholm.

Although the parties may agree on a foreign system of law to govern the contract, the law of the country in which intellectual property rights are protected is the only relevant law on questions about the existence or enforcement of these rights. Also, the question of whether a person is legally entitled to act on behalf of a company or other body is decided exclusively by the national law under which the entity was established.

Other issues for foreign owners

A foreign owner of intellectual property rights granting a licence to a Czechoslovak licensee should also consider the following issues:

- The territory in which the licence is to be effective. Can the licensee, for example, sell products manufactured under a patent licence or carrying the trade mark outside Czechoslovakia, into either Western Europe or the former Comecon territories?

- Restrictions on the use of the intellectual property rights.

- Duration of the licence and conditions for its termination.

- The licence fee or royalty. This could be a fixed sum, a per item royalty or a percentage of turnover, according to the nature of the licence. In this context the foreign licensor may be concerned to mitigate withholding tax applied to royalties.

- The obligation to pay the licence fee or royalty in hard currency, or to take goods made under the licence as a part payment.

- Whether the licensor must give a licence on up-dated or developed technology, patents or designs to the licensee, or the right to other intellectual property of the licensor.

- Whether a cross-licence relating to existing technology of the Czechoslovak licensee is required.

- Whether the licensee must transfer to the licensor all developments and alterations made to the patent or know-how, and assist in the registration of any industrial property rights in the licensor's name. An alternative is the obligation to license back such developments on advantageous or pre-agreed terms.

- Improvements to the original design of the product and alterations to the end-product.

- Marking of the products and the restrictions on use of trade marks and service marks by the licenceholder.

- Performance requirements and specifications for the end-product.

- Restrictions on sub-licensing.

- The way in which accounting for the products and its sales will be conducted between the parties.

- The requirements of confidentiality.

Impact of the Commercial Code and the Competition Act

As mentioned earlier, the Commercial Code in its final form may include provisions which will automatically apply to licence contracts unless the parties clearly exclude them. For example, the following assumptions may have to be excluded if not required:

- That the territory of the licensee extends throughout the state in which the licensee resides or has its registered office.

- That the licensee may grant sub-licences.

- That a sole licence is granted, so that the licensor is not entitled to permit anyone else to exercise the licensed rights in the territory.

- That the licensor is required to take legal proceedings to protect the licensee's rights against third parties.

- That at least one year's notice must be given to terminate the contract, if it is for an indefinite period.

The Competition Act applies to licensing. Restrictions extending beyond the strict scope and purpose of intellectual property rights may be null and void, and may lead to the imposition of fines. There are provisions for notifying licence agreements to the appropriate Office for Economic Competition and for obtaining exemptions where restrictions are indispensable to achieving a result which is in the public interest, or where certain other conditions are fulfilled. Exemptions are treated as granted if the application is not refused within two months of notification.

The effect of the Competition Act must be carefully considered when a licence agreement is being negotiated. Because there are many areas of doubt as to interpretation and future practice, it will often be advisable to seek the views of the Competition Office informally before the contract is signed and notified.

33

Establishing A Presence
KPMG Peat Marwick McLintock

Having decided to go further than a trading relationship and set up a permanent presence and office in Czechoslovakia, there are a number of issues that need to be considered. This chapter is divided into two parts: the first deals with the particular legislative considerations of setting up a representative office, and the second deals with the more practical considerations of setting up a working office in Czechoslovakia, either as a representative office or as the head office of a joint venture.

LEGISLATIVE CONSIDERATIONS

The scope of a representative office's activities is limited by Czechoslovak legislation. It is allowed to act as a sales promotion vehicle, but is not allowed to trade in its own right. Indeed, it cannot import or export goods in excess of its own operating requirements for items such as fax machines and computers. The representative office is allowed by law to sign contracts with Czechoslovaks on behalf of the mother company, but this may lead to tax complications over the office's trading status and is not recommended.

In order to set up a representative office, companies must submit an application to the relevant ministry for their particular area of business, which is normally the Ministry of Foreign Trade. In certain cases, however, it may be a different ministry (for example, foreign banks having to apply to the central bank). It is effectively a registration – if you fulfil the criteria and the minimum contents requirements laid down in the application you will be registered. There is a maximum wait of 30 days before being registered. The application must include details of:

- the company name, address and country of the main office;

- the products in which the company trades;

- the address of the representative office; and

- the names of those who will be running the operation in Czechoslovakia.

In addition, the application must be accompanied by proof of the company's credentials in its home country, and a copy of the rental agreement for office space if this has been signed before the application is submitted. Two copies of the application, either in Czech or Slovak must be submitted. Once the representative office has been registered, it must itself then register within 15 days at a tax office if it is going to be subject to Czechoslovak tax, and it must also obtain an identification number from the relevant statistical office.

Within 30 days of registration, a bank account in korunas or hard currency must be opened at a Czechoslovak bank. Since the representative office is seen as being part of the mother company, it is treated as being non-resident for foreign exchange purposes, and can therefore keep accounts in both korunas and hard currency and has no obligation to convert hard currency.

PRACTICAL CONSIDERATIONS

The following information should be seen as a guide, rather than being relied upon as a substitute for detailed research, on the ground, in Czechoslovakia. Discussions have highlighted the usefulness of a good local agent or partner who should also be able to expedite matters through contacts and through knowledge of the local situation.

Location

Most of the representative offices that have been set up are based in Prague, and the information in the rest of this section will concentrate on Prague unless stated otherwise. Prague is not the only possible location within Czechoslovakia, and Bratislava and Brno offer alternatives that are worth considering. The choice of location depends very much on what the operation is looking to achieve, and how it is planning to achieve it. Bratislava's proximity to Austria, and Brno's position, approximately mid-way between Prague and Bratislava may prove more appropriate.

Obtaining office space

Foreigners are not allowed to own property in Czechoslovakia, which precludes a representative office from purchasing its premises. However, if the foreign presence is set up through a joint venture, then, since the joint venture is treated as a Czechoslovak legal entity, it can own property. This purchase of property is governed by Decree 589 of 1990 issued by the Czechoslovak Ministry of Finance stipulating that such purchases should be at prices equivalent to those in foreign markets. The Decree does not, however, specify to which foreign markets it refers. The joint venture cannot sell on the property that it has bought to non-Czechoslovaks.

Suitable office accommodation is difficult to find in Prague, and rents vary greatly according to location and facilities. Rentals are governed by Decree 585 of 1990 issued by the Federal Ministry of Finance which fixed an annual maximum price per square metre of Kčs190. However, in several areas, like the centre of Prague, prices are not subject to an upper limit. Also, this Decree does not apply to foreign companies and joint venture companies with a foreign capital majority, and for such enterprises there is no upper rental limit. Rentals quoted range between DM30 and DM60 per square metre per month. Generally, these prices are all-inclusive of bills such as heating and lighting, but the small print of the rental contract should be studied carefully to check this.

The situation when it comes to obtaining suitable office space in the centre of Prague at a reasonable rent should improve soon as the the impact of two factors becomes fully appreciated. First, the number of companies that are reducing their activities or even going bankrupt should mean that more office space will become available. Secondly, the clarification of the restitution issue and the actual mechanics of the restitution process mean that rentals are expected to fall as those to whom property is returned put it to a more commercial use. The restitution issue has been dealt with in more depth in Chapter 12, but it remains an important consideration when dealing with the renting or buying of office space, as much as anything for the uncertainty that it has caused, merited or otherwise, over the actual ownership of the property.

Businesspeople with experience of operating in Prague have recommended that one of the best ways of acquiring suitable office space is to put an advertisement in a paper offering to pay in hard currency. However, it should be borne in mind that according to

Decree 370 of 1990 issued by the Federal Ministry of Finance, only certain groups of Czechoslovak citizens, such as auditors, lawyers, and landlords letting apartments or office space to foreigners, are legally entitled to accept hard currency payments. An alternative approach is through the Federal Ministry of Foreign Affairs' diplomatic services organisation, Správa Diplomatických Služeb.

Availability and suitability of technology

The poorly developed telecommunications infrastructure, and a lack of customer-focused technology services will undoubtedly affect any enterprise setting up an office in Czechoslovakia.

Telephone

There are currently long delays in getting telephone lines installed. The solution seems to be to rent office space that already has sufficient 'phone lines for your communications needs, not forgetting the fax machine – or to use contacts who may be able to speed the process up. If the operation is likely to expand, then it would be worth finding out from the Czechoslovak PTT about free numbers which will allow room for a relatively simple expansion.

Fax

Care needs to be taken that the chosen fax machine is compatible with the telecommunications infrastructure as some standard Western machines are not compatible, and only a few can be installed without problems.

Telex

The telex machine remains one of the least problematic to instal and one of the most reliable means of communication. Telex machines are produced locally under licence, or can be brought in from the West. As with the fax machines, though, one should check that the particular telex is compatible with local specifications before the installation phase.

Computers

Western computers and software are becoming easier to buy in Czechoslovakia, and the government has reduced customs duties on PCs and other IT products.

Staffing issues

As with the other countries in the region, a balance needs to be struck between employing native Czechoslovaks who have contacts and experience, and employing foreigners who, although more expensive, have much needed Western management and marketing skills.

Recruitment

Czechoslovakia is one of the most difficult and challenging countries in the region for recruiting suitably experienced and qualified personnel. Under the old regime, recruitment took place through the official Employment Office. This organisation no longer has a monopoly and 'head-hunting' operations are being established, but this concept is alien to most Czechoslovaks, and it will take time for the practice to become as widely accepted as it is in the UK. The most effective way to recruit staff remains the placing of advertisements in the local papers explaining the necessary qualifications and asking for applications. A good local partner or agent should have useful contacts that can speed the process and ensure that staff of the right calibre and with the right qualifications are recruited.

Remuneration

Under the traditional system, wages were determined by graded job levels based on age and experience rather than ability. The minimum salary is currently Kčs2000 per month, and an average monthly salary would be of the order of Kčs3400. Foreign language skills are at a premium, particularly English, because it is not widely spoken, and a secretary speaking Czech and/or Slovak and English would be paid in the order of Kčs36,000 per year. An accountant would be paid approximately Kčs43,200 per year. These salaries are representative for employees of state-owned companies; in the private sector it is likely that they would be doubled. It is important to remember that in addition to direct salary payments, employers also have to pay a social insurance contribution of 50 per cent of the total payroll.

34

Forming A Company
SJ Berwin & Co

Foreign investors are likely to be concerned with one of two types of Czechoslovak company. These are the joint stock company (JSC) and the limited liability company (LLC), modelled on the German and Austrian AG and GmbH and roughly equivalent to public and private companies in Britain. This chapter is mainly devoted to reviewing these two types of company. It also touches briefly on other vehicles open to foreign investors but which are less likely to be used in practice – general partnerships, limited partnerships with and without a share capital, and associations, a survival from pre-revolution days.

At the time of writing, Czechoslovak company law is in transition. JSCs are governed by the Joint Stock Companies Act (JSCA) passed in April 1990, when the rules which applied to LLCs and the above partnerships – confusingly all called 'commercial companies' – were among the amendments hastily introduced into the Economic Code to allow private enterprise to get started. Both the JSCA and the Economic Code are due to be replaced by a comprehensive Commercial Code, intended to come into force in September 1991. This will contain detailed rules for all forms of 'commercial company' and will include the present JSCA, in an amended form, in a separate chapter.

SOME KEY FEATURES OF THE CZECHOSLOVAK SYSTEM

A company or partnership comes into existence on the date of its entry in the Enterprise Register. Separate Enterprise Registers are kept for each district of Czechoslovakia. Each is maintained by the District Court located at the regional centre to which the district belongs. The Enterprise Registers are open to public inspection. The Register has separate sections for individuals carrying out entrepreneurial activities, and for companies, partnerships, state enterprises, co-operatives and certain other bodies.

Partnerships, as well as companies, have their own legal personality under Czechoslovak law. This is unlike English law where a partnership has no legal existence independently of its partners.

After contributing their capital, the shareholders of a JSC or a LLC have no further liability other than for any capital remaining uncalled. Conversely, the partners in a general partnership are exposed to unlimited joint and several liability. In a limited partnership, only general partners are exposed to these risks but limited partners, while they do enjoy limited liability, must not take any part in management. Thus, only LLCs and JSCs enable their members to enjoy limited liability coupled with freedom to manage.

Companies and partnerships are established by a written agreement signed by all the participants, followed by the filing of particulars in the Enterprise Register within 30 days. The essential information to be contained in the agreement is laid down in the legislation, such as the names and addresses of the parties, the object of the company or partnership, the method of dividing profits and losses, liquidation and general provisions to govern the relationship of the parties.

It is also possible to form a LLC and a JSC with a single founder. In such a case, a deed containing the necessary information is signed by the founder in the presence of a notary. Partnerships, however, require at least two members.

A person has authority to represent a company or partnership and to enter into legally binding agreements in its name, in four situations:

1. If he is a manager (*Jednatel*) of a LLC. In that case, third parties are allowed to assume that he has unlimited authority to conduct the company's business and to do anything on its behalf.

2. If he is a *procurist* – that is, a person who has been granted general powers to represent the company or partnership on a continuing basis. A procurist is normally authorised to conduct day-to-day business but not to enter into transactions such as selling real estate or creating mortgages, and his appointment generally requires approval at shareholder or partner level.

3. If he has a specific power of attorney, in which case his powers are limited to its express terms.

4. If he is acting in a manner necessary for the performance of his duties, or is authorised to do so by internal rules, or such representation is usual in the business.

The role of auditors in companies in which there is a foreign shareholding is covered by rules laid down by the Ministry of Finance. There are currently no rules for purely domestic companies, other than JSCs. However, a new Act which will regulate accounts and auditing for all types of commercial entity, is expected to be passed during 1991.

The minimum capital for both a LLC and a JSC is Kčs100,000. The simple structure of a LLC will often make it the most attractive vehicle for a wholly-owned subsidiary or a joint venture with a small local shareholding. A JSC requires a minimum of three directors and a supervisory board and contributions to its capital in non-monetary form have to be valued by an official expert. None of these formalities applies to a LLC. On the other hand, a LLC does not have a capital divided into shares of a fixed amount and may therefore be unsuitable where separate classes of shares are needed.

JOINT STOCK COMPANY

The summary which follows will be affected by amendments likely to be introduced in the Commercial Code.

Name and establishment

The words *akciova spolecnost* (joint stock company), or an appropriate abbreviation, must form part of the name of a JSC.

To establish a JSC two documents are required:

1. a formal shareholders' agreement (or, if there is only one shareholder, a foundation plan); and

2. the company statutes (articles of association).

The shareholders' agreement (or foundation plan) must show the name, place of business, objects and intended period of existence of the company; the issued capital and the minimum amount of the founders' shares; the number and nominal amount of the shares and, if shares of different kinds are to be issued, a description of their rights; the place and date of the first and last subscription for shares; the rules for giving notice of General Meetings; and, if any of the share subscription is to be provided in kind rather than in cash (for example, by providing land, machinery or technology), details must be given with the name of the court expert who has made a preliminary valuation of the investment (and the values attributed to these items cannot be higher than the amount shown in his valuation).

The company statutes cover the usual range of matters to be expected in articles of association, regarding the structure of the company and the conduct of its affairs. They must be signed in front of a notary public in Czechoslovakia. This can be done under powers of attorney given by the founders. If the founders of the company subscribe for all the issued capital themselves, the shareholders' agreement (or foundation plan if there is only one shareholder) and corporate statutes are lodged for registration in the Enterprise Register kept at the appropriate District Court.

If part of the share capital is to be offered for subscription to the original founder members, a formal Foundation General Meeting must be held for the subscribers to approve the terms and valuations before the company can be registered.

The Registration Court must be satisfied that all these formalities have been complied with, and that any necessary licences for the foundation of the company or the conduct of its business activity have been obtained. The company comes into existence on the date of entry in the Enterprise Register.

Capital and share structure

The issued capital of a JSC must be not less than Kčs100,000. Insofar as this is to be provided in cash, at least 30 per cent must be paid on subscription (minimum Kčs50,000). However, no minimum proportion of cash is required. Non-monetary investment is not subject to any minimum subscription rules. Property used for non-monetary contributions must be valued by a valuer whose name appears in the official list of experts kept at the District and Regional Courts. The value attributed to these contributions must not exceed the expert's preliminary valuation.

Shares may be issued at a premium (*agio*) but not at a discount (*disagio*), except in the case of employees' shares (see below). Shares are sometimes issued at a premium sufficient to cover the minimum reserve fund required by law (10 per cent of the issued capital).

Registered shares and bearer shares are permitted. The nominal value of each share must not be less than Kčs1000 and must be a multiple of Kčs1000. This rule may be removed by the Commercial Code. Different clases of shares may be created – for example, shares may be given different voting rights. The JSCA mentions in particular preferred shares, priority shares and employees' shares, but this list is not exhaustive.

Preferred shares

These give their owners priority rights to share in corporate profits. Voting rights attached to such shares may be restricted or excluded. The shares may be of several kinds, but their total nominal value must not exceed one-half of the issued shared capital.

Priority shares

Priority shares entitle the owners to a fixed rate of interest, even if the company generates no profit (and may or may not give them additional dividend rights). The combined nominal value of priority shares must not exceed 10 per cent of the issued capital. This type of share, a combination of preference shares and a debenture, may be eliminated by the Commercial Code.

Employees' shares

These may be issued to members of the company's staff on favourable terms. However, according to Section 9 of the JSCA, employees' shares may only be transferred among members of the staff and retired staff. Furthermore, the rights in these shares expire when the employee dies or his employment is terminated otherwise than through his retirement, and the shares then have to be transferred back to the company. This will normally be accompanied by repayment of the nominal value (or quoted value, if any) but these provisions can be varied in the statutes. There is a proposal in the draft Commercial Code to limit employees' shares to 10 per cent of the issued capital.

These restrictions on employees' shares have the effect of limiting their capital value to that of a conditional life annuity. They are therefore inadequate as incentives for management, but likely to be an essential component of many privatisations.

Convertible bonds

A JSC may be authorised by its statutes to issue bonds, which may be secured or unsecured, with provisions for repayment and interest and carrying the right to be exchanged for shares or the right of the first option to subscribe for new shares. Convertible bonds may be issued as registered or bearer securities. They are not treated as increasing the issued share capital and do not carry shareholders' voting or other rights.

Increase and reduction of capital

Capital can be increased by way of subscription for new shares, or by a bonus issue out of undistributed profits or, conditionally, by the issue of convertible bonds. An increase of capital requires a resolution in General Meeting on a proposal from the management board.

A reduction of capital is also possible if so resolved in General Meeting, subject to notification to the Registration Court, which advertises the resolution to give creditors the opportunity to demand payment or security in respect of outstanding claims. There are also provisions, subject to safeguards, enabling a JSC to purchase its own shares up to a maximum of one-third of its issued shared capital. Amendments to these provisions are expected in the Commercial Code.

A gradual reduction of capital is possible, subject to compensation of shareholders, to reflect a situation where a company's activity gradually uses up its capital assets (eg through the depletion of mineral deposits).

Organs of a joint stock company

The organs of a JSC are the General Shareholders' Meeting, the management board and the supervisory board.

The General Meeting

The shareholders in General Meeting are the supreme authority in the company. The General Meeting has exclusive authority to adopt or amend the statutes; to increase and reduce the issued capital; to change the rights attaching to individual classes of shares; to resolve on the dissolution of the company; to elect, remove and determine the remuneration of the management board, the supervisory board and the auditors; to approve the annual accounts and distribution of profits; to decide on the issue of negotiable or preferred instruments; and to pass resolutions on other matters within the exclusive authority of the General Meeting as specified in the JSCA or the statutes.

A majority of at least two-thirds (possibly to be increased to 75 per cent in the Commercial Code) is required for alteration of the statutes, increase and reduction of capital, changes of class rights (for which the consent of at least 75 per cent of the holders of the shares affected is also necessary) and for the dissolution of the company. Other resolutions require a simple majority unless the statutes provide otherwise.

General Meetings must be held at least once a year and can be called at any time by the management board, the supervisory board or on the requisition of the holders of one-tenth of the issued capital (who may also require any item to be included on the agenda). A quorum consists of shareholders owning more than one-half of the voting rights but the Commercial Code is likely to allow company statutes to relax this rule. Proxies are allowed but cannot be members of the management board, supervisory board or the auditors and must be appointed afresh for each General Meeting.

Management board

The Management board, elected by the shareholders in General Meeting, must consist of at least 3 and at most 11 members. The upper limit is likely to be removed in the Commercial Code. The management board exercises all the management powers of the company and has the sole right to engage and dismiss employees.

Restrictions placed on the authority of directors in the statutes are not effective towards third parties. However, members of the management board are liable for damages if they act in excess of their powers.

Supervisory board

Every JSC must have a supervisory board. This consists of at least three members, elected by the shareholders in General Meeting. The shareholders cannot appoint an employee. However, if the average annual number of employees exceeds 200 (likely soon to be reduced to 50), one-third of the members of the supervisory board must be elected by the employees. Employee representatives have no powers but, if they disagree with the majority, their opinion must be recorded.

The function of the supervisory board is to be a watch-dog ensuring the proper conduct of the company's affairs. It has a duty to check the books and accounts and to produce an annual report on the company's financial statements to the General Meeting. It also represents the company if there is litigation against the management. The members of the supervisory board take part in the General Meeting and can make proposals for the agenda.

Auditors

The JSCA requires at least one auditor of the company's accounts, who is appointed by the shareholders. Where any shares are owned by a foreign party, the number is increased to two under the terms of the Joint Venture Act. Requirements with regard to accounts and auditing are expected to be standardised in legislation now awaited.

Other matters

Conflicts of interest

The JSCA also tries to protect a JSC against conflicts of interests on the part of members of the management and supervisory boards. Board members are not only required to refrain from competing personally with the company, but are also prohibited from being a member of the senior management of another company with a similar business. On the face of it, this could even apply to directors of other companies in the same group.

The board member can be made to account for losses suffered by the company or to restore profits which he has derived at its expense, provided the claim is made within three months after the other board members become aware of the facts and within an overall time limit of one year. However, he cannot be made to resign, because the sole purpose of this rule is indemnification and restitution for the company. The Commercial Code is expected to introduce a more clearly worded non-competition clause which will apply to all forms of company and partnership.

Accounts and distribution

The management board is responsible for preparing annual accounts and proposals for distribution of profits and must report to the shareholders in General Meeting at least once a year on the business activities of the company, the condition of its property and its business policies.

The company is also required to create a reserve fund equal to at least 10 per cent of its issued capital. This may be funded out of the share premium account or may be built up to the required level by a transfer of at least 5 per cent of the annual after-tax profits.

Liquidation

The JSCA lays down the procedure for voluntary liquidation of a JSC, which requires a two-thirds majority vote from the shareholders in General Meeting and the appointment of a liquidator.

Liquidation in the case of insolvency is currently governed by

Articles 352–354 of the 1963 Civil Procedure Code, due to be replaced by comprehensive legislation on insolvency during 1991.

LIMITED LIABILITY COMPANY

While a LLC has the advantage of limited liability, its structure has the same 'personal' character as its Austrian and German equivalent, the GmbH. It is formed by a contract more akin to a partnership agreement than to the memorandum and articles of a company; its management powers are normally vested in a single manager (*Jednatel*) who has unlimited powers so far as third parties are concerned; and its capital is not divided into shares but each participant holds its proportion of the capital as a single unit, like a partnership share, and can sell or transfer it only on the conditions allowed by the agreement.

Name, establishment and capital

The name of the company must include the words *Spolecnost s rucenim omezenym* (company with limited liability, or an appropriate abbreviation such as *spol. s.r.o.*

The company is established by a written agreement, signed by all the members (or by attorneys acting on their behalf) before a notary public. Where there is a single founder, a deed containing the necessary information must be similarly signed. The foundation agreement must include the name of the company and its registered office; the object of its activity; its basic capital; the amount of each member's contribution; its organs at shareholder and management level, how they will be established and the extent of their powers; the rights and duties of the participants and consequences of breach; admission of future participants; and the method of increasing or decreasing the basic capital. The company must be registered in the Enterprise Register within 30 days after signature of the foundation agreement. Changes in the registered information must also be filed within 30 days.

The basic minimum capital at the time of establishing the company must be at least Kčs100,000 and the contribution of each member must be not less than Kčs20,000. Provided these requirements are met, the members are at liberty to agree on the amount and value of any investment in non-monetary form to be made by any of them (eg the supply of machinery or the transfer or license of patents or trade marks). Unlike a JSC, a valuation from an expert does not have to be obtained to justify the value attributed to a non-monetary investment in determining the size of the subscriber's share participation.

A participation in a LLC can be transferred by inheritance or sold. A transfer requires the approval of the members who own a majority (in value) of the share capital, unless the foundation agreement provides otherwise. Where a LLC is being set up with an existing or potential minority shareholder, it may suit the parent company not to exclude the 'majority approval' rule in the agreement as it will leave the parent company free to sell and transfer its own shares while maintaining control over transfers of the minority holding.

Organs and management

The foundation agreement must specify the organs of the company – namely, its members in General Meeting and its management.

In theory it is possible to prescribe a board of directors as the management organ. But the almost invariable practice is to appoint a manager (*Jednatel*) with full powers to manage the business – the equivalent of the German and Austrian *Geschäftsführer*. It is possible to appoint more than one manager, who will have to act jointly unless the foundation agreement states otherwise. Third parties will not be affected by internal agreements limiting the authority of any manager.

The extent of the legal risk attached to appointing a *Jednatel* in Czechoslovakia is, of course, limited to the Czechoslovak company; he will not, through his position, have authority to bind the parent company. However, if the manager has been newly recruited, the parent company may have misgivings about granting such wide powers. In that case, it may prefer to appoint one of its own executives as *Jednatel* and for him to use the machinery of a power of attorney to delegate day-to-day management powers to the Czechoslovak manager. Before these steps are taken, the parent company must check that there are no adverse tax implications.

OTHER VEHICLES

General and limited partnerships are not obvious vehicles for the foreign investor. However, as in other jurisdictions, they can be useful in the context of tax planning.

Under Czechoslovak law, a partnership has a legal existence independently of its partners (legal personality). In this respect it differs from English law, but the structure and rules of general and limited partnerships in Czechoslovakia are otherwise not unlike their English counterparts. Although the law provides a rudimentary framework (to be expanded in the Commercial Code), the details are left to be negotiated between the partners.

General partnership (Verejna Obchodni Spolecnost)
Under the present Economic Code, only individuals may be partners in a general partnership, under which all the partners have unlimited liability on a joint and several basis. However, it is illogical to exclude companies and the Commercial Code is likely to correct this.

Limited partnership (Komanditni Spolecnost)
This type of partnership comprises at least one limited partner (*Komanditista*) who has limited liability and one general partner (*Komplementar*) who has unlimited liability. Otherwise, the same rules apply as for general partnerships.

As in Britain, limited partners lose their limited liability if they take any part in the management of the partnership, which is the exclusive concern of the general partners.

Partnership limited by shares
A limited partnership may be constituted with a capital, divided into shares, to which the rules in the JSCA will apply so far as appropriate.

Associations (Sdruzeni)
A contract of association arises when parties agree to combine their efforts or resources to achieve a specific economic purpose – for example, the construction of a building. An association can be registered at the Enterprise Registry and will thereby acquire legal personality.

The laws regarding contracts of association are currently in the International Trade Code of 1963, due to be replaced by the Commercial Code. As they stand, these rules would seem to go further than a joint venture of independent parties and to amount to a partnership. The new rules in the Commercial Code will determine how far associations will remain as separate vehicles or be potentially useful to foreign investors.

35

Financing A Company
National Westminster Bank

In considering the financing of a company with foreign participation, or a joint venture, UK businesspeople should be aware of all the possibilities. From the point of view of a UK bank it will often be a more attractive proposition to lend money to a British company whom they know well, rather than to a newly established joint venture company registered in Czechoslovakia which has no published financial accounts. The amount of published information available on the Czechoslovak partner in a joint venture may be negligible and naturally this will lead potential lending institutions to tread warily.

It therefore follows that the financing of a joint venture can sometimes be more easily achieved by lending the required amount to the UK partner who will then effectively on-lend the funds to the joint venture.

When seeking loans direct for the joint venture company, the following difficulties should be borne in mind. UK banks maintain a conservative stance towards lending to commercial enterprises in the countries of Central and Eastern Europe and all have country limits which cap the amount of exposure they can have in any one country. Even if a bank were to consider providing finance to a joint venture, the cost might well be prohibitively high in order to compensate the bank for the risk it perceives that it is taking.

On the other hand, a UK company may be unwilling to take all the financial risks in what is, effectively, an equal partnership. The various alternative contributions a UK company can make to a joint venture in Czechoslovakia will be considered in this chapter, together with an outline of some of the sources of funding available.

SOURCES OF FUNDS

ECGD lines of credit

Export Credit Guarantee Department funds can be tapped to finance contracts entered into by joint venture companies in Czechoslovakia, provided that the suppliers are UK-based. The lines of credit are established between a bank in the UK and a bank in Czechoslovakia and are intended to finance the purchase of capital goods and services by various enterprises within the country, including joint venture companies. Contracts with values as low as £25,000 are acceptable under these lines of credit.

ECGD cover for the finance under these lines of credit is normally limited to 85 per cent of the UK contract value, the full amount of the balance being paid direct to the supplier by the time of delivery, with not less than 5 per cent paid within 30 days of contract signature. Funds advanced in this way from the loan are repayable by the borrower in half-yearly instalments over two to five years as appropriate to the size of the particular contract.

The borrower nominates to the lender individual contracts for financing under a line of credit; the lender (subject to the approval of ECGD) gives the go-ahead for its financing under the line; only then are they covered under the line of credit. Normally orders must be placed within 12 months of the signature of the loan agreement setting up the line of credit.

Since there is normally no direct contractual link between ECGD and the supplier, premiums are paid by the supplier to ECGD through the lending bank. Premiums for all types of buyer credit guarantees, as described above, are broadly in line with that charged for specific policies, based on ECGD's assessment of the buying country and the length of credit given for repayment of the loan. Loans made under the buyer credit and line of credit facilities carry fixed interest rates in line with the guidelines for officially supported export credit. Interest rates applying to foreign currency buyer credits and lines of credit are set at the minimum levels permitted under the international guidelines.

If it appears that you have business which could be financed under a line of credit, the appropriate bank or ECGD should be approached in order to establish whether it is acceptable (in principle) for financing and what procedure has to be followed in order to claim payments from the credit. It should never be assumed that a potential contract is eligible or that it will attract a certain credit period without first consulting ECGD or your bank.

Commercial lending

Commercial lending is a possibility, either to the UK participant in a joint venture or directly to the joint venture company itself, provided the bank is prepared to take on Czechoslovak country risk. There are a variety of lending possibilities available, some of which are outlined here.

Short-term lending

In addition to short-term finance specifically related to trade there are other short-term borrowing facilities available to companies. Short-term loans (normally any loans due for repayment within a year) are the most flexible in that they can be more easily tailored to seasonal or other cyclical requirements. Medium-term and long-term loans might be negotiated to reflect other needs. The choice of maturity will reflect your expectation of future cash flow. The maturity (ie the end of the bank's agreement to lend on the terms negotiated at the outset) will usually be geared to expected ability to repay at that time.

Additionally, the corporate treasurer will need to decide whether to go for floating or fixed rate loans, and what currencies should be borrowed. During the period of a loan, in most cases, the final rate of interest is not fixed; it varies according to market rates, often calculated as a fixed percentage above Libor (London interbank offered rate). For administration ease, however, the rate is usually fixed for short periods of, say, one or three months (the fixture period), subject to revision at the market rate at the end of the fixture period. The rate is therefore variable but fixed in the short term.

As an alternative, the corporate treasurer may decide to avoid the risk of having to bear higher interest costs than expected at the outset by fixing the interest rate throughout the life of the loan (ie until its maturity). Most banks will discuss fixed interest advances with their corporate customers but it should be borne in mind that fixed interest rates will always be higher than the variable market rates at the time of negotiation because of the rate exposure the bank will be carrying.

Medium-term Libor-linked loans

These are usually negotiated for purchases of machinery, property and other fixed capital needs; they can be made available for 'general' corporate purposes too, but usually only to large and well-established borrowers. The bank is committed to lend for a set term at an interest rate calculated at a fixed margin over Libor (whereas an overdraft would normally be linked to the bank's base rate). They are therefore floating rate loans, the rate periodically varying as Libor varies, although in practice it will be fixed for short periods (say one or three months) – the administration burden of a daily calculation would be too great. The margin will vary according to the status of the borrower, the purchase of the advance, etc – in fact the lender's perception of risk.

Typically, the minimum amount will be around £25,000, with no maximum. Normally ten years will be the maximum term, although it can be as long as fifteen years. Repayments are usually by periodic instalments over the life of the loan, although a single 'bullet' repayment at maturity can be agreed if circumstances are right. Repayment holidays can be included at the early stages of the loan, which can be useful if there is a time lag between taking out the loan and income being generated by the project or purpose for which the loan was required.

The precise terms of the repayment to which a potential lender will be most agreeable will be affected by the customer's ability to repay in the future. Quite apart from interest on the loan, fees will be payable to cover the bank's administrative costs and also to reflect its commitment to lend until maturity. Fees will usually consist of an arrangement fee to cover the bank's up-front costs; a commitment fee; a penalty fee for early repayment; and, where applicable, a non-utilisation fee. Security may be required if a large loan is syndicated (ie managed through one bank but with funds lent by a syndicate of banks). A management fee will usually also be payable in the case of syndicated loans.

Investment and project finance

There is a variety of options available to support investment in joint venture companies in Czechoslovakia. Options such as counter-trade will be more appropriately handled through joint venture arrangements where much more than a pure trading relationship will materialise.

Every investment requires an equity contribution and most require some provision of loan finance. An acceptable debt/equity ratio would need to be agreed between the joint venture partners. For a UK company contemplating how it should raise its part of the equity, the easiest option is to provide investment from its own resources. Such funds would either be provided through available funds or through borrowing in its own name from its bank. Before making any investment the UK partner must have convinced itself on risk grounds as to the viability of the underlying project.

An alternative is to consider part or all of the equity contribution through the provision of equipment and the transfer of technology. It is not uncommon for the Czechoslovak partner to satisfy its equity contribution through the provision of land, buildings and perhaps labour. The situation will become more straightforward when valuation of assets can be determined in Czechoslovakia, through the property market coming into force based on sound principles of valuation.

There are many specialised institutions which can be tapped to provide equity for a project, and these range from multilateral agencies – International Finance Corporation for the private sector, World Bank for the public sector, the European Investment Bank, and the European Bank for Reconstruction and Development – venture capital funds, commercial banks and private investors. The important role which commercial and investment banks in Czechoslovakia will play in the provision of local finance should not be forgotten.

Working capital

There are a number of ways in which working capital can be provided such as a straightforward bank overdraft or factoring (described in Chapter 28). In addition, working capital can be provided through the medium of acceptance credits.

Acceptance credits

There is an established market for bills of exchange drawn by customers on their bankers, under facilities agreed between them, to finance specific areas of their trade. This would be regarded as part of a corporate customer's working finance facilities, since the bank would be 'on risk' during the currency of the bill, which it accepts as payable at a maturity date perhaps one or three months in the future. Carrying the bank's acceptance (for which a commission is payable), the bill can be discounted at fine rates in the market to provide the customer with relatively cheap, short-term, uncommitted finance.

A refinement of this is the direct acceptance bid (DAB) under which the treasurer of a very large company might invite the treasurers of a number of banks to bid for bills of exchange he proposes to draw. Taking up the bids of the most competitive banks, the company minimises the cost of the short-term finance being raised.

REPATRIATION OF HARD CURRENCY PROFITS

The key consideration for most UK companies contemplating participation in a joint venture in Czechoslovakia is the possibility of making hard currency profits and repatriating them to the UK. The ownership and foreign exchange laws passed in Czechoslovakia at the start of 1991 have brought the country into line with international practice and increased the likelihood of growing foreign investment.

The Foreign Exchange Act, effective since 1 January 1991, fully implements internal convertibility of the Czechoslovak koruna. Prior to that date, joint venture companies were forced to segregate domestic and foreign currency reserves. Imports could be bought and profits transferred abroad in foreign currency but these would be strictly limited. There was a stipulation that joint ventures had to exchange 30 per cent of their hard currency earnings for korunas at the central bank and, after paying all their foreign currency expenses, this would invariably leave precious little in profit.

If any Czechoslovak company now requires hard currency for any purpose, it presents to its bank an order to exchange available korunas at the prevailing 'sell' rate on the date of the transaction. There are, however, two limitations. First, there is a 20 per cent surcharge imposed on the import of certain consumer goods. This surcharge should have a limited impact on joint ventures since it applies only to finished products rather than imported components and will be phased out by the end of 1991. The second limitation is that Czechoslovak companies need to apply to the central bank for special permission to buy foreign currency for purchasing immovables or securities abroad, or to receive a foreign exchange credit from a foreign bank or financial institution. While the limitations on buying foreign real estate or securities may not be of concern to most companies, the limitation on foreign exchange credit might prove to be a real issue for companies planning to rely on foreign currency financing.

Legislation on these matters is in the process of being tightened up and there is every likelihood that, as Czechoslovakia seeks to attract growing numbers of foreign investors, the ability of Western companies to repatriate hard currency earnings will be steadily enhanced.

36

Tax Issues

KPMG Peat Marwick McLintock

The form that the Western investment takes has considerable implications for the basis on which the venture will be taxed both in the home country of the investor and in Czechoslovakia.

There is an important dividing line between the Western enterprise 'trading in' or 'trading with' Czechoslovakia. Generally, when the Western enterprise is trading with Czechoslovakia, it will only be subject to tax on its profits in its own home country but may suffer withholding taxes on certain types of income remitted *from* Czechoslovakia. If, on the other hand, it is trading *in* Czechoslovakia, it can expect to be charged tax there on the profits of the enterprise. To be trading in Czechoslovakia, some form of trading entity based in the country will be required. This may be constituted in several ways. Broadly the choice is between a wholly-owned local subsidiary company or a partnership formed between the Western investing company and a local enterprise.

THE CZECHOSLOVAK TAXATION OF JOINT VENTURES

From 1 January 1991 joint ventures with a minimum of 30 per cent foreign participation are subject to profits tax at the rate of 20 per cent for profits not exceeding Kčs200,000 (approximately US$8,000), and at a rate of 40 per cent on the profits in excess of Kčs200,000. For joint venture companies with lesser levels of participation the tax rates are 20 per cent for the first Kčs200,000 and 55 per cent on the profits in excess of that. On a liquidation of the joint venture, tax at the rate of 55 per cent is required to be paid on the amount of the liquidation surplus (that is, the profits retained within the company other than amounts transferred into funds in accordance with legislation, eg the 'risk of loss reserve fund' discussed below). It should be remembered that it is possible in many circumstances to reduce the surplus, and thus the tax suffered, by making a pre-liquidation distribution (that is, by paying a dividend).

There is also the payroll tax of 50 per cent of the wages bill to be paid by a Czechoslovak joint venture company, but that is deductible in computing taxable profits for profits tax. There is no relief for losses. However, a start-up exemption or tax reduction can be granted by the Ministry of Finance of the relevant republic. All joint ventures meeting the test of having at least 30 per cent foreign equity participation are entitled to a two-year tax holiday. The tax holiday may be extended by negotiation with the Ministry of Finance in the case of joint ventures in preferred activities. Preferred areas of the economy include the production of pharmaceuticals, medical equipment, high technology industries, the production of consumer goods and industries, services connected with tourism, businesses operating to clean up the environment or to find substitutes for fossil fuels, etc. No dividends may be paid while the start-up relief applies.

The joint venture is obliged to establish a 'risk of loss reserve fund'. Five per cent of the after-tax profits of the joint venture have to be set aside annually, in this way, until the accumulated fund has reached the total prescribed in the joint venture agreement, which must be at least 10 per cent of the foundation capital. Losses made in the taxable activity have to be compensated for out of this reserve. After allocating the required sums to the loss reserve fund, (which is governed by Czechoslovak law as to the amounts required to be transferred in and as to the disposal of funds), sums may be set aside for a development fund and for any other funds the enterprise deems prudent. However, it should be noted that it is not mandatory for joint ventures to set up such funds. The balance of profits remaining after the transfers to the fund can be distributed to the partners in the joint venture.

PARTNERSHIPS

Although it is unusual for the joint venture to be formed other than as a limited liability or joint stock company, the partnership is a recognised structure in Czechoslovakia and the results of such a trade will be taxed in the same way as the joint ventures formed as corporations. The distinction between carrying on the activities in Czechoslovakia via the corporate or the partnership form of enterprise is important only where the home country of the investor taxes partnerships in a different way than it taxes corporate entities. Under many Western tax systems partners are each taxed on their proportionate shares of the underlying profits and capital gains realised by the partnership.

REPRESENTATIVE OFFICES AND AGENCIES

Non-resident taxpayers are liable to income tax on their income derived from activities carried on from permanent establishments in Czechoslovakia. The income is taxed at 40 per cent and will be computed for tax purposes by one of two methods, as agreed in advance with the finance authority. The gross representation commission method assumes that commission is earned on import sales within the range of 2 per cent to 15 per cent and this commission may not be lower than that which a Czechoslovak foreign trade corporation would achieve in similar circumstances. A deduction can be made for those related expenses which are connected with the import contracts. The second method, which is the one almost universally used, is the net representation commission basis where a net commission is assumed of 1 per cent to 2 per cent.

A foreigner will not have a permanent establishment in Czechoslovakia if he carries on business in Czechoslovakia through an independent agent.

THE ROLE OF TAX PLANNING

Although tax planning should not be allowed to assume undue importance over and above factors such as investment protection and general commercial considerations, the reality is that the after-tax return on the investment is going to be heavily influenced by the tax efficiency of the structure chosen for the investment.

It is important to ensure that the optimum structure is chosen at the outset. Once the investment has been made it is generally difficult, and often costly, to change the structure. The correct structure should ensure that not only is the maximum protection from expropriation available but that, on an eventual return of the capital invested, and on the repatriation of the profits earned, the tax suffered by way of withholding and in the home country of the investor is minimised.

The international climate is turning against abuses of the domestic direct tax system in most Western countries, particularly by the use of schemes which exploit differences between the home country tax system of the investor and the overlap with foreign tax systems – both in the countries in which the investments are being made and other countries through which the investment may be routed. One aspect of this is the potential abuse of double tax treaties to obtain advantages which would not have been available if simpler and more direct structures had been used to effect the investment. These structures often include companies based in third countries which are inserted to provide greater reliefs from withholding taxes than if no treaty, or only a less advantageous bilateral treaty, could be relied upon.

For example, if a dividend paid from Czechoslovakia to Norway suffers 15 per cent withholding tax, while the same dividend suffers 0 per cent withholding tax if paid to the Netherlands, and 0 per cent if paid from the Netherlands to Norway, assuming that there is a minimum of 25 per cent equity investment along the chain, there is an obvious saving of tax if the Netherlands is inserted into the chain. Many of the treaties now contain 'anti-treaty shopping' articles to prevent the use of treaties to reduce tax suffered in this way. However, it must be said that the policing of the treaties is not uniformly successful and structures can still be found which do provide these benefits.

Structures must be tailor-made to the requirements of the particular investment or project. These will almost certainly need to be long-term investments and the structure will therefore need to be designed so as to be sufficiently robust to meet the challenges of the economic and fiscal changes over that period.

TRADING VIA A CZECHOSLOVAK SUBSIDIARY

The majority of joint ventures take the form of participation in local companies either of the limited liability or of the joint stock type.

Considerations when investing in a joint venture company will include the following:

- the balance to be set between investing equity or loan capital (debt);

- the ability to repatriate profits by way of dividends and the cost of doing so in terms of corporate and withholding taxes;

- the tax costs of paying interest, royalties and other payments to the investor and whether these can be minimised by using treaty reliefs; and

- the tax costs of eventually disposing of or winding up the investment; and again whether this can be minimised through the utilisation of treaty reliefs.

Other tax issues may also need to be considered:

- Tax charges may arise in the investor's home country from transfers of assets to the Czechoslovak entity.

- Transfer pricing questions may arise in relation to the transfer of goods, assets (including intangibles, such as know-how) and services.

- Losses may be isolated in the separate entity without the possibility of utilising them for relief elsewhere in the group.

- There is a need to structure the investment in such a way that, should it fail, tax relief for the loss will be obtained in the home territory.

Debt or equity?

While to a large extent the debt to equity ratio of the capital invested will need to be dictated by commercial considerations, it will have important taxation implications. Interest paid by the joint venture enterprise is tax deductible. There appear to be no formal rules on the acceptable level of debt to equity ratio in funding a joint venture under Czechoslovak domestic legislation, although the level of borrowing may, of course, be limited by the need to obtain exchange control permission to make the borrowing. Most of the double taxation treaties entered into by Czechoslovakia follow the OECD model treaty closely. The interest article allows the tax authorities in the country of the payer of interest to recharacterise part or all of the amount paid to connected parties as dividend, but generally only where arm's length conditions do not apply to the borrowing, or the rate of interest is greater than the open market rate.

If the effective corporate tax rate in Czechoslovakia is greater than in the Western country and tax relief is obtained for all of the interest paid, there is an obvious saving of tax overall in taking out interest. For instance, at the 40 per cent tax rate a Kčs1,000 payment of interest to a Netherlands lender saves Kčs400 tax, but may only cost the lender Kčs350 of tax, an overall saving of Kčs50.

Where it would appear that full effective tax relief will not be obtained for the interest paid, the emphasis can be shifted to paying dividends instead. That would particularly apply where the investor's home country operates either an exemption basis of double tax relief, or where it operates a credit basis of relief for substantial participations and where the underlying tax suffered by the Czechoslovak company credited to the distribution ensures that little or no extra tax needs to be paid by the parent company in its own tax jurisdiction on receiving the dividend. This can be compared with interest income, which would be fully taxed in the Western country.

If a credit basis of relief operates in the home territory of the investor it may be possible to choose the timing of dividend remittances to achieve the best tax position. This will depend to a large extent on:

- the rules under which the investor's home country calculates the amount of the foreign tax credits which can be relieved;

- the availability of other reliefs;

- the extent to which there are restrictions to the utilisation of credit relief in the territory, for instance in the UK it may only be taken on a source by source basis; and

- whether or not excess credits can be carried forward and utilised in subsequent fiscal periods.

WITHHOLDING TAXES

In Czechoslovakia the rate of withholding tax charged on dividend, interest and royalty payments is relatively high where there is no double taxation treaty negotiated with the investor's country of residence. Dividend, interest, royalty, and rental payments are subject to 25 per cent withholding tax. Income from patents, industrial licences, know-how, and technical assistance is subject to 30 per cent withholding tax. Thus, subject to any prohibition of treaty shopping, it is usually advisable to interpose an intermediate company resident in a convenient third country in order to reduce the withholding tax cost.

The Netherlands has a comprehensive treaty with Czechoslovakia, providing for reductions of withholding tax on dividends, interest and royalties and also protection from taxation in Czechoslovakia on the eventual disposal of the participation in the Czechoslovak company (it is rarely necessary to rely on treaty protection as generally Czechoslovakia only taxes capital gains realised by persons resident in Czechoslovakia).

If the Czechoslovak company pays dividends or interest to a parent in a jurisdiction which has not entered into a double tax treaty with Czechoslovakia, tax is withheld from the payment at the rate of 25 per cent. However, if the company had invested through its Netherlands subsidiary having a 'participation privilege', the rate of withholding tax suffered would be reduced to 0 per cent for a participation of 25 per cent or more, and a dividend could be paid on, only suffering withholding tax in Holland, and that could be substantially reduced if relief were available under the extensive Dutch double tax treaty network. Owing to its extensive network of double tax treaties and the benefits of its holding company tax regime, Holland has become a favoured route for investment into Czechoslovakia where there is either no double taxation treaty in place or another treaty is less favourable than the Dutch treaty. Other jurisdictions which also offer a favourable holding company tax regime, such as Austria and Cyprus, suffer a 10 per cent minimum withholding tax on dividends paid from Czechoslovakia, making it difficult for them to compete with the Netherlands for tax efficient dividend routeing from Czechoslovakia.

A double taxation agreement was signed between Czechoslovakia and the UK in November 1990. It has not yet been formally ratified, but is expected to be implemented soon. Under this treaty it is expected that the effective rate of withholding tax from dividends will be 5 per cent in respect of UK investors who hold at least 25 per cent of the voting rights of the company making the payment, or 15 per cent in all other circumstances. It is also expected that the withholding tax rate on interest will be nil, and that the rate on industrial royalties will be 10 per cent.

37

Accounting Issues
KPMG Peat Marwick McLintock

Accounting practices in Czechoslovakia have been geared to the need to supply information to the state authorities for taxation and central planning purposes. As a result, the financial statements of a Czechoslovak company will not necessarily provide a fair indication of its performance, its efficiency or, indeed, of its value.

Czechoslovak accounts follow standard formats laid down by law. The system of financial accounting reflects the principal Western accounting concepts – that is, the 'going concern' basis, prudence, consistency and the accruals (as distinct from cash) basis. Assets and liabilities are shown at cost and it is not the practice to revalue balance sheet items. Legislation is due to come into force in 1993 to change the accounting regulations to meet the new requirements and demands for information, particularly with respect to the new tax structure that is due to come into effect at the same time.

PRINCIPAL ADJUSTMENTS

Given that it is likely that a potential investor in a Czechoslovak company will be presented with information on that company, including the company's financial statements, it is important that the potential investor is aware of the principal areas where adjustments to the financial statements may be needed to restate them into Western format. These are:

- fixed assets (rates of depreciation and valuation);
- stock (provisions against slow-moving or obsolete stock and valuation);

- debtors (provisions against bad and doubtful debts and valuation); and

- reserves (pre-tax/post-tax adjustments and corresponding balance sheet classifications).

Fixed assets

Depreciation

Rates of depreciation are established by law and the management of a company does not have the opportunity to set the rates which it might consider to be most appropriate to its particular business. Generally these prescribed rates appear low compared with Western rates. However, it must also be appreciated that many businesses invest substantially in repairs and maintenance expenditure each year to ensure that older plant and machinery continues to be operational. Some of the plant may be fully written down and, more importantly, the charge for repairs and maintenance expenditure needs to be aggregated with the depreciation in order to gain a better understanding of the state of affairs. Depreciation is charged in accordance with Decree 586 of 1990.

The valuation of fixed assets

These observations on the annual depreciation charge impact directly on the question of the net value of fixed assets. The key consideration is the likely continuing use of the assets concerned. For example, if a potential investor is considering taking a substantial shareholding in a business, it may be on the basis that the route to future profitability lies in the early replacement of existing plant with more modern technology. In such circumstances, the potential investor will have only relatively limited interest in the book-value of existing assets because, as far as he is concerned, the relevant value is that of the second-hand or even scrap market.

The financial statements of most businesses will not show any value for the land on which the fixed assets are situated. In the past, all land was deemed to belong to the state, and the 'means of production' could never be privately owned. As the use of the land was often acquired by the business for nil consideration there would be a nil cost to put into the balance sheet.

Stock

Provisions against slow-moving and obsolete stock

Provisions against stock may only be made with the agreement of the Ministry of Finance. Experience has been that the financial statements of a company do not usually show a provision against slow-moving and obsolete stocks, and it is rarely possible to comment in detail on the adequacy of provisions without a detailed technical review of the stock itself.

The valuation of stock

The adequacy of, or lack of, provisions against slow-moving and obsolete stock are clearly of fundamental importance to its balance sheet valuation. Current practice is to value stock at individual or average acquisition cost, and an item would remain at that value until it is sold, irrespective of how long that might take or its storage condition.

Debtors

Provisions against bad and doubtful debts

As with stock, provisions may only be made with the agreement of the Ministry of Finance. This practice may have been reasonable in the past, especially as regards domestic debtors where government policy tended to provide continuing financial support to businesses which were facing economic difficulties, but it is unlikely to be acceptable in the future. In the case of foreign debtors, the burden of collection may well have been assumed by a government agency but, where this is not the case, there would seem to be a need to distinguish carefully between established OECD trading partners on the one hand, and less developed countries on the other.

The valuation of debtors

The adequacy, or otherwise, of provisions against bad and doubtful debts are clearly important to the balance sheet valuation of debtors. It may be noted that it is somewhat easier to form a view on this item than on stock because of the availability of 'cash after date' verification tests.

Reserves

The net assets of the company are reflected in several 'funds' which are the equivalent of its share capital and reserves. Appropriations of post-tax profits are made to these funds but, in certain cases, these appropriations are, in effect, the post-tax charging of an expense item which would normally fall to be charged in arriving at the profit before tax.

An example of this might be an employee benefit, such as an

annual bonus, paid from a special fund. Although in such circumstances the payment might be discretionary, the fact is that it is nevertheless a cost of employment because it forms part of the overall remuneration of employees. In these circumstances, these funds should be seen as provisions in Western terms, and shown as liabilities quite separate from the other funds, and the corresponding charge should be shown in arriving at the profit before taxation.

Certain other expenses may be covered by allocations of post-tax profits, and it is therefore usually necessary to review the movements on each fund during each period in order to identify any potential adjustments.

PROBLEMS OF VALUING PROPOSED INVESTMENTS

One of the major difficulties in assessing a potential investment is valuing the company. Past earnings are unlikely to be a reliable guide to the future value and potential of the business in a market-driven economy. Reliable future earnings forecasts are difficult to produce because of the inherent economic uncertainties. Particular problems can arise from the differing perceptions of a company's value that a potential investor will have when compared with the perceptions of the company's owners or management. The large sums invested in plant and machinery in the past may well exceed the valuation given to the company. However, if these assets are producing goods which are not saleable, or are not competitive with goods produced elsewhere, then they will have only limited value. Ultimately, the value of a company is what a purchaser is prepared to pay for it, as distinct from some notional value ascribed to it. In the early stages of the privatisation process, this could be a particular problem and could lead to substantial political and/or bureaucratic opposition to a privatisation.

Part IV

Case Studies

Case Study 1

Chequepoint International

A report of a conversation with Kathryn Rae, business development director.

In early 1990, despite the round of revolutions which had rocked Eastern Europe during the previous year, and which had opened up the possibility of new markets for Western firms in the former communist bloc, Czechoslovakia seemed to attract relatively little commercial attention. Hungary, Poland and the former East Germany were generating far more interest with their ambitious privatisation programmes.

Chequepoint International, the largest privately owned *bureau de change* company in the world, was excited by the possibilities for new business in Eastern Europe as a whole, but saw no particular attraction in Czechoslovakia. Lord Shepherd, the non-executive chairman, had suggested, however, that the region was certainly worth serious investigation.

It was decided that Chequepoint's business development director, Kathryn Rae, an Australian corporate lawyer, should visit each Eastern European country to assess the possibilities. At that stage, Chequepoint had no experience in Eastern Europe, largely because tourism, on which *bureaux de change* are heavily reliant, was still an undeveloped sector.

Kathryn Rae, together with two former Euro MPs and a Harvard economist, travelled through Eastern Europe in February 1990. Her brief was simply to 'have a look', to assess the tourist infrastructure and potential, and to scout out possible joint venture partners. Her travelling companions had a useful network of contacts in the region and, between them, spoke most of the necessary local languages. Together they met government officials, bankers, representatives of foreign trade organisations, politicians and aspiring entrepreneurs. Kathryn Rae was convinced that, of all the countries she visited, Czechoslovakia offered the best immediate prospects for Chequepoint: 'In my view, Czechoslovakia was the best place to start', she says. 'First, because of its central location and proximity to Germany, Austria and Northern Italy. Second, its immense beauty was bound to attract tourists – I knew that the Italians would flock there. Third, Prague struck me as being very like Paris – the sort of place where people would go for weekends.'

There were two other significant factors which helped to convince Chequepoint that it should establish its first East European *bureau de change* in Czechoslovakia. The first was that the time was right. It was evident that Western firms, which were prepared to take a risk and to commit themselves quickly to investment in Czechoslovakia before the results of the federal assembly elections became known, would secure an important advantage over their competitors. 'One of the main reasons why we were successful was that we got into Czechoslovakia before the elections', says Kathryn Rae. 'Despite the risks, it was a golden opportunity and many German and even Italian firms knew it. The Czechoslovaks could not understand why more British and US firms were not moving in. The reason was that they were being over-cautious, waiting for the election results.'

Perhaps they were right to be cautious. The political situation at the time was still fluid. The coalition government was led by Marian Čalfa and the Communist Party still had a strong base of support, particularly in the rural areas. The communists even managed to win 12 per cent of the vote in the elections. However, Kathryn Rae is convinced that it was Chequepoint's willingness to take a risk and to commit itself to Czechoslovakia early on that really paid dividends: 'As soon as the elections were over, all the other Brits and Americans were out there but we were treated as pioneers. The Czechoslovaks were delighted by our vote of confidence and couldn't have been more helpful.'

What finally influenced her decision in favour of Czechoslovakia, however, was the quality of Chequepoint's potential joint venture partners: 'We were very careful with the people we looked at. Of all the potential joint venture partners I talked to on my tour through Eastern Europe, the Prague people struck me as being the ones who could move quickest.' Indeed, Chequepoint's partner, the Ceskoslovenska Obchodni Banka, was ready to move with such speed that the first *bureau de change* was up and running within five months of Kathryn Rae's first visit. The two sides signed a letter of intent in early April 1990 and a full joint venture agreement in May. On 25 June, the first *bureau de change* opened in Prague. By the end of September, there were three more in operation.

Kathryn Rae attributes much of the progress so far to the Czechoslovak team: 'There are some very bright people over there. Many of them are coming out of the universities and the state jobs they had before the revolution, looking for work in the new private sector. Our Czechoslovak staff are very impressive. We have spent a lot of time training them and they are as good as Chequepoint staff anywhere. In the future, they may be used in Western Europe or as part of our management pool anywhere in the world.'

Despite the speed with which Chequepoint managed to establish itself in Czechoslovakia, it was by no means plain sailing all the way. Coming to terms with doing business in a country which, only six months earlier, had been one of the most rigidly centralised states in Europe, was difficult. A multitude of complex problems had to be sorted out. Kathryn Rae decided that the only way to ensure the joint venture's success was by means of Chequepoint's 'hands-on management' in Prague. She recognised that she would be unable to establish such a complicated project from the company's London base, with only occasional trips to Czechoslovakia. A Chequepoint management team would have to be sent to Czechoslovakia to oversee the establishment of the first *bureau de change* and the selection and training of local personnel. 'In the end, I lived over there most of the last year', she says, 'and we put in a Chequepoint team of three for the season'.

Chequepoint's partner, the Ceskoslovenska Obchodni Banka, helped to overcome many of the most serious problems. In those early days it was extremely helpful and, for example, provided legal advice, office facilities and premises for the recruitment and training of staff.

The problem of repatriating profits from East European countries whose currencies are not fully convertible has often discouraged potential Western investors in the region in the past. According to Kathryn Rae, however, Chequepoint has had very little difficulty in this respect. 'There was no problem with repatriating profits at all when we signed the deal,' she says.

Ceskoslovenska Obchodni Banka also helped to overcome another problem which has traditionally undermined Western companies. Czechoslovakia has been much slower than many of its neighbours to reform the communist legal system governing the ownership of property. Chequepoint and its partner, however, decided that they did not need to acquire the freehold properties for their *bureaux de change* – it was more convenient simply to lease them.

'Chequepoint's most important contribution to the joint venture was know-how', says Kathryn Rae. 'We showed them how to run a *bureau de change*. We brought in computers and modern technology.' Chequepoint also arranged the fitting out of the first *bureau de change*, preferring to entrust the task to a Dutch team rather than local Czechoslovak labour. Subsequent *bureaux de change*, however, have been fitted out by a team of 'local mixture'.

The joint venture's original purpose was to satisfy demand within the growing tourist market to enable easy access to hard currency. Chequepoint has now been given permission to sell hard currency for korunas to Czechoslovak citizens.

'When we first started, we did not have permission to sell hard currency to the Czechoslovaks,' Kathryn Rae explains. They wouldn't let us do it to start with; now, we sell hard currency without difficulty.'

When one considers that when Chequepoint and the Ceskoslovenska Obchodni Banka signed their letter of intent in April 1990, Czechoslovakia was still just beginning to teeter towards major currency and price reforms, the scale of their achievement in establishing a thriving currency exchange business becomes apparent. Kathryn Rae attributes Chequepoint's success to a conviction that Czechoslovakia is a 'golden opportunity', and to a determination, despite all the obstacles, to do business: 'Someone who has been doing business in the area for many years gave me the best advice I know about Eastern

Europe', she says: 'If you see a deal coming – stay.'

Chequepoint certainly looks set to stay in Czechoslovakia. The venture has been for them a greater success than was expected.

Case Study 2

Berox Machine Tool Co Ltd

A report of a conversation with Jaroslav Beran, managing director.

Jaroslav Beran is a Czech who moved to England in 1966. He started Berox in 1971, specialising in East–West trade in computer numerically controlled machine-tools and measuring machines. As a Czech with many years' experience in the field, one might expect that Beran could deal better than most with the complexities of Eastern European joint ventures. This has been true of some cases, but the company has had its fair share of false starts.

Beran's overall strategy is to construct a network of small individual business units in Czechoslovakia which, taken together, might eventually cover the key stages of a trade deal; from initial design, to production, transportation and a final market in the West. Berox has four operational joint ventures in engineering/production and supporting services. Two in development involve road haulage and air transport companies. In addition to these there have been at least two 'complete fiascos', one of which is discussed below, by necessity in terms which are somewhat vague since there is a strong possibility of legal action over the case.

The two ventures on which we focus here stand on their own as examples of what can go right, and disastrously wrong, with joint ventures in Czechoslovakia. Both began with the same background conditions which accompany all such deals; paperwork, bureaucracy and, above all, uncertainty at a time of legislative and economic change. One of these ventures, Berox Metrology Division, has now borne fruit in the form of a signed, sealed and delivered shipment of goods to a prominent German company, with more sales to come. The other, a joint venture with a state enterprise has, by contrast, produced only a complete severing of relations between the original partners.

The Berox success story has been Berox Metrology Division (BMD), a joint venture with private shareholders in Northern Bohemia producing tool-setting and coordinate measuring machines. The company is an offshoot of a state enterprise, which Berox had successfully dealt with in the past, in a co-operative arrangement which lasted four years. Although this co-operation had been 'successful from our point of view', Beran had more recently tried and failed to move the existing management towards new product markets. Aware of the technical capabilities of the workforce, Beran decided by March 1990 to offer a deal to what he considered to be the company's key personnel. In essence, he suggested that the chief designer and others leave the unwieldy machinations of the state enterprise structure and go into business with him in their own right. It was crucial for Beran that they put their own savings into the venture. Thus, while Berox began by owning 51 per cent of the embryonic BMD, the remaining 49 per cent was spread among the workforce.

These more or less hand-picked workers already had ideas about a new product which Beran felt could be marketed in the West. Rather than twiddle their thumbs through the long process of officially establishing the new company, they therefore opted to hand in their notice to the state firm early on in order to begin working on the prototype. Initially, this took place in the workers' own homes, but in June 1990 Beran began renting the empty premises which had been chosen for the new enterprise. The workforce were able to continue working on the new machine with support from the foreign partner, which included basic office equipment and key components from external sources.

Maintaining the momentum of the project in this way enabled BMD to exhibit a new optical precision tool setting machine at the Brno Engineering Fair in September 1990, the very same month in which the new company had received its formal registration documents from the authorities. Exposure at this make-or-break event in turn led to a concrete order from a German company. The first 20 machines were shipped out in May 1991, and the company's full capacity output of 200 machines has now been sold to the Germans, who have taken full responsibility for marketing of the product.

The BMD project owes its success to a number of factors, the most important of which may have been insider knowledge: 'You cannot start that kind of joint venture coming as a greenhorn to the market. I started there because, first, I knew the field. I had dealt with the state enterprise for a number of years, and I knew the people personally.' The Czechoslovak partners were themselves in the know when it came to a further aspect of the deal, namely those Czechoslovak companies in related fields who could be trusted to produce components for BMD. Second order know-how of this kind was the key to the other side of BMD's strategy – knowing its own limits. 'We did not try to manufacture everything ourselves. Rather, we aimed to build strength on design, and co-ordination of the entire production process. Everything else was run on the basis of sub-contracting.'

Contracting-out is still a pretty alien concept to a business culture so long used to fully integrated central planning. Yet, apparently, it can work, as long as you have the personnel on the ground able to keep a watchful eye on the proceedings. BMD's small workforce of around 20 people is divided into two parts: the primary design workers, and a second group of all-round 'co-ordinators', who have the technological and local knowledge to be able to find suitable sub-contractors, and ensure that they have (or acquire) the capability to produce precisely the right goods for BMD. 'Everything needs watching. Czechoslovak factories are now so keen to get work that they'll agree to anything. Months later you discover their machines never had the required accuracy, or the operators the required skill, to really make what you needed.'

The BMD experience lies in contrast to at least one of Berox's other Czechoslovak ventures, a joint venture to produce hydraulic operated loaders with the subsidiary of a large state company. Beran was initially drawn to the firm as a compact outfit of 400 relatively skilled employees, well-separated from its rather monolithic parent. Berox had assessed its potential over a two-year period, and in January 1990, articles of association were eventually drawn up to produce a particular kind of loader for sale in the UK. Drawings of a prototype were sent to Slovakia and at the same time managers from the enterprise came over to Britain, receiving advice on how the firm could best be restructured for greater efficiency.

Things began to go wrong in the summer of that year, when new laws concerning state enterprises came into force. On paper at least, these changed the status quo such that the joint venture ceased to exist. Beran was loathe to abandon the project: 'Nothing is forever. We could have spent months waiting for the legal situation to be clarified, only to find that in the meantime our march on the market had been lost.' It was therefore decided that work on the product should continue, in what was now something of a legal vacuum. The result was a prototype shown at the 1990 Brno fair. Yet by this stage the Czech design team had moved away from the exact specifications which had been agreed in January. Over the months which followed, relations between the partners steadily deteriorated. Deadlines were missed, as the factory failed to produce the machine for which Berox had established British orders. At the end of the year, Beran demanded the original drawings and prototype back from the Czechoslovak team, having found another firm in Bohemia willing to make the same product. Meanwhile, 'the Czechoslovak company repudiated all involvement with Berox, and put on the market a very similar machine, which they planned to sell independently to Germany and other Western markets.'

Beran draws two central lessons from the experience: 'Avoid state enterprises as much as possible, and above all, make sure that you can trust your partners. I misjudged the people, and did not expect the legislation to penalise joint ventures with enterprises as much as it did.' For both mistakes he paid a heavy price, not least in his relations with the British companies whose orders he was left unable to fill.

The issue of land ownership apparently impinges on all aspects of Czechoslovak joint ventures, whether successful or not. The fact that Berox did not (and could not legally) own any part of the loader factory in the last case was one of the reasons why the Czechoslovak company was able to renege on their side of the deal.

On the more positive side, the BMD case shows that legal uncertainty need not rule out a successful deal. There, the fact that the Czechoslovak workforce was committed to the project, and willing to work for a company which did not yet legally exist, allowed the co-operation to move along an altogether more profitable path for all concerned.

Does Beran have any general words of advice for British companies considering joint ventures with Czechoslovak companies? 'Prior experience of the field is absolutely essential. I don't think I can stress that enough.' In the same vein, Beran warns against 'arriving in the country with a suitcase full of banknotes. Where possible, you should try to borrow money from Czechoslovak banks on behalf of the new venture.' He does not think that today's high nominal interest rates make this unfeasible, given that future inflation and exchange rates are so uncertain, and are likely to devalue the real cost of repayment. Unsurprisingly, Beran would also advise foreigners to avoid state enterprises: in his view, the privatisation programme, along with worries about 'selling off the family silver', mean that in practice officials try to make foreign involvement in state firms as difficult as possible. Instead, Beran encourages a focus on individual Czechoslovaks in joint ventures: 'Work with private shareholders you can trust, who have made their own financial commitment to the success of the project.'

Case Study 3

Emmex Consultants

A report of a conversation with Emmex's chairman, Mike Chamberlin.

Emmex Consultants was established by Mike Chamberlin with the express purpose of trading with Eastern Europe, and in particular with Czechoslovakia, although its operations have since spread to Hungary and more recently into Poland. From small beginnings in 1974 it has grown steadily until in 1990 turnover reached £4 million. Cranes, compressors and foundry equipment form the core of the operation but many other sorts of general engineering equipment and miscellaneous items have been traded.

The removal of the communists from power in 1989 presented a massive challenge to the survival of Emmex. Previously, the company had been able to use its knowledge of the Czechoslovak bureaucracy and economy to establish a strong position in a niche market and the planned economy provided a relatively stable economic environment. Moreover, Emmex's particular market was particularly secure because heavy engineering equipment was at the heart of the Czechoslovak economy and because, as import licences were only granted for goods not manufactured by Czechoslovak companies, domestic competition was non-existent.

As Czechoslovak firms were either unwilling or unable to spend scarce hard currency reserves, Emmex often had to use counter-trade as a form of payment. This exercise required both persistence and ingenuity. A search had to be made for items of sufficient quality to be saleable in the West and then a Western buyer had to be found. It was by such a route that Emmex found itself importing weight-lifting weights. However, opportunities for market development were fairly limited. It was only following a slight relaxation of economic controls in the early 1980s that Emmex was able to employ a 'handyman' from the state-owned Prague Information

Services to act as a translator and information gatherer. However, this helper could not sell direct himself – he could only provide a list of possible future customers to visit. Furthermore, he was rather expensive to employ.

In the initial period after the events of 1989, as a result of the considerable 'over-hang' of contracts, Emmex did not experience a dramatic change in its business. Some contracts lasted for many months and the Czechoslovak companies concerned had in many cases already ordered and put in place the necessary hard currency. This situation helped Emmex to maintain turnover in 1990 at 1989 levels. However, in the last six months things have tightened up considerably and turnover has been down by around 50 per cent. An important cause of the downturn has been the decimation of Czechoslovak export markets in East Germany and the USSR which are now based on hard currency trade. Thus, Czechoslovak engineering companies either do not want to invest in heavy machinery because of the lack of demand for the final product, or they just cannot afford to because of a lack of investment funds. Moreover, the many liquidations taking place in the context of the lack of a proper system of credit rating means that Emmex now has to demand payment up front. Recently a Czechoslovak company went into liquidation owing Emmex £35,000. Fortunately, at the time of its liquidation, it was owed £33,000 *by* Emmex.

Emmex has set about tackling its difficulties in a number of ways. First, it has attempted to remedy its short-term cash flow problems by widening the range of goods supplied. All restrictions on imports, profit repatriation, and who you can do business with have been removed and thus there are many opportunities during the transition period for the astute businessman. For example, Emmex has recently sold a £5,000 consignment of perfume to a Czechoslovak company. In addition, it is still as far as possible tapping the sources it has previously identified while establishing countertrade transactions. However, at this stage Mike Chamberlin sees these measures as being purely temporary because such opportunities will only last as long as the economy is in significant difficulty and, moreover, Emmex will be best placed if it concentrates in the medium-to-long term on its core markets where its principal expertise lies.

Secondly, Emmex has decided to reshape the structure of its operations. Now it has to place a much greater emphasis on going out and actually generating business and to that end it is necessary to have a significant presence on the ground in Czechoslovakia. Its medium-term strategy is to have an Emmex trading company firmly established in Prague to take advantage of the turn up in trade that will undoubtedly take place in the next few years. Chamberlin draws comfort from Hungary which began the liberalisation process a number of years earlier and is now 'past the worst'. Thus, in April 1991 Emmex Praha AS was registered as a Czechoslovak company. Registering Emmex Praha AS was a relatively straightforward and cheap procedure requiring only that the registration be put forward by a local legal representative. The next step is the leasing of a warehouse and showroom.

The costs of such local operations are not perceived as being a problem. After an initial price surge, fuelled to a large extent by speculation, office space in Prague has become relatively cheap as the central bureaucracy has been slimmed down and some companies disappear. Furthermore, real wage levels have risen only slightly since 1989.

Emmex sees little advantage in establishing a joint venture with an existing Czechoslovak company. There is little in the way of knowledge and expertise that Emmex lacks that could be usefully supplied by such companies. Moreover, most Czechoslovak companies are still not sufficiently imbued with the entrepreneurial 'spirit' necessary for survival in such a rapidly changing environment. Far better to make a fresh start with a new Czechoslovak company.

Thirdly, Emmex is endeavouring to widen slightly the focus of the company to include more emphasis on the retail side. There are a range of goods that it was previously prevented from importing that lie within the core area of its business. These tend to be smaller items that could already be manufactured in Czechoslovakia and such items are precisely those that typically require a more 'retail' style of operation. Moreover, Emmex expects that the recovery of the economy will be, at least initially, concentrated in the smaller industrial sectors and thus trade in light engineering equipment can be expected to be particularly buoyant.

One idea currently under investigation is the establishment of a hiring company aimed at small companies needing small items of machinery but unable to afford the larger outlay required to buy the equipment outright. As the economy picks up this will also provide a useful source of contacts for the sale of other items.

Lastly, Emmex is widening the geographical scope of the operation. It set up an office in Hungary in 1990, and is currently in the process of establishing one in Poland. In Hungary (in contrast to Czechoslovakia) a joint venture company has been established because of Emmex's relative lack of experience and also tax considerations.

FUTURE PROSPECTS

Chamberlin expresses great confidence in Emmex's future in Czechoslovakia, citing as evidence his company's ongoing investment at a time when the economy is depressed. Nevertheless, as a prudent measure this investment is being internally financed. Should the upturn take slightly longer than anticipated he doesn't want Emmex to be saddled with debt obligations. He readily acknowledges the difficulty of the task that lies ahead.

One particular problem is the lack of an adequate trade press. Until one is developed, communication of the firm's presence and product availability will be particularly difficult and Emmex will have to rely on informal contacts and mail shots. Also troublesome for a relatively small company is the lack of a properly developed banking sector in Czechoslovakia. Sometimes, for no apparent reason, Emmex has had to wait several weeks for the transmission of funds.

Domestic competition has certainly been slow to emerge. However, vigorous competition is expected from Germany and Austria which are geographically adjacent and tend to regard Czechoslovakia as their own back yard. The current investment in the Czechoslovak operation is to some extent a pre-emptive strike against such competition.

It is apparent that a major factor shaping the prospects of Western companies in Czechoslovakia will be their ability to identify growth areas in the economy, get close to their customers and work extremely hard to follow a quickly changing situation. As long as it can survive the current downturn, Emmex would appear to be extremely well placed. The market for engineering machinery is bound to one of the first to pick up. Moreover, Mike Chamberlin has long experience of trading with Czechoslovakia and has a close knowledge of the country (he speaks fluent Czech and has been Chairman of the Czechoslovak section of the London Chamber of Commerce for the last ten years). As he candidly observed: 'Czechoslovakia now has the fewest barriers of any country I know and we have everything to play for.'

Case Study 4

Nuclear Electric PLC

A report of a conversation with Dr Richard Garnsey, safety and technology branch manager.

The development of an efficient, clean and safe energy industry is a major priority for the Czechoslovak government. Indeed, the success of the government's political and economic reform programme depends, to a large extent, on its ability to solve energy-related problems.

The first of these problems is the appalling legacy of environmental degradation left by the communists; the second is the economy's dependence on energy from the Soviet Union; and the third is the need to earn hard currency through the sale of energy to finance economic regeneration.

Nuclear Electric PLC became involved in helping to find solutions to the last two of these problems after another company, Fuel Tech, had been invited to help with the first, by suggesting ways of reducing environmental damage caused by brown coal production. On its own privatisation in the UK, Nuclear Electric had taken on much of the CEGB's international consultancy portfolio. Nuclear Electric visited Czechoslovakia, together with the Atomic Energy Authority, in 1990 to assess the potential for collaboration with the Czechoslovak nuclear industry. They soon realised that nuclear energy was destined to become one of Czechoslovakia's growth industries. Despite Chernobyl and international green pressure, the Czechoslovaks readily understood the benefits of nuclear power.

'The Czechoslovak economy is very dependent on energy and it is very energy inefficient', says Dr Richard Garnsey of Nuclear Electric's PWR project group. 'They have heavy industries which use a lot of power and they want to use energy more efficiently. They are also very dependent on brown coal production, which is causing devastation in the north of the country. Even their Green Party has accepted that nuclear power is the lesser of two evils compared with brown coal. So, they want to expand the nuclear industry to reduce their dependency on brown coal and to increase energy efficiency.'

The other factor which makes nuclear power so attractive to the Czechoslovaks is its potential as a hard currency earner. 'They know they can sell power', says Dr Garnsey. 'They are already exporting it to Switzerland and they are looking at selling it to northern Italy, southern Germany and Austria. There is a huge market for energy generation in this area.'

However, Czechoslovakia's nuclear industry had grown up in the era of Comecon. It was heavily dependent on Soviet design and fuel technology.

Their priorities now are to increase safety and efficiency and reduce dependence on the Russians. 'They wanted to get away from dependence on the Russians, particularly for design', says Dr Garnsey. 'But they were also dependent on them for the purchase and enrichment of uranium, the fabrication of fuel and the reprocessing of fuel. The Russians were ready to continue to supply fuel and to take away spent fuel but they had increased the price because they now expected payment in hard currency. BNFL could now meet the price.' Indeed, Garnsey is sure that there is 'really big money in reprocessing there and a lot of business for BNFL to get into'.

Nuclear Electric decided, however, that its own prospects in the short term in Czechoslovakia were more modest, although there might be opportunities in the longer term to develop new business in fuel management and the supply of software for waste management. The key was to develop a continuing relationship with an existing Czechoslovak organisation. 'Czechoslovakia is looking for potential joint venture partners' says Dr Garnsey. 'They're not so keen on turn-key projects'. CEZ, the Czechoslovak power company, is responsible for large power stations and projects at Dukovany and Temelin, which is a pressurised water reactor (PWR), type VVER 440.

At the time of the revolution, it was proposed to build 4 new units of 1000MW each at Temelin and the first unit was well under way. About 50 per cent of the concrete had been laid and the cooling towers had been built. It was clear that CEZ was committed to Temelin and it wanted support to continue its construction, although only two rather than four units were approved. Dukovany is an earlier design and is producing electricity very satisfactorily.

In Slovakia, the station at Bohunice, which is the oldest design of

VVER, was a cause for concern, particularly to the neighbouring Austrians. These concerns are understood by the Slovak power company. The Slovaks also wanted first to replace an unsatisfactory Soviet control system at Mochovce. By the middle of 1990, however, they had already settled on a Siemens system. Nuclear Electric, therefore, concentrated its attentions on CEZ. As Sizewell B was at the same stage as Temelin, Nuclear Electric was well placed to provide consultancy and advice on the acquisition of a suitable control system. This would help to establish the possibility of a longer-term partnership in power station design, construction and operation.

Nuclear Electric's main task was to assist Skoda, the Czechoslovak engineering company, which had been appointed general supplier to CEZ, with the evaluation of tenders for the provision of a top-level computer. It was also formally agreed that Nuclear Electric would act as advisers to CEZ in the following fields:

1. Assessment of technical design, specification and performance requirements.

2. Commercial aspects of plant procurement and assessment of tenders, including administration of contracts, claims and variations.

3. Safety assessment and plant improvements.

4. Quality assurance.

5. Project construction, planning and management.

6. Operator and staff training.

7. Computer and office systems.

'The Czechoslovaks did not appreciate how to put out an enquiry document to a Western organisation', says Dr Garnsey. 'We were able to help them to write a specification to get value for money – that was the major element. The next phase was going through the tenders in detail to ensure there were no snags. That sort of detailed evaluation is much more time-consuming and a lot of sophisticated negotiation with the suppliers is also required.'

Dr Garnsey describes Nuclear Electric's contract as 'small beer compared with the contract to provide a control system' but he is convinced that it is the beginning of a profitable partnership in the future. With that in mind, Nuclear Electric has been keen to participate in personnel exchanges with CEZ and has agreed to have a Czechoslovak operator working over in the UK. Richard Garnsey's biggest disappointment in his experience of dealing with Czechoslovakia has been the lack of support from the UK know-how fund and the EC for nuclear upgrading in Eastern Europe. He describes the know-how fund as 'a dead loss'. 'I suspect that the know-how fund's priorities have changed', he says. 'They are interested in small enterprise stuff, not the potentially large-scale governmental activity that an agreement between Nuclear Electric and CEZ would involve.' The European Commission realises the importance of nuclear power for the economies of Eastern Europe as well as for the environment. It is, therefore, keen to help with upgrading but its own bureaucratic infrastructure and lack of experience appear to stifle initiative.

'Nuclear safety comes under DG11, which deals with the environment', says Dr Garnsey. 'But research is funded by DG12, and DG17 – energy – is also involved. They are still arguing among themselves and not an Ecu has yet come out of the PHARE fund to support nuclear upgrading.'

Nuclear Electric has been involved in the establishment of a European Economic Interest Group (EEIG) with nuclear concerns from other European countries, which would act as the EC's agent to distribute money for nuclear upgrading, particularly VVERs. The company's involvement in upgrading in Eastern Europe is about more than just good business. 'Nuclear power is dead in this country if there's another nuclear accident in Russia or Eastern Europe', he says. 'It's no good screaming that we would have done it differently. There's a real requirement for nuclear energy in Eastern Europe and we have got to make it work.'

Case Study 5

Baker Street Trading Overseas Ltd

A report of a conversation with Ivan Schwarz, company director.

Baker Street Trading Overseas Ltd (BSTO) was formed in 1956 to promote small mechanisation in the construction industry in Eastern Europe. Company director, Ivan Schwarz, is of Czechoslovak origin, but since its establishment the company has been based in North London. BSTO have been distributors providing a full range of export services for UK companies wishing to sell their products in Czechoslovakia. The radical changes in the business environment have led BSTO itself to pursue a more ambitious range of projects in Czechoslovakia.

As distributors, BSTO undertook various activities. At the outset of a project, it would talk with the clients (the Czechoslovak authorities), and discuss the requirements of the Czechoslovak enterprises. Details would be reported to the principal, a UK company, ensuring that the request could be met. The exporting, licensing, pricing, delivery and invoicing was all performed by BSTO, who also provided an after sales service.

Schwarz feels that the reforms cannot allow his business to continue in its present form. The opportunities provided by the changes are so great that the company needs a firmer base in Czechoslovakia. As distributors, BSTO needed very few assets in order to go about their business. Contacts with bureaucrats and local knowledge were far more important. Schwarz sees this situation changing, implying changes for BSTO as a whole. He says, 'now we must become actors – we must build up capital ourselves'.

BSTO deals with Czechoslovak engineering and manufacturing companies, but under the old regime, these companies 'were not allowed to have initiatives' says Schwarz. Plans for manufacturing came from the centre, implying that bureaucracy was responsible for determining the precise materials and tools used for a project. Before a component or tool was ordered from any Western firm, the Foreign Trade Organisation had to be convinced that there was no suitable alternative available in an Eastern European country. If no alternative existed, three competitive quotes for similar products had to be presented to the authorities who would then decide on the suitable product. The choice of input was purely political – it seldom matched the precise requirements of the manufacturing enterprise.

Such bureaucracy put BSTO at risk from bankruptcy. Irrespective of the quality of the products they represented, or the performance of their sales staff, the company could not be guaranteed a stable day-to-day (or even year-to-year) cash flow. To succeed, they had to seek the approval of the bureaucrats.

So what has happened in the last two years? Firms can now determine the product required for their plans. This development has changed the way that BSTO must go about its business. End-users of products are no longer out of reach. Previously, to find favour with buyers (the Czechoslovak authorities) it paid to keep a low profile and gain business through 'politicking'. Now, for the first time, BSTO has felt the need to 'sell itself' to Czechoslovak companies. Marketing and advertising has superseded politicking as the method of boosting sales. As distributors responsible for the principals' sales, BSTO must incur advertising expenditure if it wants to develop and keep ahead of its rivals. But, even if advertising is effective, Schwarz still sees problems in generating a stable cash flow for his company. 'Today's problem is that firms are no longer guaranteed by the government. Previously, if you were awarded a contract, at least you knew that you would get paid one day.'

Under the new system, Czechoslovak companies and small enterprises will have to secure their own equity capital. They will now be subject to a bankruptcy constraint. The liberalisation of the economy will create enormous problems for enterprises of all sizes. No one pretends that solving these problems will be easy, but in attempting to help small businesses, a company with knowledge of the Czechoslovak market and bureaucratic process could create many openings for itself. This strategy of providing assistance to small businesses offers exciting development opportunities, but requires BSTO to invest.

Small, or indeed any, businesses have little experience in preparing analyses of future earnings, a task now required to be included in any project proposal. BSTO decided that helping businesses to prepare forecasts and presentations was a useful method of teaching them the alien concepts of efficiency, productivity and cash flow requirements. The company is committed to providing further support in terms of material inputs. Schwarz is convinced that the skills of small tradesmen are the key to economic redevelopment for Czechoslovakia. 'Over the past 40 years skilled tradesmen were not allowed to function fully. This has created a tremendous deficiency in services to the general public, as well as in industrial requirements.' In this way, unemployment could be beneficial. 'The breaking up of complexes, I hope, will release skilled persons, who will be prepared to take the plunge and set up in business on their own.'

To aid this process, BSTO has used its contacts with tool suppliers in the UK to set up a number of plant hire shops nationwide in Czechoslovakia. Self-employed workers will be able to lease, or buy through hire purchase, the equipment needed to maintain and furnish a growing business. The deals will be on favourable credit terms. In some cases, BSTO may be willing to enter markets as joint venture partners, providing equipment to skilled tradesmen. The firm's commitment to this scheme is evidenced by the setting up of a Czechoslovak registered company – BSTO Praha Ltd. From June 1991 it will operate with capital of Kčs0.5 million. BSTO London will hold 80 per cent of the shares, and provide the new company with tools for hire and leasing in Czechoslovakia.

A pioneering scheme to install water filters in buildings across the nation will also help skilled tradesmen. The environmental situation in the country gives great cause for concern and political parties will have to take action to bring about improvements. One of the crucial factors affecting the quality of life is water supply. The scheme involves installing filters which will remove impurities common in the Czechoslovak water supply: lead, aluminium, herbicides, pesticides and chlorine. The risk of typhoid and cholera would also be reduced. As Schwarz elaborates, it becomes clear that complex problems need to be solved if the project is to be successful. Due to a lack of planning or materials in the years of the communist regime, the plumbing system differs from building to building. There is no uniformity in the designs. How can BSTO devise a water filter suitable for pipes of varying diameters and quality? The answer is to employ specialist plumbers to install each filter individually.

In the large monolithic factories of the communist years, each worker was assigned to a trade, first serving a long apprenticeship before becoming a specialist. Workers who trained as plumbers are the targets of Ivan Schwarz. 'We must advertise for these workers to come forward. We must tell them why we need them, and make them our sales agents'. In exchange for their skills, the plumbers will be taught how to cost and estimate jobs, something they never learned under the inefficiencies of the previous regime.

Other dilemmas face BSTO concerning the manufacture of the fittings. In this venture it is likely some parts will be manufactured in Czechoslovakia. A substantial investment is required from BSTO in the near future if the decision is taken to set up a manufacturing base in that country. Such an initiative would be a new experience for BSTO.

Changes in the political and economic climate have brought both opportunities and risks to firms in the market. If opportunities are to be seized upon, the lesson is that corporate change must occur. All the developments noted above - advertising and marketing, consultancy advice for small businesses, plant hire shops, and a manufacturing capacity for water filters - require a more proactive role in Czechoslovakia, and far more investment in capital than this trading company has ever experienced. Czechoslovakia hopes to see more firms develop strategies similar to BSTO. Success for the company will be reflected in a more widespread and efficient small business sector - an essential component of any plans for sustained economic regeneration.

Appendices

Opportunities by Sector
Cerrex Ltd

TRANSPORT INFRASTRUCTURE

Czechoslovakia needs to modernise its communication networks not only to meet its own increasing internal needs but also those of the international community, and incorporate the country into the existing European transport and communication systems.

Transport was heavily subsidised under the old regime but is generally ill-equipped to meet rising demand. Substantial fare increases in 1990 failed to make road transport and railways self-sufficient and the need remains for new buses and locomotives as well as for spares and repair facilities. For 1991 some Kčs3.4 billion is earmarked for projects involving modernisation of the Czechoslovak railway network, the electrification of selected parts including Brno, Olomouc and Ceske Budejovice, and data transmission information systems. A Bratislava-Wienna rail connection is now under consideration and there has been some discussion about the possible construction of a rapid transit rail system in Bratislava involving seven kilometres of rail and nine stations.

Requirements for new motorways and maintenance of existing ones is expected to cost some Kčs20 billion. Both Prague and Bratislava airports require heavy investment for modernisation, new machinery, new terminals and safety equipment. Total investments in air transport is expected to be some Kčs13.8 billion by the year 2000, while water transport investment requirements are estimated at Kčs5 billion.

RESEARCH AND TECHNOLOGY

Czechoslovakia has had a very high percentage of the population employed in research and scientific development, particularly in the mechanical engineering sector, and the quality of the work undertaken has often been very high. The country has, however, failed to capitalise or to apply such research to manufacturing. Under the new system, the strong control which the ministries and the State Commission for Science, Technology and Investment used to have over the research institutes will be weakened, and will be integrated more into state, university and private business sectors and many institutions are to work more on a self-financing basis.

During 1991, aid of over ECU100 million has been allocated for some 18 projects. Several Czechoslovak organisations hope that Western firms will be willing to sub-contract research to organisations in Czechoslovakia, especially in the fields of materials testing, water and engineering in order to use the skills that already exist. Government R&D priorities are education, improvement and protection of the environment, waste recycling, public health and health care and nutrition standards, new materials technologies and fibre optics. There are hopes that a major design centre will be established in the country.

ENVIRONMENT

Action against air, water and other environment problems which stemmed mainly from the pollution caused mainly by agriculture and by the chemical, mining and steel industries is now a major priority within the country. Most serious are levels of nitrogen oxide, hydrocarbons, carbon monoxide and sulphur dioxide in the air around Prague, Northern Bohemia, Bratislava, Ostrava-Karvina and the valley of the Vah. Further problems exist with drinking water, river contamination, solid waste dumps and pesticide and fertiliser contamination.

The agreed policy is to introduce measurement and control technology in industry, power generation, agriculture and transport, to implement international agreements on pollution including the reduction of sulphur dioxide emissions by 30 per cent and to establish centres for the disposal and/or recycling of toxic waste.

Opportunities are expected under the Czechoslovak ecological programme to occur in systems for monitoring and improving the quality of air and soil, river water pollution, protection of ground water from industrial and agricultural pollution and the reduction of vehicle emissions. Equipment is needed for controlling waste gases and pollutants emitted from production processes, nuclear safety, waste disposal and recycling, desulphurisation of power stations, for the construction of waste water treatment plants and the provision of alternative sources of energy. Typical are the plans for desulphurisation of flue gases at Pocerady, water supply schemes at Kolin, Hradec, Pardubice and Zlin, waste water treatment plants and sewerage network at Hradec Kralove, Usti nad Labem, and Decin and equipment for processing household and industrial waste in Bratislava.

Plans covering the next two decades are budgeted to involve expenditure of some Kčs600 billion. Substantial funds have been allocated by the federal and Republic authorities and under aid funds. Environment expenditure under the EC PHARE (Year 1) programme was ECU30 million including waste, air, water and energy pollution, projects on toxology centres, and ground water centres. Details of the aid allocation for environmental purposes for coming years are not clear, but are expected to include more under the PHARE programme and World Bank funds for priority projects including promotion of consultancy. Western companies that acquire shares in manufacturers causing pollution will be expected to invest in pollution control equipment.

Engineering firms are turning to production for ecological equipment programmes. Vitkovice Zelezarny for example has developed equipment for reducing emissions from metallurgical and coking plants, for dry cooling of coke, dust collection devices, coke oven desulphurisation and for improving the technical and ecological standards of other plants. They have developed co-operation programmes with Holter (Germany) and Clecin (France) covering emissions and dust removal. They are also concentrating on sewage and refuse treatment plant production and anti-pollution equipment for agricultural use.

AGRICULTURE AND FOOD PROCESSING

The main question mark overhanging the sector is the pace and manner of privatisation of the state-owned and co-operative sectors, the opportunities for the expansion of private farms, leasing, joint stock companies and the sale of land. With increased costs for energy and the abolition of a wide range of subsidies, demand has dramatically decreased particularly for some kinds of meat and dairy products. All sectors will require more modern methods of farming, improved crop strains and fertilisers.

Most food processing firms suffer from a lack of modern

machinery and equipment but have advantages in the form of local suppliers of food for processing, increasing demand locally for higher quality products and an international market. It is estimated that a quarter of all equipment used is over 25 years old and only 5 per cent of the industry is fully automated. This has led to the lack of variety in processed foodstuffs as well as shortages of instant and long life foods. There is also a shortage of modern packaging materials and of storage and warehousing capacity. Meat processing appears more advanced than processing of fruit or vegetables and cereals. The sugar industry has its own particular problems with low yields and very high energy costs, although it is expected that the government will continue to support the industry. Best opportunities appear to be in the deep freezing and canning industries, breakfast cereals, fish, cereals, meat, spices, vegetables and instant foods, and those areas where the government is keen to see increased production.

Koospol, now in competition with private sector companies, still handles 50–60 per cent of all foodstuffs traded. Many of the big UK brand names are already sold into Czechoslovakia and others such as Weetabix, Cadburys and Johnny Walker are also starting to make an impact.

BREWING

Czechoslovakia claims some 100 breweries, often based solely on a local area. Many are combined with restaurants and have become tourist attractions. Most beer produced is for local consumption but around 10 per cent – about 2.8 million hectolitres annually – is exported, with Hungary and the USSR traditionally the major markets. Pilsner (Plzen) and Budvar (at Ceske Budejovice) have a very good international reputation and sell well in the West, especially in Germany and Austria.

An investor interested in co-operation with a Czechoslovak firm in bottling under licence would enjoy the benefits of access to Eastern European markets, low costs and a traditional product of high reputation. Plans for the industry include increasing exports to both the East and West. Opportunities for co-operation would need to take account of purity laws and sensitivity in certain parts of the EC over competition.

Other opportunities include increasing production and modernisation of hop rooms and plants, improving the shelf life of beers, advanced bottling techniques and replacing bottles with cans which are at present more rare. The plant at Choteborske Strojirny has production programmes covering bottling equipment for beverages (but extending also to dairying). ZVU (Hradec Kralove) manufactures beer equipment, bottle loaders and conveyancing.

MINING

Czechoslovakia mines substantial amounts of both hard and brown coal, and to a lesser extent iron, uranium, lead, zinc and gold. For many years energy has been derived primarily from coal (the country has no major deposits of oil or gas), but the tonnage mined has now fallen to about 100,000 tons as the country has turned more to other sources including nuclear power for its energy needs.

During 1991 mining will face a completely new situation. Much mining has been open-cast and, combined with sulphur emissions from the coal-fired power stations, has led to environmental problems which must be tackled. A new Bill enacted during 1991 will enable participation of Western companies in the industry, and the sector will be gradually privatised and subsidies from the state will be withdrawn leaving prices of coal no longer controlled by the state.

Exploitation of some small sites only can be expected for non-ferrous metals, uranium ore and some others. The future of gold mining is also in the balance. Czechoslovakia will continue to mine several ceramic raw materials and materials for the building industry.

Investment opportunities are in waste removal, anti-pollution (desulphurisation equipment), separation technology, deep mining technology and associated equipment including cleaning technology, transport and conveyancing equipment.

METALLURGY

Czechoslovakia ranks about tenth in world steel production and is one of the largest per capita producers accounting for some 10 per cent of Czechoslovak industrial output. Production costs are however among the highest in the world, and much of the capacity is out of date and inefficient and due to be closed down in the mid-1990s.

Total reconstruction of the metallurgy sector is one of the overall aims of the government through progressive cuts in heavy manufacturing to reduce energy consumption, development of a processing industry that will give added value, and modernisation especially of stainless steel and alloy production. Over the next ten years Czechoslovakia is expected to narrow its production range, concentrate on steel flat products, profiles, welded pipes, steel products with anti-corrosion treatment and thereby aim to gain a larger share of the Western European market for finished products. New equipment may well be installed at Kosice, Kladno and Ostrava, and at other sites involving continuous and rolled steel production, installation of furnaces, anti-pollution and work dust equipment.

The Czechoslovaks are seeking co-operation with Western firms to introduce new technologies. Voest Alpine (Austria) has set up a joint designing company with Hutni Projekt in Prague and Kosice.

The Poldi Steel Works at Kladno boasts integrated production using imported machinery ranging from raw steel to finished products. Specific projects under consideration include crankshaft production for tractor engines at Poldi and, at ZTS Martin, the reconstruction of the metallurgical base of the weapons industry castings. Skoda Rolling Mills is one of the largest European heavy engineering enterprises and supplies products from its hot and cold rolling mills to Europe, Africa and Latin America.

ENGINEERING

In the late 1980s this was the largest industrial sector in the country employing about 1 million people in over 300 major companies and accounting for 20-25 per cent of industrial output and about 50 per cent of total exports. It divides into some eight sectors, of which the most important are automobiles, railway equipment, construction and agriculture, heavy engineering including mining, transport, armaments, power pumps and turbines and industrial processing including textile machinery. To date, sales have been aimed mainly at the Comecon and Soviet markets. Much of the equipment manufactured is of early 1960s design and the average age of machinery used is estimated at 18-24 years. There is little specialisation within each sector, but freedom from central control is expected to result in a massive reorganisation. The requirement therefore is to update the sector to world standards, and there will be many opportunities for investment and co-operation as well as expertise and technology transfer. (ASEA Brown Boveri are one of the early companies to be involved.)

Some of the more promising sectors appear to be aluminium

components for the motor and compressor industries (although pollution is a problem here), aeronautical engineering (where Pratt and Whitney and United Technologies are already involved), vehicles and vehicle parts, trailers, agricultural machines, textile machinery, optics, boats, railway vehicles, hydraulic motors, industrial heating equipment, machine tools and robotics (where German and Austrian influence is strong).

Czechoslovakia used to be the supplier to Comecon of agricultural machinery, pumps and turbines and other heavy engineering equipment and therefore established strong export links, but their future will depend very much on the willingness of the USSR and Western Europe to open up their markets and inject capital and technology. The textile machinery sector is considered to be highly competitive on a world-wide basis, as to a lesser extent are the leather and footwear equipment sectors.

Firms such as ZTS (Martin) and ZVS (Brno) will be looking to convert former military production to civilian use. Proposals for these plants include the development of small tractors, the reconstruction of the metallurgical base to castings for diesel engines, earth moving equipment and for the automobile industry and the manufacture of construction equipment, but such conversions would not be without difficulties. Projects which have been given recent publicity include production of hermetic compressors and refrigeration equipment at Calex, ball bearing production and the development of forging capacity at ZVL Kysucke Nove Mesto, industrial heating equipment at Povazska Bystrica, turbines, energy and gas production at Kovosvit, aeronautics at Aero Prague and agricultural machines at Agrozet, Brno.

ELECTRONICS

The electronics sector had high priority and was the major recipient of investment in the 1986–90 period. The target growth rate of 10 per cent, however, did not materialise and the industry failed to make a significant contribution to saving raw materials and fuel, or to the development of engineering at which it was aimed. Its major export market in the USSR has declined rapidly, few Czechoslovaks firms are competitive, and many are faced with the need to take on new technology in order to help establish new markets, or go under. Several companies which were part of the former Tesla group will present opportunities for takeovers.

Sales of computer and high technology products in general are limited by a shortage of hard currency rather than demand. Locally produced electronics products and systems of Western quality are rare and will have to be improved especially if industrial capacity is to be updated. PCs for example are in great demand and the local market has become highly competitive with many Far Eastern companies selling there having set up local assembly operations with joint venture partners. Relaxation of the CoCom rules has encouraged increased interest from IBM (including computer systems for higher education), Philips, ICL and others, and the high level of education and research ability, cheap labour costs and raw materials plus access to major markets have made the country a cost-effective location for components manufacturers. Management skills and knowledge of the world market are in short supply locally.

A mission to the UK in 1990 identified priority areas for encouragement of foreign co-operation as components and control systems, electronic data transmission systems, co-operation in TV and radio communications technology, application of science to health systems, software and semi-conductors. In industrial applications, priority will be the development and manufacture of new technology (mainly waste and biotechnologies), energy and materials-saving designed for environmental protection.

There are also plans to improve production of electronic consumer products including microwave ovens and colour TVs. Percentage ownership of TVs and, to a lesser extent, refrigerators and washing machines is comparable with most Western countries (although colour TVs and videos are comparatively rare), but products are generally old-fashioned and lack Western sophistication.

Projects of interest recently publicised include pcb development at CKD Polovodice and the Krizik Works in Prague and current breakers and other components at the EJF Brno Electrical Works.

TELECOMMUNICATIONS

Telecommunications in Czechoslovakia were probably the most developed of the three Central European states but, none the less, well behind Western standards. In mid-1990, Rude Pravo stated that the fax and telephone network required an investment of Kčs2 billion to enable it to cope with the expected increase in domestic and international traffic.

To meet initial demand, the Czechoslovak government has encouraged joint ventures and co-operation agreements covering the manufacture of digital telephones (Siemens RFA and Tesla Karlin), public data networks, and the manufacture of satellite and TV systems. In 1990, the US companies, US West and Bell Atlantic won a contract to develop data transmission and radio telecommunications systems. Other firms such as BT have been looking towards management of the system.

The first part of the plans to expand and modernise the basic telecommunication network involves an investment between 1992 and 1994 of some $500 million directed at the construction of basic remote digital equipment, international transit exchanges and local exchanges in areas where industry is concentrated.

Investment in telecommunications is one of the sectors covered under the PHARE programme and is also expected to be a World Bank priority. In addition, it seems likely that EBRD and EIB money could be available for financially viable projects.

CHEMICALS AND ALLIED TRADES

In 1988–89, chemical production was some 10–15 per cent of total industrial output, making it the third largest in the country. Production of chemicals was closely integrated with other Comecon countries under the specialisation and co-operation agreements.

During the 1970s the government put substantial financial assistance into the expansion of the industry, especially in Slovakia. However, it developed in relative isolation from the world market and is one of the sectors that might benefit substantially from an improvement in international distribution. The industry is highly diversified and ranges from modern refinery and petrochemical complexes to very out-dated facilities. Petroleum processing and petrochemicals including base plastics account for about 40 per cent of total production, but Czechoslovak firms are also strong in biotechnology, pharmaceuticals and agricultural technology, including vaccines and blood products. Previous plans envisaged a steady investment in the chemical industry as a whole while emphasis was put on speciality and polymer chemicals, plastics and synthetic resins, fertilisers and pesticides. There has been a deliberate policy to move away from bulk raw materials and energy-intensive chemicals towards non-bulk speciality products, and this is expected to continue under the present regime.

Opportunities are expected to include the development of fertilisers, 'environment friendly' chemicals, detergents, low lead petrol, printing materials and paint, synthetic fibres and substances for plant protection. All investments must take account of the need to meet the pollution requirements for the sector. The sector has been the most energy intensive in the country and will face problems as a result of the ending of the cheap energy agreement with the USSR. Modernisation of the chemical industry is expected to be one of the aid-supported sectors under the PHARE programme.

PAPER AND PULP

The pulp and paper industry uses locally produced wood and waste paper. Many of the paper mills are obsolete, due mainly to a shortage of hard currency required to buy modern equipment. Plans include that between now and 1995 production of paper and pulp is to be increased by some 30–40 per cent. It seems likely that there will continue to be a long-term shortage of paper and paper products on the Czechoslovak market, and opportunities include waste paper, newsprint, corrugated cardboard, food cartons, paper bags and cartons and speciality papers (such as photocopying and cling papers). Plastic packaging is also expected to develop.

In the pulp sector, opportunities may well cover chemicals required in the industry, extraction of acids from waste paper, processing of waste into marketable end-uses including animal feed. Western technology will be required for such production, especially at Biocel Paskov.

WOOD, WOODWORKING AND FURNITURE

The woodworking industry has an importance in the Czechoslovak economy comparable with glass and porcelain. It employs some 100,000 people. About 30 per cent of production has been exported (a high proportion to the West especially Austria, Germany and the UK), mainly in the form of raw timber and processed woods like boards and furniture.

Available investment for this sector was put into equipment for board making and furniture and the timber industry has remained very labour-intensive with demand expected for sorting, sawing, finishing and drying machines.

Opportunities comprise timber products for housing, processed wood boards and particle boards where the formaldehyde content has been a problem. The industry will also aim to improve the surface quality of its boards, as well as fire resistant and waterproofing techniques, in order to increase exports to the West.

To date, the furniture industry has been a large importer of machinery and equipment from the West. It is hoping to modernise and improve the quality of its furniture output, especially upholstered and bedroom furniture. A large number of private companies established in the sector remain short of finance and are looking to encourage investment from overseas.

VEHICLES

Motor vehicle production has a long and relatively successful history. Skoda was Eastern Europe's largest car manufacturer and road vehicles were the country's largest export to the UK.

During 1988-89, Czechoslovakia produced annually some 200,000 cars, about 50 per cent going to the West. To meet the substantial waiting lists for new cars – most are over 10 years old – and increase exports further, Skoda made plans to double the production of family cars during the 1990s and this will require substantial investment and modern technology which Volkswagen, who now own a large part of the company, is expected to provide. The expansion will provide a stimulus for sales of parts and components. Continental (Germany), for example, has an agreement with Barum which has traditionally sold tyres to Skoda and other Czechoslovak companies. As regards truck production (about 50,000 pa), approximately 60 per cent was exported, the vast majority to the USSR and the Eastern bloc, but this area has been steadily drying up as a source of earnings.

The future of the BAZ (Bratislava) plant remains uncertain, although now less so since they are producing gear boxes (130,000 pa) and, under a deal with Volkswagen, they are to assemble Passat cars. It also seems possible that the heavy engineering works at Martin (previously known for military output) will manufacture engines for vans to be produced at Bratislava in 1993.

In the motorcycle sector, where Jawa and CZ (currently negotiating with Cagiva – Italy) are well known, there are plans to modernise the industry to world levels. There are also plans to supply parts for cars, railway coaches and tram cars at Ziar nad Hronom, small planes at the Aero Aircraft works in Prague, modernisation of diesel electric locomotives, tram car manufacture at CKD Prague and trolley buses at Skoda (Plzen).

GLASS

The main sectors of the glass industry include fine glass (eg Bohemian Crystal and Crystalex) and industrial glass/flat glass and safety glass. During 1988–89 the industry employed some 80,000 people. Production had been estimated at some £500 million pa.

Czechoslovakia has traditionally exported substantial volumes (to approximately 90 countries) of high quality glass, jewellery, and decorative porcelain. Technology is claimed to be the equal of, or superior to, the Western product. Companies in both Slovakia and the Czech lands are seeking to increase exports and co-operation with Western firms. Glaverbel (Belgium) has taken a controlling share in Sklo Union Teplice, the country's major producer of flat glass, and is expected to dominate that sector.

The 1985–90 plan laid down targets to increase sheet glass production by 40 per cent and also to expand production of glass, fibre optic glass, toughened glass for cars as well as mirrors and glass for colour TV sets.

Demand is expected to increase for glass for hotels (which are to be modernised and privatised), toughened glass, utility glassware, glass for bottling, modernisation of production of safety glass and glass fibre at Trnava. There also appear to be opportunities for glass technology research.

TILES, CERAMICS AND BUILDING MATERIALS

After a period during which these sectors had little investment, the country aims to expand production of floor, wall and roof tiles, cement, brick and masonry materials and insulating plaster mixtures.

This could be an area of considerable potential, bearing in mind the requirements for cement etc. in new construction, hotel building and modernisation of the road infrastructure. It will also probably be one of the more promising sectors when enterprises are to be sold off under the large-scale privatisation scheme. Some products, such as tiles, may have considerable export potential if the country could guarantee the standard of the final product.

Among the modernisation plans, tile production at Novy Hrad, cement-making and updating of kilns at Horne Srnie, and bricks and tiles at the East Slovak brickworks at Kosice have been pushed most strongly.

LEATHER, FOOTWEAR, LEATHER GOODS

Czechoslovakia is one of the world's largest suppliers of cheap shoes. Production totals some 100 million pairs annually and uses two-thirds of all domestic leather. Traditionally, about 10–15 per cent of all footwear was exported to the West (the UK was the largest market after the USSR): the remainder was retained either for home consumption or export to the Eastern bloc.

Production per employee compared to Western European firms is relatively low and restructuring of the industry to phase out the most inefficient plants with the least export potential has been proposed. Under the privatisation plans, plants will be split into a larger number with independent production according to styles and different channels of sale. Foreign companies are being sought for co-operative ventures that can offer capital injections, distribution networks, help with improvement in quality, design technology, waste reduction, training and marketing. BATA, for example, is planning to modernise and co-operate with local enterprises in the design and manufacture of footwear.

Opportunities exist in the leather sector for the supply of equipment and expertise for the manufacture of shoes with direct moulded soles, automatic stretching and industrial sewing machines, raw materials and semi-finished products for the shoe industry, improvements in the quality of leather production and the means of using waste from the leather process. Some major companies involved are at Zlín/Otrokovice and Partizanske and Kozeto (Fancy Goods) at Prerov.

TEXTILES AND CLOTHING

The industry is concentrated in north west Bohemia and Moravia, although it is spread throughout the country. Textiles and clothing, mainly cotton cloth and yarn, knitted goods and under-garments account for approximately 8 per cent of total industrial production in Czechoslovakia. It has exported very considerable amounts, especially cotton thread and clothing under-garments, suits and carpets to hard currency markets. The quality of the products is generally very high, due in part to the investment in very modern Swiss-made machinery.

Opportunities in this sector lie mainly in the expansion of manufacture of men's and women's clothing, fibre and yarn production (both synthetic and natural), hotel and hospital linen and towelling, dyeing and knitted apparel, and probably in specialities – heavy overcoats and hats, ready-to-wear and sports clothes where Puma (Germany) is already established. The Czechoslovaks are optimistic about prospects for high fashion goods and the use of foreign design skills and supplying for 'own label' distributors.

Main production was traditionally at Hradec Kralove (cotton), Trutnov (linen), Brno (wool), Pisek (knitted goods) and at Trencin in Slovakia, although each of these has now been broken into several independent companies. Companies looking for Western associates include Bavlnarske Zavody at Ruzomberok (cotton thread and ready to wear goods) and Kara at Trutnov (finished garments, semi finished goods). Worth a special mention is textile machinery, where Elitex is a competitive manufacturer on a world-wide scale and one of the successes of the Czechoslovak economy.

ENERGY

Czechoslovakia has the doubtful distinction of being a super-power in terms of per head energy consumption. Its energy intensive steel and petrochemical industries have traditionally relied on domestically mined brown and hard coal. Over 50 per cent of Czechoslovak power requirements are generated by coal-fired thermal plants, some 30 per cent gas, oil and nuclear, and the remainder from hydroelectric power. Production of oil and gas is insignificant, requirements having been met from the USSR with small amounts from the Middle East and North Africa. With the demise of Comecon and the transferable rouble, Czechoslovakia now has to pay hard currency for its oil and gas imports. With no sea ports or existing pipelines linking Czechoslovakia with East European countries, massive investment will be needed to find new ways to transport oil from non-Soviet sources. Membership of the Alps Danube Co-operation Group could result in the extension of a gas pipeline to North Africa and transport of gas across Italy.

Between 1985–90 approximately 15 per cent of Czechoslovak investment was put into the energy sector and electricity generation has been rising steadily throughout the period mainly because of the growth of nuclear power. Plans were that, by 1996, nuclear power would account for about 40 per cent of the total power generation capacity, but the policy of extending its nuclear power capability will meet opposition on pollution and safety grounds. Much of the existing capacity is expensive to run and has a low level of life expectancy, being based on out-dated technology.

The Czechoslovaks are concerned about the harmful effects of their previous fuel policy and future projects concentrate on the modernisation of existing plants by the reduction of power and material intensive raw materials, up-grading of technical standards, introduction of new power saving manufacturing methods, changing the energy balance through a shift towards a greater use of natural gas and new and renewable sources of energy.

Major projects include the expansion of power plants at Melnik and Chvaletice (respectively to supply the increasing requirements for Prague and Kolin), modernisation of the nuclear power plant at Temelin and the extension of the power line from Hradec to the border with Germany.

The energy sector is expected to be well supported with aid funds.

HEALTH AND MEDICINE

A survey of health standards for 27 European countries showed Czechoslovakia placed tenth in 1960/64, falling dramatically by the 1980s, with the rate of infant mortality decreasing more slowly than in other countries. Lack of status of the medical profession, diet and lack of health education were among the factors responsible. A new health care system was put forward in late 1990 with the aim of being in operation in 1992. This will include decentralisation, the creation of a territorial network of health care facilities, the establishment of new bodies and professional institutions, changes in structure and financing, the introduction of a compulsory insurance system and education of medical workers.

Opportunities will exist for co-operation in updating equipment and instruments for use in research institutions, medical schools and in the new health care facilities, treatment of the handicapped, improvements in nutrition standards, co-operation in bio-medical technology and spa development, treatment of cardiovascular diseases, tumours, cancer and stomach ailments and in medical administration and insurance. Medical care research and biotechnology appear to be advanced (the Czechoslovaks claim to have developed soft contact lenses) and this may be a field for joint activity.

Organisations for joint co-operation and production in this sector (although names and organisation may change over the period of privatisation) include Chirana (medical equipment) in Slovakia, Leciva in Prague (medical drugs), Farmakon at Olomouc (vitamins), Biotika at Slovenska Lupca (antibiotics and stimulators) Slovakofarma at Hlohovec (gelatine, vitamin oils and disinfectants) and at Hradek nad Nisou (surgical goods and protective devices). Three major institutes include Jilove u Prahy (antibiotics), the Research Institute for Pharmaceuticals at Modra (new drug research) and the Institute of Sera and Vaccines, which acts as a centre for the modernisation of bacterial and viral vaccine production, blood products and allergy research.

TOURISM

Tourism is an important generator of hard currency and substantial investment in new hotels, restaurants, and Western style department stores is planned in the main cities (eg Prague, Bratislava, Piestany, Kosice and Ruzomberok). Czechoslovakia offers insufficient hotel beds that meet European standards – it is estimated, for example, that more than three-quarters of the tourists visiting Czechoslovakia come to Prague yet the capital can only offer only 20 per cent of beds. Most existing hotels are 60–90 years old and need extensive modernisation. Many Western firms have already negotiated joint ventures and others are searching for suitable space. Spa towns (for example, Karlovy Vary, Marianske Lazne, Teplice, Podebrady, Jachymov and Frantiskovy Lazne) are prime locations for foreign participation. Outside the main cities, there is a need for smaller family run hotels and hostels which the authorities hope to see developed once the privatisation law is fully operative and attitudes towards speculative ventures change. While the number of tourists visiting Prague has doubled since 1988 to over 50 million, their spending is low. Cinemas, theatres, cultural centres, sporting facilities (ski resorts and golf courses), spas and casinos all provide opportunities for development or modernisation which will need to be funded by private enterprise, bearing in mind that government or aid funds for this sector are unlikely to materialise.

SERVICES

In the average world economy, services now account for 60 per cent of the total labour force in contrast with only 40 per cent in Czechoslovakia. The Czechoslovaks have traditionally been less willing to bring foreign professional expertise and management skills into the industrial sector, but this is now changing. Initial UK successes have been in business management, financial and management know-how, banking, accountancy and training. Other opportunities for which aid could be available include the transfer of scientific expertise, education services and the establishment of professional bodies of all kinds.

In the education and cultural field, the renovation of historical monuments and buildings, archaeological sites and museums will help to encourage tourism. Universities and other bodies are interested in satellite broadcasting, computer and reprographic technology and setting up film production facilities.

Western firms have shown an interest in establishing advertising, property and architectural services but, as such services are not traditional to the country, initial sales will probably be more towards Western organisations wishing to promote their interests in the country and aid-supported projects. The media, including newspapers (publishing, printing equipment) local television, etc, and communication services have also expanded and they offer opportunities for Western companies.

Appendix 2

Legislation

1. Relations with the EC
Agreement between EEC, EAEC and CSFR on Trade, Commercial and Economic Co-operation, 7 May 1990. Association Agreement – a major agreement between EEC and Czechoslovakia is expected to be adopted in the summer of 1991.

2. Legal and government structure
Constitution of Czech and Slovak Federative Republik No.100/1960. Constitutional Law on Czechoslovak Federation No.143/1968 and post-revolutionary constitutional laws amending the Constitution: Nos. 14/1990, 45/1990, 46/1990, 81/1990, 100/1990, 101/1990, 102/1990, 158/1990, 159/1990, 160/1990, 161/1990, 294/1990, 295/1990, 296/1990, 376/1990, 556/1990, 23/1991, etc.

3. Basic Laws for transition to a market economy
Constitutional Amendments Law No. 100/1990. Economic Code Amendments Act No. 103/1990. Private Enterpreneurial Activities of Individuals Act No. 105/1990. State Enterprise Act No. 111/1990. Joint Stock Companies Act No. 104/1990. Agreed Prices Act No. 35/1990. Prices Act No. 26/1990. Act on Protection of Economic Competition No. 63/1991.

4. Foreign investment and joint ventures
Agreement between the UK and and CSFR for promotion and protection of investments, 10 July 1990. Enterprise with Foreign Participation Act (Joint Ventures Act) No. 173/1988, as amended by Act No. 112/1990 and subsequent regulations. Act on Economic Relations with Foreign Countries No. 113/1990 and subsequent implementary regulations: regulation on authorisation for carrying out foreign trade activities, carrying out foreign trade activities without authorisation or registration and carrying out foreign trade activities by foreigners No. 533/1990 as amended by the Regulation

No. 27/1991. Regulation on Exports and Imports Requiring Authorisation No. 256/1990. Foreign Exchange Act No. 528/1990. Customs Act No. 44/1974 as amended by subsequent regulations (the most recent being No. 5/1991). Ministry of Trade Act No. 266/1990.

5. *Banking and financial services*
Act on Czechoslovak State Bank No. 130/1989. Act on Banks and Saving Banks No. 158/1989.

6. *Restitution*
Act on Relieving the Consequences of Some Property Injuries No. 403/1990, as amended by subsequent regulations: No. 458/1990 and No. 137/1991 (Small Restitution Act). Act on Out-of-Court Rehabilitations (Large Restitution Act) No. 87/1991.

7. *Privatisation: the legal aspects*
Act on Transfer of State Property with Regard to Some Objects to Other Legal or Physical Persons (Small-scale Privatisation Law) No. 427/1990, as amended by Act No 541/1990. Act on the Conditions of Transfer of Property of the State to Other Persons (Large-scale Privatisation Law) No. 92/1991.

8. *Commercial law*
Act on Economic Arbitration No. 121/1962, as amended by subsequent Acts (the most recent being Act No. 106/1990). Act on Legal Relations in International Business Transactions (International Trade Code) No. 101/1963. Commercial Code – complex law regulation – is at the time of writing in proposal stage and is expected to come into effect in September 1991.

9. *Real estate*
Act on Adjustment of Ownership Rights to Land (Land Law) of 21 May 1991. Act on Letting and Sub-letting of Business Premises No. 116/1990, as amended by subsequent regulations.

10. *The environment*
Act on Waste of 22 May 1991. Environment Framework Law – currently being negotiated in the Federal Assembly.

11. *The labour market*
Act on Employment No. 1/1991. Act on Collective Negotiation of 4 December 1990. Labour Code No. 167/1991.

12. *Insurance*
Act by Slovak National Council on Insurance No. 24/1991.

13. *Technology licensing*
   Act on Inventions, Industrial Designs and Innovations (Rationalisation Proposals) No. 527/1990. Act on Trade Marks No. 174/1988. Act on Literary, Scientific and Artistic Works (Copyright Act) No. 247/1990.

14. *Agencies, distributorship and franchises*
   Act on Legal Relations in International Business Transactions (International Trade Code) No. 101/1963.

15. *Establishing a presence*
   Act 42 of 1980, as amended by law 113 of 1990 Economic Relations with Foreign Countries, Articles 37–39. Decree of the Ministry of Foreign Trade 265 of 1990. Decree of the Ministry of Foreign Trade 533 of 1990 as amended by Decree 27 of 1991.

16. *Forming a company in Czechoslovakia*
   Regulation on Establishing and Functioning of Representative Offices of Foreign Persons No. 265/1990. Act on Employment No. 1/1991. Government Ordinance regulating conditions for granting approval to newly established joint ventures No. 132/1991.

17. *Taxes on companies with foreign participation*
   Income Tax Law No. 157/1989 and subsequent amendments and regulations: Income Tax Law Amendments Act No. 108/1990 amending simultaneously also Act on Agricultural Tax No. 172/1988 and Act on Activity of Organisations with Foreign Element No. 116/1985. Regulation No. 193/1989 implementing Income Tax Law (full text published as Regulation No. 214/1990). Turnover Tax Law No. 73/1952 and subsequent amendments and regulations: Turnover Tax Law Amendments Act No. 107/1990 (the most recent amendment); Regulation No. 560/1990 implementing Turnover Tax Law. 'Tariff of rates of Turnover Tax' effective since 1 January 1991 No. 453/1990. Wages Tax Law 76/1952 as amended by subsequent decrees. Government Ordinance No. 15/1991 on Regulative Levies in the Area of Wages No. 15/1991 as amended by Government Ordinance No. 139/1990. Citizens Income Tax Law No. 389/1990. Bilateral agreements for the avoidance of double taxation.

18. *Accounting*
   Decree 586/1990 on rates of depreciation. Law on Enterprises with Foreign Capital Participation 173/1988 as amended by Law 112/1990.

Czech and Slovak Federal Republic No. 1 (1990)

Agreement

between the Government of the
United Kingdom of Great Britain and Northern Ireland
and the Government of the Czech and Slovak Federal Republic

for the Promotion and Protection of Investments

with Protocol

Prague, 10 July 1990

[the Agreement is not in force)

*Presented to Parliament
by the Secretary of State for Foreign and Commonwealth Affairs
by Command of Her Majesty
November 1990*

LONDON : HMSO
£1.75 net

**AGREEMENT
BETWEEN THE GOVERNMENT OF THE UNITED
KINGDOM OF GREAT BRITAIN AND NORTHERN
IRELAND AND THE GOVERNMENT OF THE CZECH AND
SLOVAK FEDERAL REPUBLIC FOR THE PROMOTION AND
PROTECTION OF INVESTMENTS**

The Government of the United Kingdom of Great Britain and Northern Ireland and the Government of the Czech and Slovak Federal Republic;

Desiring to create favourable conditions for greater investment by investors of one State in the territory of the other State;

Recognising that the encouragement and reciprocal protection under international agreement of such investments will be conducive to the stimulation of business initiative and will contribute to the development of economic relations between the two States;

Acting in the spirit of the principles of the Final Act of the Conference on Security and Co-operation in Europe signed at Helsinki on 1 August 1975[1];

Have agreed as follows:

ARTICLE 1

Definitions

For the purposes of this Agreement:

(a) the term "investment" means every kind of asset belonging to an investor of one Contracting Party in the territory of the other Contracting Party under the law in force of the latter Contracting Party in any sector of economic activity and in particular, though not exclusively, includes:

(i) movable and immovable property and any other related property rights including mortgages, liens or pledges;

(ii) shares in and stock and debentures of a company and any other form of participation in a company;

(iii) claims to money or to any performance under contract having a financial value;

(iv) intellectual property rights, goodwill, know-how and technical processes;

(v) business concessions conferred by law or, where appropriate under the law of the Contracting Party concerned, under contract, including concessions to search for, cultivate, extract or exploit natural resources.

A change in the form in which assets are invested does not affect their character as investments within the meaning of this Agreement. The term "investment" includes all investments, whether

[1] Cmnd. 168

made before or after the date of entry into force of this Agreement;

(b) the term "returns" means the amounts yielded by an investment and in particular, though not exclusively, includes profit, interest, capital gains, dividends, royalties and fees;

(c) the term "investors" means:

   (i) in respect of the Czech and Slovak Federal Republic:

      (aa) all legal entities established under Czechoslovak law;

      (bb) all natural persons who, according to Czechoslovak law, are Czechoslovak citizens and have the right to act as investors;

   (ii) in respect of the United Kingdom:

      (aa) physical persons deriving their status as United Kingdom nationals from the law in force in the United Kingdom;

      (bb) corporations, firms and associations incorporated or constituted under the law in force in any part of the United Kingdom or in any territory to which this Agreement is extended in accordance with the provisions of Article 12;

(d) the term "territory" means:

   (i) in respect of the Czech and Slovak Federal Republic: the territory of the Czech and Slovak Federal Republic;

   (ii) in respect of the United Kingdom: Great Britain and Northern Ireland, including the territorial sea and any maritime area situated beyond the territorial sea of the United Kingdom which has been or might in the future be designated under the national law of the United Kingdom in accordance with international law as an area within which the United Kingdom may exercise rights with regard to the seabed and subsoil and the natural resources and any territory to which this Agreement is extended in accordance with the provisions of Article 12.

Article 2

Promotion and Protection of Investment

(1)   Each Contracting Party shall encourage and create favourable conditions for investors of the other Contracting Party to invest

capital in its territory, and, subject to its right to exercise powers conferred by its laws, shall admit such capital.

(2) Investments of investors of each Contracting Party shall at all times be accorded fair and equitable treatment and enjoy full protection and security in the territory of the other Contracting Party. Neither Contracting Party shall in any way impair by unreasonable or discriminatory measures the management, maintenance, use, enjoyment or disposal of investments in its territory of investors of the other Contracting Party.

(3) Investors of one Contracting Party may conclude with the other Contracting Party specific agreements, the provisions and effect of which, unless more beneficial to the investor, shall not be at variance with this Agreement. Each Contracting Party shall, with regard to investments of investors of the other Contracting Party, observe the provisions of these specific agreements, as well as the provisions of this Agreement.

ARTICLE 3

National Treatment and Most-favoured-nation Provisions

(1) Each Contracting Party shall ensure that under its law investments or returns of investors of the other Contracting Party are granted treatment not less favourable than that which it accords to investments or returns of its own investors or to investments or returns of investors of any third State.

(2) Each Contracting Party shall ensure that under its law investors of the other Contracting Party, as regards their management, maintenance, use, enjoyment or disposal of their investments, are granted treatment not less favourable than that which it accords to its own investors or to investors of any third State.

ARTICLE 4

Compensation for Losses

Investors of one Contracting Party whose investments in the territory of the other Contracting Party suffer losses owing to any armed conflict, a state of national emergency, or civil distrubances in the territory of the latter Contracting Party shall be accorded by the latter Contracting Party treatment, as regards restitution, indemnification, compensation or other settlement, no less favourable than that which the latter Contracting Party accords to its own investors or to investors of any third State. Resulting payments shall be freely transferable.

ARTICLE 5

Expropriation

(1)   Investments of investors of either Contracting Party shall not be nationalised, expropriated or subjected to measures having effect equivalent to nationalisation or expropriation (hereinafter referred to as "expropriation") in the territory of the other Contracting Party except for a public purpose related to the internal needs of that Party on a non-discriminatory basis and against prompt, adequate and effective compensation. Such compensation shall amount to the genuine value of the investment expropriated immediately before the expropriation or before the impending expropriation became public knowledge, whichever is the earlier, shall include interest at a normal commercial rate until the date of payment, shall be made without delay, be effectively realisable and be freely transferable. The investor affected shall have a right, under the law of the Contracting Party making the expropriation, to prompt review, by a judicial or other independent authority of that party, of his or its case and of the valuation of his or its investment in accordance with the principles set out in this paragraph.

(2)   The provisions of paragraph (1) shall also apply where a Contracting Party expropriates the assets of a company which is incorporated or constituted under the law in force in any part of its own territory, and in which investors of the other Contracting Party own shares.

ARTICLE 6

Repatriation of Investment and Returns

Each Contracting Party shall in respect of investments guarantee to investors of the other Contracting Party the unrestricted transfer of their investments and returns. Transfers shall be effected without delay in the convertible currency in which the capital was originally invested or in any other convertible currency agreed by the investor and the Contracting Party concerned. Unless otherwise agreed by the investor transfers shall be made at the rate of exchange applicable on the date of transfer pursuant to the exchange regulations in force.

ARTICLE 7

Exceptions

The provisions of this Agreement relative to the grant of treatment not less favourable than that accorded to the investors of either Contracting Party or of any third State shall not be construed so as to oblige one Contracting Party to extend to the investors of the other the benefit of any treatment, preference or privilege resulting from:

(a) any existing or future customs or economic union or similar international agreement to which either of the Contracting Parties is or may become a Party, or

(b) any international agreement or arrangement, or any domestic legislation, relating wholly or mainly to taxation.

ARTICLE 8

Settlement of Disputes between an Investor and a Host State

(1) Disputes between an investor of one Contracting Party and the other Contracting Party concerning an obligation of the latter under Articles 2(3), 4, 5 and 6 of this Agreement in relation to an investment of the former which have not been amicably settled shall, after a period of four months from written notification of a claim, be submitted to arbitration under paragraph (2) below if either party to the dispute so wishes.

(2) Where the dispute is referred to arbitration, the investor concerned in the dispute shall have the right to refer the dispute either to:

(a) an arbitrator or *ad hoc* arbitral tribunal to be appointed by a special agreement or established and conducted under the Arbitration Rules of the United Nations Commission on International Trade Law; the parties to the dispute may agree in writing to modify these Rules, or

(b) the Institute of Arbitration of the Chamber of Commerce of Stockholm, or

(c) the Court of Arbitration of the Federal Chamber of Commerce and Industry in Vienna.

(3) The arbitrator or arbitral tribunal to which the dispute is referred under paragraph (2) shall, in particular, base its decision on the provisions of this Agreement.

ARTICLE 9

Disputes between the Contracting Parties

(1)   Disputes between the Contracting Parties concerning the interpretation or application of this Agreement should, if possible, be settled amicably.

(2)   If a dispute between the Contracting Parties cannot thus be settled, it shall upon the request of either Contracting Party be submitted to an arbitral tribunal.

(3)   Such an arbitral shall be constituted for each individual case in the following way. Within two months of the receipt of the request for arbitration, each Contracting Party shall appoint one member of the tribunal. Those two members shall then select a national of a third State who on approval by the two Contracting Parties shall be appointed Chairman of the tribunal. The Chairman shall be appointed within two months from the date of appointment of the other two members.

(4)   If within the periods specified in paragraph (3) of this Article the necessary appointments have not been made, either Contracting Party may, in the absence of any other agreement, invite the President of the International Court of Justice to make any necessary appointments. If the President is a national of either Contracting Party or if he is otherwise prevented from discharging the said function, the Vice-President shall be invited to make the necessary appointments. If the Vice-President is a national of either Contracting Party or if he too is prevented from discharging the said function, the Member of the International Court of Justice next in seniority who is not a national of either Contracting Party shall be invited to make the necessary appointments.

(5)   The tribunal shall determine its own procedure. The arbitral tribunal shall reach its decision by a majority of votes. Such decision shall be binding on both Contracting Parties.

(6)   Each Contracting Party shall bear the cost of its own member of the tribunal and of its representation in the arbitral proceedings; the cost of the Chairman and the remaining costs shall be borne in equal parts by the Contracting Parties. The tribunal may, however, in its decision direct that a higher proportion of costs shall be borne by one of the two Contracting Parties, and this award shall be binding on both Contracting Parties.

ARTICLE 10

Subrogation

(1) If one Contracting Party or its designated Agency ("the first Contracting Party") makes a payment under an indemnity given in respect of an investment in the territory of the other Contracting Party ("the second Contracting Party"), the second Contracting Party shall recognise:

(a) the assignment to the first Contracting Party by law or by legal transaction of all the rights and claims of the party indemnified, and

(b) that the first Contracting Party is entitled to exercise such rights and enforce such claims by virtue of subrogation, to the same extent as the party indemnified.

(2) The first Contracting Party shall be entitled in all circumstances to:

(a) the same treatment in respect of the rights and claims acquired by it by virtue of the assignment, and

(b) any payments received in pursuance of those rights and claims,

as the party indemnified was entitled to receive by virtue of this Agreement in respect of the investment concerned and its related returns.

(3) Any payments received in non-convertible currency by the first Contracting Party in pursuance of the rights and claims acquired shall be freely available to the first Contracting Party for the purpose of meeting any expenditure incurred in the territory of the second Contracting Party.

ARTICLE 11

Application of Other Rules

If the provision of law of either Contracting Party or obligations under international law existing at present or established hereafter between the Contracting Parties in addition to the present Agreement contain rules, whether general or specific, entitling investments by investors of the other Contracting Party to a treatment more favourable than is provided for by the present Agreement, such rules shall to the extent that they are more favourable prevail over the present Agreement.

ARTICLE 12

Territorial Extension

At the time of entry into force of this Agreement, or at any time thereafter, the provisions of this Agreement may be extended to such territories for whose international relations the Government of the United Kingdom are responsible as may be agreed between the Contracting Parties in an Exchange of Notes.

ARTICLE 13

Entry into Force

Each Contracting Party shall notify the other in writing of the completion of the constitutional formalities required in its territory for the entry into force of this Agreement. This Agreement shall enter into force on the date of the latter of the two notifications.

ARTICLE 14

Duration and Termination

This Agreement shall remain in force for a period of ten years. Thereafter it shall continue in force until the expiration of twelve months from the date on which either Contracting Party shall have given written notice of termination to the other. Provided that in respect of investments made whilst the Agreement is in force, its provisions shall continue in effect with respect to such investments for a period of fifteen years after the date of termination and without prejudice to the application thereafter of the rules of general international law.

In witness whereof the undersigned, duly authorised thereto by their respective Governments, have signed this Agreement.

Done at Prague this Tenth day of July 1990 in duplicate in the English and Czech languages, both texts being equally authoritative.

For the Government of the United Kingdom of Great Britain and Northern Ireland:

NICHOLAS RIDLEY

For the Government of the Czech and Slovak Federal Republic:

VACLAV KLAUS

PROTOCOL
RELATING TO THE AGREEMENT BETWEEN THE GOVERNMENT OF THE UNITED KINGDOM OF GREAT BRITAIN AND NORTHERN IRELAND AND THE GOVERNMENT OF THE CZECH AND SLOVAK FEDERAL REPUBLIC FOR THE PROMOTION AND PROTECTION OF INVESTMENTS

On the signature of the Agreement between the Government of the United Kingdom of Great Britain and Northern Ireland and the Government of the Czech and Slovak Federal Republic for the Promotion and Protection of Investments the signatories below being duly authorised thereto by their respective Governments, have agreed as follows:

"The provisions of Article 6 of the Agreement shall be applied, in respect of the Czech and Slovak Federal Republic, so that unrestricted transfer of payments relating to returns and loan repayments, shall only be permitted in any one year up to a maximum of 20 per cent of the value of the investment of the investor of the United Kingdom, that value being the value of the investment at the date of the admission of the investment to the Czech and Slovak Federal Republic.

All transfers effected from the convertible currency account of a company in which an investor owns shares are excluded from the above mentioned restriction."

This Protocol shall form an integral part of the above mentioned Agreement. Unless the Contracting Parties agree in writing on an earlier term, the validity of this Protocol will be terminated on 31 December 1994.

Done at Prague this Tenth day of July 1990 in duplicate in the English and the Czech languages, both texts being equally authoritative.

For the Government of the United Kingdom of Great Britain and Northern Ireland:

NICHOLAS RIDLEY

For the Government of the Czech and Slovak Federal Republic:

VACLAV KLAUS

Appendix 3

Bibliography and Sources of Further Information

BIBLIOGRAPHY

Books

Czechoslovak Enterprises Directory, Czechoslovak Chamber of Commerce, Prague, 1991.

Czechoslovakia: Paving the Way to a Free Economy, a Guide to Legislation Governing the Establishment of Companies and Investment in Czechoslovakia, KPMG, London 1991.

Doing Business in Eastern Europe, Karen Liebrich, BBC, London 1991.

Doing Business with Eastern Europe, A Handbook for the 1990s, Peter Danton de Rouffignac, Pitman Publishing, London, 1991.

Europa World Year Book, (annual), Europa Publications Ltd, London.

Guide to Czechoslovakia, Simon Hayman, Bradt Publications UK, 1990.

Statisticka Rocenka, Statistical Yearbook (annual), Prague.

Your Trade Partners in Czechoslovakia, Czechoslovak Chamber of Commerce, Prague, 1990.

Periodicals and journals

Business Eastern Europe, fortnightly, Business International, London.

Central European, monthly, Euromoney Publications, London.

Czechoslovak Financial Review, fortnightly, Cohfin in association with PPS Publications, Prague.

Czechoslovak Foreign Trade, monthly, Czechoslovak Chamber of Commerce and Industry, Prague.

Czechoslovakia Country Report, quarterly and *Czechoslovakia Country Profile*, yearly, Economist Intelligent Unit, London.

Czechoslovakia Market Newsletter, monthly, Prague.

East Europe Business Focus, monthly, WLP Newsletters Ltd, London.

East European Banker, monthly, Lafferty Group of Publications, Dublin.

East European Markets, fortnightly, FT Business Information Ltd, London.

Economic Digest, Czechoslovak Chamber of Commerce, Prague.

Finance East Europe, fortnightly, FT Business Information Ltd, London.

Image-International Magazine for Eastern Europe, quarterly, KPMG, Amsterdam.

Insight-East European Business Report, Insight Publishing Ltd, London.

News from Prague, monthly, Trade Links, Prague.

Opportunities Briefing, IFF Publications, London.

PlanEcon Business Report, fortnightly, PlanEcon Inc, Washington DC.

Soviet and East European Report, monthly, Gostick Hall Publications.

SOURCES OF FURTHER INFORMATION

Julian Lew/Michael Rose
SJ Berwin & Co*
236 Grays Inn Road
London WC1X 8HB
Tel: 44 (71) 278 0444
Fax: 44 (71) 833 2860
* With associates in Prague and
  Bratislava

Maurice Childs
Head of East European
  Department
CBI
Centre Point
103 New Oxford Street
London WC1A 1DU
Tel: 44 (71) 379 7400
Fax: 44 (71) 240 1578

Michael Gibbins
Eastern Europe Practice Group
KPMG Peat Marwick
1 Puddle Dock
London EC4V 3PD
Tel: 44 (71) 236 8000
Fax: 44 (71) 248 6552

Paul Lom/Jan Zurek
KPMG Reviconsult
Vaclavke Namesti 41
11283 Prague 1
Czechoslovakia
Tel: 010 42 (2) 265 242
Fax: 010 42 (2) 264 131

David Butler
National Westminster Bank plc
National Westminster Tower
Level 26
25 Old Broad Street
London EC2N 1HQ
Tel: 44 (71) 920 5354
Fax: 44 (71) 920 1627

Michael Bird
Cerrex Ltd
Morley House
314–322 Regent Street
London W1R 5AG
Tel: 071-637 1312

Simon Goode
Saatchi & Saatchi Advertising
    Worldwide
80 Charlotte Street
London W1A 1AQ
Tel: 44 (71) 636 5060
Fax: 44 (71) 436 8905

Jordan Stojanov
BSB Saatchi & Saatchi Creative
    Communications
Zdikovska 39
CS-15000 Prague 5
Czechoslovakia
Tel: 010 42 (2) 524 445
Fax: 010 42 (2) 526 133

Department of Trade and
    Industry
Czechoslovakia Desk
1 Victoria Street
London SW1H 0ET
Tel: 44 (71) 215 5152

East European Trade Council
Suite 10
Westminster Palace Gardens
Artillery Row
London SW1P 1RL
Tel: 44 (71) 222 7622

London Chamber of Commerce
East European Section
69 Cannon Street
London EC4N 5AB
Tel: 44 (71) 248 4444
Fax: 44 (71) 489 0391

Export Market Information
    Centre
1 Victoria Street
London SW1 0ET
Tel: 44 (071) 215 5444/5445

Export Intelligence Service
Lime Grove
Eastcote
Middlesex HA4 8RS
Tel: 44 (81) 866 8771

Technical Help to Exporters
BSI
Linford Wood
Milton Keynes
MK14 6LE
Tel: 44 (0908) 220022

Simpler Trade Procedures
Venture House
29 Glasshouse Street
London W1R 5RG
Tel: 44 (71) 287 3525

CoCom
Department of Trade and
   Industry
Kingsgate House
66–74 Victoria Street
London SW1E 6SW
Tel: 44 (71) 215 8032

ECGD
Export House
50 Ludgate Hill
London EC4M 7AY
Tel: 44 (71) 382 7000

EBRD
Level 7
6 Broadgate
London EC2M 2QS
Tel: 44 (71) 496 0060

European Investment Bank
London Office
68 Pall Mall
London SW1 5ES
Tel: 44 (71) 839 3351

European Investment Bank
100 Boulevard Konrad
   Adenauer
L2950 Luxembourg
Tel: 010 35 243 791

International Finance
   Corporation
European Office
New Zealand House
Haymarket
London SW1Y 4TE
Tel: 44 (71) 930 8741

Know-How Fund
The Joint Assistance
Unit
Eastern European Department
Foreign and Commonwealth
   Office
King Charles Street
London SW1A 2AH
Tel: 44 (71) 270 3470

Overseas Projects Fund
Projects and Export Policy
   Division
DTI
Second Floor
1–19 Victoria Street
London SW1H 0ET
Tel: 44 (71) 215 5076

PHARE
World Aid Section
DTI
Room 402
1 Victoria Street
London SW1H 0ET
Tel: 44 (71) 215 4255/5369

Czechoslovak Embassy
Commercial Section
26 Kensington Palace Gardens
London W8 4QY
Tel: 44 (71) 727 4918

British Embassy
Commercial Section
Blanicka 13/11
Prague 2
Czechoslovakia
Tel: 42 (2) 258 685
Fax: 42 (2) 250 986

Federal Agency for Foreign
Investment
tr. kpt Jarose 1000
170 32 Prague 7
Czechoslovakia
Tel: 42 (2) 389 1111
Fax: 42 (2) 376 063

Federal Ministry of Finance
Letenska 15
118 10 Prague 1
Czechoslovakia
Tel: 42 (2) 514 1111
Fax: 42 (2) 535 759

Federal Ministry of Foreign
Trade
Politickych Veznu 20
112 49 Prague 1
Czechoslovakia
Tel: 42 (2) 126 1111
Fax: 42 (2) 322 868

Czech Ministry for the
Administration and
Privatisation of National
Assets
Senovazne Nam. 32
113 87 Prague 1
Czechoslovakia
Tel: 42 (2) 236 2065
Fax: 42 (2) 236 8945

Slovak Ministry for the
Administration and
Privatisation of National
Assets
Drienova 24
820 09 Bratislava
Czechoslovakia
Tel: 42 (7) 234 332

Czechoslovak Chamber of
Commerce and Industry
Argentinska 38
170 05 Prague 7
Czechoslovakia
Tel: 42 (2) 872 4111
Fax: 42 (2) 879 134

Slovak Chamber of Commerce
Gorkeho 9
81603 Bratislava
Czechoslovakia
Tel: 42 (7) 58 681

Index

acceptance credits 301-2
accountancy 82, 150, 182, 191-2, 192, 292, 311-14
  principal adjustments 311-14
  debtors 313
  fixed assets 312
  reserves 313-14
  stock 312-13
  valuing proposed investments 314
acquisitions
  of Czechoslovak assets 81
  and other options 211-12
Act on Out of Court Rehabilitations (1991) 105, 107-8, 224
Act on Protection of Economic Competition (1991) 138-44, 258, 267, 277-8
advance purchase 247
advertising 221-2, 332
  television 219-20
Advokatni poradna c.1/c.10 (Law and Patent Bureaux Nos 1/10) 271
agencies 212, 258-61, 363
  brokers 259
  commercial representatives 259-61
  contract check-list 261
  legal regulations 257-8
  taxation of 305
Agency For Foreign Investment and Assistance 48, 56, 211
agriculture 36, 63, 201
  and food processing 345-6
aid 41, 193-202, 357
  EBRD 155, 195-6, 301, 351
  EIB 200-2, 351

IFC 198-200, 237-8, 301
Overseas Projects Fund (OPF) 194-5
PHARE Programme 61, 155, 184, 197-8, 336, 345, 351, 352
UK government Know-How Fund 55, 193-4, 336
air pollution 41, 152, 160, 344
air travel
  cargo services 170
  internal 38, 172
  to/from Czechoslovakia 171-2
akciova polecnost see joint stock companies
Akciova spolecnost (joint stock company) 79
anti-dumping regulations 64
anti-trust law 138-44
  abuse of a monopoly/dominant position 141-2
  control of mergers 141, 143
  escape clauses 140-1
  exemptions 139-40
  the Office: extent of power 142
  purpose and scope 138-9
  cartel agreements 139, 140
  some general comments 142-4
arbitration 83, 369-70
  state 75
Association of Accountants and Auditors of Slovakia (AAAS) 192
Association Agreements 28, 60-5, 364-73
  with the EC 60-5
  agriculture, industry and fishery 63
  approximation of laws 64

back-up provisions 63
economic co-operation 63-4
financial assistance 64-5
free movement of goods 62-3
free movement of workers,
services, capital 63
state aids/anti-dumping 64
structures/institutional framework
61-2
with Hungary and Poland 60-1
Association of Entrepreneurs 48
associations (*Sdruzeni*) 79, 295

Baker Street Trading Overseas (BSTO)
337-40
banking and financial services 80,
97-102, 194, 362
commercial banks 98, 301
the financial system 100-1
foreign banks 100
interest rates 102
monetary policy 101-2
specialised banks 98-100
Ceskoslovenská Obchodni Banka
98
Investicni Banka 99
savings banks 99-100
Zivnostenská Banka 98
Statni Banka Ceskoslovenska
(Czechoslovak State Bank) 80,
97-8
see also aid
bankruptcy and liquidation 31
barter 245-6
BC-Net (EC database) 54, 198
Berox Machine Tool Co Ltd 210-11,
323-7
big ticket leasing 242
'black triangle', pollution 152
BRE (EC database) 54
breach of contract 135
brewing industry 38, 346-7
British Embassy, Prague 55-6
British International Freight
Association 54
brokers, agency 259
building industry 354-5
building permissions 129
buses 173-5

business culture, Czechoslovakia's 45-9
current players 46-7
the private sector 47
state enterprises 46-7
foreign involvement 47-8
management culture 49
Business Eastern Europe 53
business plan 212-13
business strategies, implementing
315-40
buy-back 245, 247-8

capital
JSCs 288-90
markets 110-11
cartel agreements 139, 140
case studies 315-40
Baker Street Trading Overseas
337-40
Berox Machine Tool Co Ltd 210-11,
323-7
Chequepoint International 317-21
Emmex Consultants 329-32
Nuclear Electric plc 333-6
ceramics 38, 39, 41, 354-5
Ceskoslovenská Obchodní Banka
(CSOB) (foreign trade bank) 98,
226, 318, 320
Ceskoslovensko radio station 220
chemicals and allied trades 154, 351-2
Chequepoint International 317-21
cinema advertising 221
citizens' income tax 148
civil courts 74-5
Civil Procedure Code 31, 126
'classic a' forfait 239
clothing industry 355-6
co-operative land, transfer of 126
Co-ordinating Committee for
Multilateral Export Control
(CoCom) 164, 225
Collective Negotiation Act (1991) 32
commercial banks 98-101, 301
Commercial Code, draft 69, 131, 133,
137, 275, 276, 277-8
commercial courts 31-2
commercial law 30, 131-6, 362
the law of contract 132-5
liability for damage to others 135-6

damages 135-6, 161, 264
    product guarantees/breach of
        contract 135
    unjust enrichment 135
commercial lending 299-300
    medium-term Libor-linked loans
        299-300
    short-term 299
communications 37-9, 163-8, 282, 350,
    359
    computer hardware and
        manufacturing 166-7
    maintenance and support services
        168
    people – the hidden IT resource 166
    software 120, 167-8, 282
    the technological heritage 164
    telecommunications 165, 282, 350-1
companies
    financing 297-302
        commercial lending 299-300
        ECGD lines of credit 298
        investment and project finance
            300-1
        repatriation of hard currency
            profits 302
        working capital 301-2
    forming 285-95, 363
        joint stock companies 287-93
        key features of Czechoslovak
            system 285-7
        limited liability companies 293-4
        other vehicles 294-5
    see also establishing a presence;
        foreign investment
company law 30, 79, 285, 363
compensation trading *see* barter
competition 137-44
    anti-trust law 138-44
        abuse of a monopoly/dominant
            position 141-2
        control of mergers 141
        escape clauses 140-1
        exemptions 139-40
        the Office: extent of power 142
        purpose and scope 138-9
        some general comments 142-4
    unfair competition 137-8
Competition Act (1991) *see* Act on

Protection of Economic
    Competition (1991)
Computer Aided Design (CAD) 164,
    167
computer hardware and manufacturing
    166-7, 282, 359
Computer Integrated Manufacturing
    (CIM) 164, 167, 348
'confiscation' insurance 254-5
conflicts of interest 83, 292, 369-70
Constitution, the 70-1, 117
    Constitutional Court 74
consultancies 48, 119, 190
consumer markets 216-19
    labelling/health and safety/the
        environment 218
    market research 217
    retail and distribution 218-19
consumer prices *see* pricing
'contract frustration' insurance 254
contract law 132-5
    specific types of contract 134-5
contractual joint ventures 84
convertibility of the Koruna 18, 29,
    87-91, 245, 302
    convertible bonds 289-90
    currency debt 21
    rationale 87-8
    the risks of 90-1
    the road to 88-90
copyright 120, 167, 274-5
    software 167
corporate joint ventures 84-6
    additional documents 85-6
counterpurchase 246-7
countertrade 243-8, 300
    advance purchase 247
    barter 245-6
    buy-back 247-8
    counterpurchase 246-7
    Czechoslovakia's attitude to 244-5
    form of 245-8
        barter 245-6
    offset 248
    types of transaction 243-4
country indicators 209
Country Profile (DTI) 53
courier services to Czechoslovakia 170
courts, the 74-5

credit assessment 226-7
credit insurance 249
  ECGD-supported finance schemes 55,
    236-7, 250-4, 298
  amount of insurance 253-4
  eligible investors and enterprises
    252-3
  Overseas Investment Insurance
    Scheme 251-2
  unfair calling cover 251
  private market insurance 254-6
  deprivation of collateral insurance
    255-6
  risks insured 254-5
customs 55, 232
  customs-free zones 83
Customs Act (1974 amended 1990)
    31
Czechoslovak Chamber of Commerce
    (CCC) 53, 56
  database 56
Czechoslovak Confederation of Trade
    Unions 182
Czechoslovak Enterprises Directory
    (CCC) 56
Czechoslovak State Bank 80; *Statní
    Banka Ceskoslovenska*
Czechoslovakia, a business revolution?
    15-65
  businesss culture 45-9
  and its trading partners 57-65
  map 59
  market intelligence 51-6
  market potential 35-43
  political and economic
    transformation 17-25
  recreating a market economy 27-33

damage liability 135-6, 161, 264
databases 54, 56, 198, 217, 222, 351
debtors, accounting for 313
Department of Trade and Industry
    (DTI) 53
diesel vouchers 175
direct mail 222, 332
discounting 102, 235-6, 241
dispute resolution 83, 369-70
distance learning 190
distribution 168, 169, 218-19, 363

distributorship 261-4
  areas of particular concern 264
  legal regulations 257-8
documentary credits 227, 231-6
  discounting 235-6
  examples of 233-5
dominant position, abuse of 141-2
double taxation treaties 306, 308-9

easements/servitudes 129
East European Trade Council 53
Eastern Europe, Czechoslovakia's trade
    with 17, 57-60
EBRD *see* European Bank for
    Reconstruction and Development
EC Tempus programme 184
ECGD *see* Export Credits Guarantee
    Department
Economic Code 69, 126, 131
Economic Daily 56
Economic Digest (CCC) 53
Economic Supplement (Brit. Embassy,
    Prague) 54
economic transformation,
    Czechoslovakia's 17-25
  external debt 21-5
  ingredients of reform 18-21
Economist Intelligence Unit (EIU) 52
education 180-1, 350
  distance learning 190
effective purchase 121
EIB *see* European Investment Bank
electronics industry 349-50
emergency telephone numbers 175
Emmex Consultants 329-32
employment *see* labour market
energy 37, 40, 58, 151-4, 201, 216, 333,
    356-7
Energy Efficiency Centre, Prague 155
engineering 182, 191, 348-9
Enterprise with Foreign Property
    Participation Act (1988) ('JVA')
    78, 82, 83
environment, the 32-3, 41, 159, 194,
    218, 264, 333, 339, 344-5, 350, 362
  guidance for investors 158-61
  key sectors 158-9
  who to talk to/steps to take 159-61
  the legal structure 153-8

authorities responsible 154
draft framework law 155-8
the future 154-5
issues for the investor 161
priorities 151-3
  air pollution 152
  waste and soil contamination 41,
    153, 156, 157, 334, 344, 347
  water pollution 41, 152-3, 154, 157,
    339, 344
Esomar (trade directory) 53
establishing a presence 279-83, 293-4,
  363
  legislative considerations 279-80
  practical considerations 280-3
    availability/suitability of
      technology 282
    location 280
    obtaining office space 281-2
    staffing issues 282-3
  see also foreign investment
European Bank for Reconstruction and
  Development (EBRD) 155, 195-6,
  301, 351
European Community (EC)
  Czechoslovakia's relations with 28,
    60-5, 361
  PHARE Programme 61, 155, 184,
    197-8, 336, 345, 351, 352
European Economic Interest Group
  (EEIG) 336
European Environment Agency 155
European Investment Bank (EIB)
  200-2, 351
  a complementary source of finance
    202
  types of project 201-2
exchange rate system *see* convertibility
Exhibition Bulletin 52
expatriates, taxation of 146, 148, 305
Export Credits Guarantee Department
  (ECGD) 55, 236-7, 249-54, 298
  amount of insurance 253-4
  eligible investors and enterprises
    252-3
  lines of credit 298
  Overseas Investment Insurance
    Scheme 251-2
  unfair calling cover 251

export and import 223-9
  by sector 42-3
  current situation 226-9
    buying from Czechoslovakia 228
    credit assessment 226-7
    FTOs and agents 226
    planning 227-8
    selling to Czechoslovakia 228-9
  foreign trade liberalisation 224-5
    legislation 224-5
  situation pre-liberalisation 223-4
  see also trading partners,
    Czechoslovakia's
Export Intelligence Service 55
Export Market Information Centre
  (DTI) 54
external debt, Czechoslovakia's 21-5

factoring 240-2
fax machines 282
Federal and Republic authorities 71-3
female labour force 178, 183, 192
fibre optics 40
finance, trade and project 231-42
  documentary credits 231-6
    discounting 235-6
  ECGD - supported schemes 236-7
  factoring 240-2
  forfaiting 238-40
  leasing 242
  limited recourse finance 237-8
financial services *see* banking and
  financial services
fiscal framework 145-50, 363
  the Czechoslovak tax system 145-9,
    303-9
  main taxes 146-9
  tax reform 32, 150
  see also taxation
fixed assets 312
flights to/from Czechoslovakia 171
food processing 345-6
footwear industry 355
Foreign and Commonwealth Office 55
foreign exchange 24
Foreign Exchange Act (1990) 29, 268,
  302
foreign exchange, convertibility of 18,
  19, 29, 87-91, 245, 302

foreign investment 29, 47–8, 77–86, 111, 361–2
  accounting practice 82
  reserve fund 82
  applicable law/dispute resolution 83
  customs-free zones 83
  employment law 81
  forms of participation 80–1
  framework for 78–9
    main features of FPCs 79
  investment protection 82–3
  negotiating joint ventures 83–6
  obtaining authority to invest 79–80
Foreign Investment Advisory Service (FIAS) (IFC) 200
Foreign Property Companies (FPCs) 79
Foreign Trade Act 268
foreign trade liberalisation 224–5
  legislation 224–5
  other aspects/issues 225
Foreign Trade Organisations (FTOs) 28, 223–4
  and agents 226
forfaiting 238–40
franchises 212, 264–5
  legal regulations 257–8, 363
freight transport 169–70
funds, sources of 298–302

GATT (General Agreement on Trade and Tariffs) 31, 225
general partnerships 295
glass industry 38, 39, 41, 111, 354
'global loans scheme', EIB 202
grants 41, 193–202, 357
  EBRD 55, 195–6, 236–7, 249–54, 298
  EIB 200–2
  IFC 198–200
  Overseas Projects Fund (OPF) 194–5
  PHARE Programme 61, 155, 184, 197–8, 336, 345, 351, 352
  UK government Know-How Fund 193–4
Green Circle environmental group 151
gross representation commission 305
Group of 24 *see* Organisation for Economic Co-operation and Development
group relief of losses 150

hazardous wastes 41, 153, 160, 161
health and medicine 217, 357–8
health and safety 218
Hungary, trade with 60, 61, 329, 332
hydropower 153

IFC *see* International Finance Corporation
impact assessments, environmental 160
import charges on consumer goods 218, 225
improvements, protecting intellectual property 273, 277
income tax *see* taxation
Industrial Designs and Innovations (Rationalisation Proposals) 269
industrial designs, protecting 272–3
inflation 23, 90–1, 102, 216
information sources 53–6, 376–9
Information Technology *see* technology and communications
infrastructure, business 67–202
Institute for Labour, Nuremberg 185
Institute for Technical Development and Information (UTRIN) 271
Institutes of Management (IOMs), Prague/Bratislava 56, 190
insurance 362
  credit 249
  ECGD-supported finance schemes 250–4
  private market insurance 254–6
intellectual property rights 85–6, 120–1, 139, 167, 264
  protecting 268–72
  improvements 273, 277
  local laws/international conventions 269–70
  means available to foreign proprietors 271–2
  registration of rights 270–1
interest rates 102
internal flights 172
International Bank for Reconstruction and Development (World Bank) 22, 90, 196, 198, 201, 301, 345, 351
International Chamber of Commerce, Zurich 83, 232, 276
international conventions 269–70

International Court of Arbitration 83
International Finance Corporation
    (IFC) 198–200, 237–8, 301
    what it does 199–200
International Labour Organisation
    (ILO) 182
International Monetary Fund (IMF) 22,
    33, 90
International Trade Code (1963) 129,
    131, 295
Interprogram radio station 220
Investicni Banka 99, 110
Investment Bank *see Investicni Banka*
investment, foreign 47–8, 77–86
    investment vouchers 112–13, 121–2
    obtaining authority to invest 79–80
    trade and project finance 231–42,
        300–1
        documentary credits 231–6
        ECGD – supported schemes 55,
            236–7, 249–54, 298
        factoring 240–2
        leasing 242
        limited recourse finance 237–8
    valuing proposed investments 314
    see also UK/Czechoslovak
        Agreement on Investment
        Protection (1990)

Jednatel (manager) *see* management
job centres 185
Joint Assistance Unit 194
Joint Stock Companies Act (JSCA)
    (1990) 285
joint stock companies (JSCs) 287–93
    capital and share structure 288–90
    name and establishment 287–8
    organs of 290–2
    other matters 292–3
Joint Venture Act (JVA) *see* Enterprise
    with Foreign Property
    Participation Act (1988)
joint ventures 47–8, 210–11
    negotiating 83–6
        contractual joint ventures 84
        corporate joint ventures 84–6
        partnership arrangements 84
        Treaty of Rome 86
        taxation of 149, 303–4, 363

Kancerlárské Stroje state distributors
    168
know-how
    protecting 275
    see also intellectual property
    second order know-how 325
    UK government Know-How Fund 55,
        193–4, 336
Komanditni Spolecnost see limited
    partnerships
Komercní Banka (Commercial Bank)
    98, 99, 100, 110
Kovo state import organisation 168

labelling 218
Labour Code 32, 81
labour market 18, 96, 177–85, 362
    basic education indicators 180–1
    other recruitment issues 185, 283
    sectoral distribution 179–80
    skills strengths and weaknesses
        181–2
    trade unions and wage bargaining
        182–3
    training 46, 47, 184–5, 194, 221, 268
    unemployment and social security
        benefits 183–4
    working population 177–9
        female labour force 178, 183, 192
land dealings 32, 125–8, 326
    land registration 125–6
    transfer and use of state land 126
    see also real estate; restitution
Large Privatisation Act (1991) 117–22,
    124, 189, 210, 354
    miscellaneous provisions 122
    the privatisation project 118–19
    transition to funds 119–22
        effective purchase 121
        intellectual property 120–1
        investment vouchers 121–2
Large Restitution Act (1991) *see* Act on
    Out of Court Rehabilitations
    (1991)
Law Society 55
lawyers 182, 191, 211
leasing 242
leather, footwear, leather goods 355

legal framework, the 18-19, 27, 69-75, 361
the Constitution 70-1
the courts 74-5
the civil courts 74-5
Constitutional Court 74
state arbitration 75
federal and Republic authorities 71-3
local government 74
the legal system 69-70
legislative process 73-4
legislation 361-73
Acts of Parliament *see* by name
agencies, distributorships and franchises 257-8, 363
banks and financial services 362
commercial law 30, 131-6, 362
company law 30, 79, 285, 363
competition 137-44, 277-8
customs law 31
employment law 32, 81
on the environment 32-3, 156-61, 362
establishing a presence 279-80, 363
foreign exchange 29, 268, 302
foreign investment 77-86, 361-2
on insurance 362
on intellectual property 269-70
labour market 32, 362
on privatisation 28, 46, 115-22, 362
property law 32, 95-6, 105-8, 362
real estate 362
relations with EC 361
restitution 95-6, 105-8, 362
technology licensing 363
trade liberalisation 224-5, 361
see also Association Agreements; legal framework, the
letters of credit *see* documentary credits
letting/sub-letting of business premises 126-8
liberalisation 19, 159, 361
export/import 223-4
foreign trade 224-5
legislation 224-5
other aspects/issues 225
Libor-linked loans 299-300
licensing 47, 211, 267-78, 363

considerations 275-8
Commercial Code and Competition Act 277-8
other issues for foreign owners 276-7
new opportunities in Czechoslovakia 267-8
protecting intellectual property rights 268-72
specific rights 272-5
improvements 273
industrial designs 272-3
know-how 275
patents 272
trade/service marks 273-4
limited internal convertibility 88-9
limited liability companies 293-4
name, establishment and capital 293-4
organs and management 294
limited partnerships 295
limited recourse finance *see* trade and project finance
liquidation 31
JSCs 292, 303
local government 74
London Commerce (LCC) 54

management 286, 290, 293, 294, 350
consultancies 190
culture 49
and the professions 187-92
level of management skills 187-8
local professions 191-2
management ethos 188-9
management training 56, 189-91
market economy, recreating a 27-33, 109-10
outlook 33
progress to date 28-33
bankruptcy and liquidation 31
commercial law 30
company law 30
customs law 31
employment law 32
the environment 32-3
foreign exchange convertibility 29
foreign trade 28-9
land ownership 32

private enterprise 28
privatisation 29–30
removal of price and wage controls
    31
securities market and stock
    exchange 30–1
tax reform 32
market intelligence 51–6
    information sources 53–6, 376–9
        in Czechoslovakia 55–6
        other sources 376–9
        in the UK 53–5
    market research and surveys 53
    sources of statistics 51–2
    trade fairs 52
market potential, Czechoslovakia's
    35–43
    background 35–6
    resources 36–9
        agriculture 36
        communications 37–9
        energy 37
        raw materials 36–7
    some major opportunities 39–41
        problem areas 40–1
    UK trade with Czechoslovakia 41–3
marketing 215–22
    advertising 221–2
    consumer markets 216–19
        labelling/health and safety/the
            environment 218
        market research 217
        pricing 218
        retail and distribution 218–19
    direct mail 222, 332
    media 219–21
        outdoor 220–1
        print 220
        radio 220
        television 219–20
media 219–21, 359
    cinema 221
    outdoor 220–1
    print 220, 332
    radio 194, 220
    television 219–20
mergers 141, 143
metallurgy 347–8
metro system 173

mining industry 347
monetary policy 101–2
monopolies 141–2, 267
moral suasion 101–2
mortgages 128–9

national insurance *see* payroll tax
National Trade Union Centre 182
net representation commission 305
Nezavisle Radio 220
Nuclear Electric plc 333–6
nuclear power 37, 154, 344

Office of Geodesy and Cartography 125
office space, obtaining 281–2
Offices for Economic Competition 138
offset 245, 248
oil 39, 58, 154
OPF *see* Overseas Projects Fund
opportunities by sector 343–59
options for British business 203–314
Organisation for Economic Co-
    operation and Development
    (OECD) 60, 197
Our Common Future (World
    Commission report) 157
Overseas Development Agency 55
Overseas Investment Insurance Scheme
    251–2
Overseas Projects Fund (OPF) 194–5
ownership of land 32, 103–8, 124–5,
    281, 326

packaging, draft law on 160, 218, 352
paper and pulp 41, 352
partnerships, taxation of 304–5
patent agents 271
payment in kind *see* barter
payroll tax 147
periodicals and journals 51–6, 220, 232,
    270, 375–6
petrol 175, 217
PHARE Programme 61, 155, 184,
    197–8, 336, 345, 351, 352
Plan Econ (USA) 52
planning 205–13, 227–8
    the business plan 212–13
    formulating a strategy 205–9
    mode of entry 209–12

acquisitions and other options
211-12
joint ventures 210-11
role of tax 305-6
Poland, trade with 60, 61, 329, 332
political transformation,
Czechoslovakia's 17-25
ingredients of reform 18-21
pollution *see* environment, the
population, Czechoslovak 36
poster sites, outdoor 220-1
Prague airport 171
pricing 218
controls on prices and wages 31,
93-6, 218, 225
transfer 150
print media 220
private enterprise 28, 47, 138
Enterprise Registers 285-6, 288
Private Enterprise Act (1990) 28
private market insurance 254-6
deprivation of collateral insurance
255-6
risks insured 254-5
privatisation 18, 29-30, 194, 362
the economics of 109-13
capital markets 110-11
foreign investment 111
the market economy 109-10
the process of 115-22
Large Privatisation Act (1991)
117-22, 124, 189, 210, 354
Small Privatisation Act (1990) 46,
115-17, 126
progress to date 111-13
large privatisation 112-13, 117-22,
124, 189, 210, 354
small privatisation 111-12
product guarantees 135
professions, the 182, 187-92
level of management skills 187-8
local 191-2
accountants 191-2
engineers 191
lawyers 191
management ethos 188-9
Profit Weekly 56
profits tax 146-7

Programme A environmental policy
document 157-61
project finance *see* trade and project
finance
property 85, 216
real estate 123-9
building permissions 129
easements/servitudes 129
land dealings 125-8
mortgages and other security
128-9
ownership 32, 124-5, 281
rents 95-6
valuation of 105
see also intellectual property;
restitution
Protection of Commercial Agents, EC
Directive on 261
public transport 37, 173-5, 216

qualifications, Czechoslovak
educational 180-1

R&D (Research and Development) 39,
198, 220
and technology 343-5
radio 220
rail services
domestic 37, 173
to/from Czechoslovakia 172
raw materials, Czechoslovakia's 36-7
real estate 123-9, 362
building permissions 129
easements/servitudes 129
land dealings 125-8
land registration 125-6
letting/sub-letting of business
premises 126-8
transfer and use of state land 126
mortgages and other security 128-9
ownership 32, 124-5
recruitment *see* labour market
remuneration *see* wages
rents, prices and wages 93-6, 108
repatriation of hard currency profits
302, 308
representative offices 212, 279, 305
reserve fund 82
reserves, accounting for 313-14

resources, Czechoslovakia's 36–9
  agriculture 36
  communications 37–9
  energy 37
  raw materials 36–7
restitution 103–8, 281, 362
  the legislative framework 105–8
    Large Restitution Act (1991)
      107–8, 224
    Small Restitution Act (1990)
      105–7
  political and commercial
    considerations 103–5
Restitution Bill (1991) 95–6
retail and distribution 218–19
revolution in Czechoslovakia, a business
  15–65
  business culture 45–9
  its trading partners 57–65
  market intelligence 51–6
  market potential 35–43
  political and economic
    transformation 17–25
  recreating a market economy 27–33
Rhine-Main-Danube canal link, new
  170
road network, Czechoslovak 37–8, 175

savings banks 99–100
Sdruzeni see associations
second order know-how 325
sectoral distribution, labour market
  179–80
securities market and stock exchange
  30–1
service marks, protecting 273–4
services industry 41, 359
Simpler Trade Procedures Board
  (SITPRO) 55, 232
Small Privatisation Act (1990) 46,
  115–17, 126
  mechanics of 116–17
Small Restitution Act (1990) 105,
  105–7
  Restitution Bill (1991) 95–6
Small- and Medium-sized Enterprises
  (SMEs), funding for 202, 338–9
social security benefits 183–4, 283
Société Général 100

software 120, 167–8, 282, 334
speed limits 175
Spolecnost s rucenym omezenim (plc
  limited by shares) 79, 293
Správa diplomatickych sluzeb
  diplomatic services organisation
  282
'stabilisation fund' 90
staffing issues 282–3
state aid 64
state arbitration 75
State Bank *see Statní Banka
  Ceskoslovenska*
state enterprises 46–7, 72, 138
state land, transfer and use of 126
Statisticka Rocenka (statistical
  yearbook) 51
Statní Banka Ceskoslovenska
  (Czechoslovak State Bank) 80,
  97–8
stock, accounting for 312–13
stock exchange 30–1
strategic planning 205–13
  the business plan 212–13
  formulating a strategy 205–9
  mode of entry 209–12
    acquisitions and other options
      211–12
    joint ventures 210–11
subrogation 371
subsidiaries, Czechoslovak 306–8
supervisory boards, JSC 291
surveys, market 53
switch trading 248

tariffs 225
taxation 145–9, 303–9, 363
  citizens' income tax 148
  collection and administration of 149
  and Czechoslovak subsidiaries 306–8
    debt or equity? 307–8
  of expatriates 148
  future developments 150
  of joint ventures 303–4
  of partnerships 304–5
  payroll tax 147
  profits tax 146–7
  representative offices and agencies
    305

role of tax planning 305-6
tax reform 32, 150
turnover tax 149
wage tax 31, 147-8
withholding taxes 149, 277, 303,
    308-9
    treaty shopping 308-9
Technical Help to Exporters 55
technology 40, 187-8
    and communications 37-9, 163-8,
        282, 350
        computer hardware and
            manufacturing 166-7
        maintenance and support services
            168, 359
        people - the hidden IT resource
            166
        software 167-8
        the technological heritage 164
        telecommunications 40, 165, 282,
            350-1
    electronics 349-50
    and R&D 343-5
telecommunications 40, 165, 282,
    350-1
telephones 164, 282
television advertising 219-20
telex 282
'ten-by-six' forfait 239
textiles and clothes 38, 355-6
tiles, ceramics and building materials
    354-5
TOP Weekly 56
tourism 201, 346, 358
Trade and Co-operation Agreements
    (1988) 61
trade fairs 52
Trade Marks Act (1988) 269, 273-4
trade and project finance 231-42, 300-1
    documentary credits 231-6
        discounting 235-6
    ECGD - supported schemes 55,
        236-7, 249-54, 298
    factoring 240-2
    forfaiting 238-40
    leasing 2422
    limited recourse finance 237-8
        borrower's objectives 238
        role of the banks 238

'trade secrets' *see* know-how
trade unions and wage bargaining
    182-3
trading partners, Czechoslovakia's 28-9,
    57-65
    relations with Eastern Europe 17,
        57-60
    relations with the EC 60-5, 361
        the future 65
        a new direction 60-4
        some key issues 64-5
    UK trade with Czechoslovakia 41-3
training 46, 47, 184-5, 194, 221, 268
    management 56, 189-91
transfer pricing 150
'transferable roubles' 58
transport 40, 169-75
    courier services to Czechoslovakia
        170
    freight 169-70
    infrastructure 343
    travel to/from Czechoslovakia 171-2
        air travel 171-2
        rail services 172
    within Czechoslovakia 172-5
        domestic rail travel 37, 173
        internal flights 38, 172
        public transport 37, 173-5, 216
        the road network 37-8, 175
Treaty of Rome 86
treaty-shopping 306
turnover tax 149

UK/Czechoslovak Agreement on
    Investment Protection (1990) 82,
        364-73
    application of other rules 371
    compensation for losses 367-8
    definitions 365-6
    dispute settlement 369-70
    duration and termination 372
    entry into force 372
    exceptions 369
    expropriation 308
    national treatment/MFN provisions
        367
    promotion/protection of investment
        366-7
    Protocol 373

repatriation of investment and return 308
subrogation 371
territorial extension 372
underground railway system 173
unemployment 91, 177-80, 184, 248, 339
    and social security benefits 183-4
unfair competition 137-8
Uniform Customs and Practice for Documentary Credits (ICC) 232
Union of Czechoslovak Accountants (UCA) 192
unjust enrichment 135
US Agency for International Development 155

valuations 105, 301, 312, 313, 314
Value Added Tax (VAT) 150
vehicles 353-4
'Velvet Revolution, the' 17, 103, 223, 259
Verejna Obchodni Spolecnost (general partnerships) 295
Vestnik Uradu (intellectual property bulletin) 270
vouchers
    diesel 175
    investment 112-13, 121-2, 124

Vseobecná Uverová Banká (General Credit Bank) 98

wages 96, 283
    controls *see* taxation
    prices and rents 93-6
    and trade unions 182-3
waste and soil contamination/ treatment 41, 153, 156, 157, 334, 344, 347
water pollution/treatment 41, 152-3, 154, 157, 339, 344
withholding taxes 149, 277, 303, 308-9
without recourse discounting 238-9
wood, woodworking and furniture 41, 352-3
working capital 301-2
working population 177-9
World Bank *see* International Bank for Reconstruction and Development
World Environment Centre, New York 155
Worldwatch Institute, Washington 151

Your Trade Partners in Czechoslovakia (CCC) 53

Zivnostenská Banka 98